The Eggs Benedict Option

# The Eggs Benedict Option

— RAW EGG NATIONALIST —

*Foreword by Noor Bin Ladin*

ANTELOPE HILL PUBLISHING

Antelope Hill Publishing
www.antelopehillpublishing.com

Paperback ISBN-13: 978-1-956887-26-6
EPUB ISBN-13: 978-1-956887-27-3

*For my family and friends, and the future you really deserve*

# CONTENTS

**Part One: Great Resets Old and New**

Chapter 1: Welcome To 2030 BC: The Original Great
Reset?

# WE WILL NOT EAT THE BUGS, KLAUS!
## A FOREWORD BY NOOR BIN LADIN

*"Food and medicine are not two different things: they are the front and back of one body. Chemically grown vegetables may be eaten for food, but they cannot be used as medicine."*

— Masanobu Fukuoka, *The One-Straw Revolution*

In 1974, *Foreign Affairs* (CFR) published an essay entitled "The Hard Road to World Order" by Richard N. Gardner, who stated that:

*In short, the "house of world order" will have to be built from the bottom up rather than from the top down. It will look like a great "booming, buzzing confusion," to use William James' famous description of reality, but an end run around national sovereignty, eroding it piece by piece, will accomplish much more than the old-fashioned frontal assault.*

For many people, the world changed completely in 2020 when the COVID-19 pandemic was declared. For others like myself, the drastic dissolution of our freedoms and Western society's accelerated decay were the mere continuation of a long-standing, methodical plan.

Eroding our national sovereignty piece by piece—and with it our individual sovereignty—is precisely what the globalists were working towards long before Gardner's words were even printed. To achieve their goal of a "world order," a multitude of chaos-triggering events were weaponized, aided by mass manipulation techniques and followed up with coordinated policy-making at national and international levels.

The playbook isn't new: under the guise of "health" and "safety," those who rule over us have systematically used our "security" as a justification to undermine our personal sovereignty. Manufacture a problem via a conscious and intelligent fear campaign, in order to offer a "solution"—*their* solution. Yet each time these "solutions" are implemented, our genuine problems only deepen.

This latest "crisis" was no exception. The suicide rates, vaccine side effects, cognitive impairment of children locked up and masked, abuse of the elderly, and the general dehumanization of our society—these are but a few of the immediate outcomes. The decimation of the middle class and private businesses has left many destitute, with people struggling to make ends meet and feed their families. We must expect more to come.

These were not unintended consequences: they are deliberate, and they have succeeded in making us more vulnerable than ever. The objective? Accelerate and herald the final stages of a societal overhaul coined "The Great Reset," which is, in reality, the globalists' latest iteration of the New World Order: a global governance system to centralize every aspect of our lives. And they are incredibly close to reaching their goal: due to technological progress and the advent of 5G, which has made possible the Internet of Things, we are on the cusp of having our every move recorded and tracked. The idea is to measure everything we do, everywhere, all the time. Just like in China, a social credit score system for each individual will be tied to a digital ID. Rations of food, energy, and consumer goods will in-evitably follow, leaving us at the mercy of a ruling class intent on removing our most basic right as humans: our free will.

Like many others who openly call out these machinations, REN and I have been labeled conspiracy theorists by those seeking to obfuscate their motivations and discredit our evi-dence-based claims. But this is not a conspiracy *theory*, for the globalists' agenda has been thoroughly documented through-out the years. And that which is not hidden, is not a *conspiracy*. Though the globalists use certain smokescreens, most of their attacks are done in plain sight, and the evidence of what they have done is often readily available. Documenting the full ex-tent of the social engineering forced upon us, right through the twentieth century and up to the present day, would fill a size-able library. For much has been done to render us compliant to the point of losing ourselves in a transhumanist matrix of per-petual serfdom.

This has been achieved through the capturing of entire in-dustries that operate as cartels, the usurpation of our political systems, and the infiltration of our institutions, like the educa-tion or medical systems and governing bodies such as the FDA, the FCC, or the WHO. In addition, the creation of international organizations dictating the global agenda was an essential part of pushing both narratives and policies upon individual na-tions. This of course was enabled by an almost total strangle-hold over the media, entertainment, tech sector and academia. And all of this was underpinned by the financial structure headed by the central banks that ensure and perpetuate the citizens' enslavement via debt and usury. The use of popula-tion-manipulation techniques, the rewriting of history, the dumbing-down of society and, last but not least, the infliction of trauma were all indispensable to facilitate the herding of the masses blindly towards the slaughterhouse.

Indeed, looking at the past one hundred years, it is clear for those of us who have gone down the rabbit hole: the people at the very top of the pyramid have gone to great lengths to deliberately poison us—mind, body and soul. Weak populations are easier to control.

*The Eggs Benedict Option (EBO)* is the first book that focuses on the poisoning of our body via the food we consume in the context of today's Great Reset. REN does an outstanding job at giving a concise yet well documented overview of precisely how the globalists consolidated their dominion over the world's food supply chain, leaving us reliant on a handful of companies to feed ourselves. Through the meticulous study of the corporatization of agriculture and the industrialization of the farming system, the *EBO* exposes one of the most fundamental ways we've been robbed of our independence, and how we've been harmed as a result. The key to a healthy life—our food—is no longer in our possession.

As REN correctly points out several times, it's not a question of *when* these supply chain changes—and thus changes in food quality—will occur. They already have been implemented to a large extent, and the effects have been devastating. The stunting of our growth and marring of our physiognomy, the downgrading of our DNA, the increase of degenerative diseases and other physical ailments—all are without question largely the result of our impoverished diet. At this point, it is only a question of *degree*—from quasi-total to total control of the food production and distribution system.

Again, this isn't conjecture, as you will find out in the first part of the *EBO*.

REN identifies the globalists' key players and policies you need to know about, starting with the World Economic Forum (WEF) and Klaus Schwab. Also covered are the other usual suspects: the Rockefeller Foundation; the UN and partner organizations such as the EAT Foundation; chemical and food processing corporations; pharmaceutical companies; and "esteemed" "health" commissions or so-called scientific publications like *The Lancet*. All working hand in hand towards the completion of the Great Reset and the UN's 2030 Sustainable Development Goals.

Looking at the news currently, you can see their concerted programming playing out in real time: the celebrities eating bugs; the push for fake meat; the promotion of processed foods along with the vilification of healthy foods and glorification of plant-based diets. It is worth stressing that our regulatory and medical authorities seem to support harmful practices by choice, making them fully complicit in our ill health. We are told to "trust the science," but they are lying to us.

Also painfully obvious is the engineered scarcity, whether by the destruction of an inexplicable number of food processing plants or the staged conflict in the Ukraine, and, of course, by the manufactured economic pressures via regulations on farming, leaving independent small-scale farmers unable to earn a living. Economists and forecasters agree, an unprecedented famine is about to hit us as a result.

Another chapter in the crisis playbook is the environmental justifications to reduce our consumption of nourishing foods and monitor our "carbon footprint." The narrative is well underway to use "climate change" to implement rations, quotas, and absurd "recommendations," including upcoming "climate lockdowns." In other words, expect more doomporn of an even more terrifying sort.

The globalists are using all their might to complete the centralization of the food supply chain. They will stop at nothing to capture the last remaining pockets of production that aren't fully under their control—and according to their own timeline, these Malthusian psycho freaks are on a mission to complete their plan by 2030.

One of the most vocal academics who rejected the overpopulation narrative was Julian Simon, famous notably for challenging famed eugenicist and population-control charlatan Paul Ehrlich. It was Ehrlich who in 1969 stated to the United States Commission for UNESCO that "the Government might have to put sterility drugs in reservoirs and in food shipped to foreign countries to limit human multiplication."

Needless to say, Julian Simon was on the right side of history and had a very good grasp on the false paradigm we've been taught:

> *Not understanding the process of a spontaneously-ordered economy goes hand-in-hand with not understanding the creation of resources and wealth. And when a person does not understand the creation of resources and wealth, the only intellectual alternative is to believe that increasing wealth must be at the cost of someone else. This belief that our good fortune must be an exploitation of others may be the taproot of false prophecy about doom that our evil ways must bring upon us.*

He also understood the true nature of our predicament: "The world's problem is not too many people, but a lack of political and economic freedom."

It is easy to feel discouraged when realizing how badly we've been poisoned throughout the years, but it is only by naming and framing the problems in the first place that an opportunity arises to solve them. After a brilliant albeit depressing exposé of the globalists' machinations, REN manages to be incredibly motivating by sharing viable solutions that have been tried and tested. And while REN doesn't reinvent the wheel—nor does he purport to—we can be thankful for the invaluable guidance he provides us at this juncture. By reintroducing us to household gardening, also known as backyard agriculture, with which we have lost touch here in the West, REN reorients us towards our environment, our ancestors, the treasure trove that is traditional knowledge and, thus, our humanity.

Drawing from the leading figures in the field of regenerative agriculture such as Joel Salatin in America and case studies of Russian gardens or "dachas," the *EBO* shows us the alternative paths to explore in lieu of the current system, providing us with a great starting point for further research. Once you read this book, you'll understand the urgency and necessity of reclaiming our independence from this corporatized food supply system. I have no doubt it will inspire you to start digging. Quickly, you'll realize that many elegant—and even profitable —solutions abound. From the teachings of Joel Salatin to those of figures such as André Voisin, Alan Savory, Darren Doherty, Sepp Holzer, David Holmgren, and Richard Perkins, to name a few, you'll find the world of regenerative agriculture in general is fascinating—and it makes sense. Growing nourishing food based on your direct environment and exchanging produce locally should be the standard, or as Darren Doherty said years ago, "this needs to be the New Normal." Yes, not the ridiculous New Normal the globalists are trying to enforce!

The beauty of these solutions is that they are actually beneficial for the environment where they are implemented. In the words of Michael Pollan in an interview for *Polyfaces* (2015), a documentary on Joel Salatin's farming methods:

> *The idea that we could take beautiful food off of the land and heal it at the same time . . . that's a very hopeful lesson, because it's bigger than food or farming. It suggests that as long as the sun shines, there is a free lunch. And that you can capture that energy and run it through a system, and not diminish the world.*

As noted above, this message is the exact opposite of the narrative we've been fed ad nauseam about our supposedly finite resources, which are used to justify horrendous measures implemented to our detriment. In the WEF's words, "you'll own nothing and you'll be happy," which translates to *you'll own nothing—not even your health—but we'll own everything including you,* enslaved to a system that weakens us to a point where we neither have the physical strength to break away nor the will to contemplate emancipation, transformed into com-

xvi | *The Eggs Benedict Option*

pletely malleable creatures devoid of inner and physical fortitude, disconnected from ourselves and others. Their plan has worked brilliantly so far—one need only look at the state of our society. We are sick and divided, ready to be conquered.

But there is another plan, and thanks to REN's work, many will be awakened to the truth and will thus be able to reject this evil premise in favor of a promising new way of life, a path where we return to methods that foster our independence from overarching governing structures, nurture cooperation with our fellow man, and cultivate the building of communities around the most essential need that joins us together: food.

It is of utmost importance that we urgently look to these tried and tested alternatives to the current poisonous system closing in on us. Fighting for our independence over what we put into our bodies is an essential front in this war. We owe it to ourselves, and our children, to stop this assault on our physical integrity and reclaim our sovereignty. For if we do not even have autonomy over our own health, what freedom do we have?

The time to change course is now. The right option is *The Eggs Benedict Option.*

Noor Bin Ladin
July 2022

# PREFACE

This is a book about food and social control. Although this might seem like an unlikely pairing, in truth the two things go together like peas and carrots. And it's been that way for a very long time.

During his famous trip down to the Piraeus, as imagined in Plato's *Republic*, Socrates and his young companions Glaucon and Adeimantus begin to consider how justice first arises in a community (Book II). After both of the young men have had their chance to speak at some length, Socrates proposes that, in order to pursue their inquiry further, they should take the development of a city as a kind of metaphor for the individual's moral development. The three men discuss how, from the start, a division of labor is necessary to supply the community with food, shelter, and clothing, how the functions of each different class of worker are complementary to one another, and how goods will be exchanged, through marketplaces where they are bought and sold. Then the conversation turns to the lifestyle of the ordinary people of this imagined community, including the kinds of foods they might eat. Socrates continues:

*So let us consider first how our citizens, so equipped, will live. They will produce corn, wine, clothes, and shoes, and will build themselves houses. In the summer they will for*

> *the most part work unclothed and unshod, in the winter they will be clothed and shod suitably. For food they will prepare wheat-meal or barley-meal for baking or kneading. They will serve splendid cakes and loaves on rushes or fruit leaves, and will sit down to feast with their children on couches of myrtle and bryony; and they will have wine to drink too, and pray to the gods with garlands on their heads, and enjoy each other's company. And fear of poverty and war will make them keep the numbers of their families within their means.[1]*

Young Glaucon is quick to object that this is "pretty plain fare for a feast," which leads Socrates to concede that the ordinary people would be allowed "a few luxuries." These consist of:

> *Salt, of course, and olive oil and cheese, and different kinds of vegetables to make various country dishes. And we must give them some dessert, figs and peas and beans, and myrtle-berries and acorns to roast at the fire as they sip their wine. So they will lead a peaceful and healthy life, and probably die at a ripe old age, bequeathing a similar way of life to their children.*

But even these "luxuries" aren't enough for Glaucon: "That's just the fodder you would provide if you were founding a community of pigs!" The ordinary people must be allowed to recline on couches, eat off tables, and they must "have the sort of food we have today," meaning meat and fish as well.

Socrates agrees that allowing these things too might actually prove useful to the discussion, but not without introducing an important caveat. Whereas the community that he had been describing was "the true one, like a man in health," this new society is "one in a fever." This fevered state needs more than

---

[1] Plato, *The Republic*, 59–61 (for all quotes).

mere "necessaries" and must be enlarged considerably as a result—in occupations, to produce the new goods its people desire, and in territories, to yield more land for pasture and
plough as the population increases. And if the neighboring
states are also in a fevered condition, as is likely, then war will
follow, since the neighbors will also want to expand beyond
their original borders. So now our imagined state requires an
army—a new class of "guardians." The discussion continues.

Interesting, isn't it, that even in the mid-fourth century BC,
when Plato was writing *The Republic*, diet was thought to have
profound enough effects that a widespread change could turn a
once-peaceful, harmonious society on its head? Although it's
clear that the republic that is described in the rest of the book
is not a strictly vegetarian one, it's equally clear that Plato—or
rather, Plato's Socrates—believed the truly ideal community
would be one where the workers did not consume meat of any
kind.

Plato was one of the first social planners—Karl Popper saw
him as the father of modern totalitarianism—and today his
heirs in organizations like the World Economic Forum have
very similar ideas about the necessity of feeding ordinary people, the world over, a plant-based diet in the name of utopia.
This would be something unheralded, a first in human history.
They call it the Great Reset, with good reason. While these proposals for a global food transformation are clothed in today's
familiar garb of sustainability, equality, health, and well-being, the truth is that the logic is not so far from that underlying
the claims Socrates made about the "true" community. A
global, plant-based diet is indeed the right food for a quiescent
lower class—and not just because of the physical and mental
effects of not eating meat either. This global food transformation will be brought about through a corporate takeover of
the entire food supply that will leave the people totally alien-
ated from the production of the food they eat. We will be totally
at the mercy of corporations whose only real concern is not our
health nor well-being, nor indeed our rights, nor the proper

stewardship of the environment, but their own bottom line, plain and simple. This will be a disaster—and it's only the beginning of the twisted system of control the globalists want to establish.

Although this plan is well advanced and has the backing of many of the most powerful individuals and organizations in the world, we still have a chance to stop it. My hope is that this book will not only alert people to the true nature of the problem, but also get them to think about and mobilize effectively against it. Even if you don't agree with all of my ideas, I hope you can agree at least with this one: that we must start to imagine a new way of living, and we must do so fast. Because if we don't, there are others who are more than happy to do so for us instead. And they have a lot to gain at our expense—the whole world, in fact.

RAW EGG NATIONALIST

# INTRODUCTION

## Welcome to 2030

"Welcome to 2030," the headline reads. "I Own Nothing, Have No Privacy and Life Has Never Been Better." Published across multiple sites on November 10th, 2016, this World Economic Forum "thinkpiece" and its title in particular has come to be emblematic of what the Great Reset means, at least to its opponents. This will be our departure point.

The piece, written by Ida Auken, a female Danish politician, imagines a 2030 that has been transformed beyond recognition by the advent of the much-hyped Fourth Industrial Revolution, as new technologies like AI, gene editing, advanced robotics, and the Internet of Things create a new hyper-connected, "smart" global society. We meet a nameless denizen of a nameless city who explains to us just how much things have changed between then and now:

*Welcome to the year 2030. Welcome to my city—or should I say, "our city." I don't own anything. I don't own a car. I don't own a house. I don't own any appliances or any clothes.*

Everything that was once a product has now become a service—transportation, accommodation, food, communication, energy, "all the things we need in our daily lives." After communication and energy became free, the die was cast, and the rest inevitably followed. Nobody needs to own a car when a driverless vehicle or flying car can be called, for free, in a few minutes. And why own or rent a house, when you can just use spaces in the city as and when you need them? "My living room is used for business meetings when I am not there." You don't even need to own cooking equipment, since a "pasta maker or crepe cooker" can be delivered near-instantaneously when you need it—again, for free.

The economy is now totally "circular." Planned obsolescence—the short lifespan that is built in to consumer products today—is no more. Instead, things are made to last and to circulate among people, rather than just going in the bin. Materials are recycled and reused efficiently and cleanly. Indeed, there are now no environmental problems, "since we only use clean energy and clean production methods." There is clean air, clean water, and large parts of nature have been circumscribed because of their value to human well-being. Cities are now much greener places than they ever were before.

But how was all this possible? As well as the discovery of cheap, plentiful forms of renewable energy, this social revolution owes its existence to robots and AI, which have eliminated the need for most work. Labor now has no real value, since more or less all socially necessary work can be done by a machine. What little "work" humans do hardly merits the name. "It is more like thinking-time, creation-time and development-time." This benevolent AI is so powerful that it can make choices for us, since, in a world where everything is data, the AI knows our tastes and preferences as well as, if not better than, we do; in fact, it even knows *when* we want to have things. This can actually be a liberation, we are told, when choosing for ourselves ceases to be fun.

But not everything is well here, if you couldn't have guessed. While the abandonment of ownership and choice have had untold benefits, another form of abandonment pains our nameless guide, although perhaps, it was no less necessary or inevitable all the same. As if to anticipate the backlash that the article itself was about to draw, we're now told about a less fortunate, less enlightened group of people: "those we lost on the way." "Those who felt obsolete and useless when robots and AI took over big parts of our jobs. Those who got upset with the political system and turned against it." Like Aristotle's gods and beasts who live outside the *polis* (city-state), or the strange primitives in Michel Houellebecq's novel *The Possibility of an Island*, these dissenters "live different kinds of lives outside the city," lives that are more or less incomprehensible to those within it. While some have organized and "formed little self-supplying communities," other groups simply inhabit the ruins of the old world, living in "the empty and abandoned houses in small 19th century villages."

These people, presumably, were the ones who refused to believe "that we could not continue with the same model of growth," who didn't realize "that we could do things differently." Maybe—*maybe*—there's some kernel of truth to their protest. It's annoying not to have any real privacy, we're told, annoying not to be able to go anywhere without it being registered somewhere by someone. Even our thoughts and dreams aren't safe—or, at least, it feels that way sometimes. Then again, what was the alternative? After all, these drastic changes were the only way we, as a species, could deal with the witch's brew of threats we'd been facing, almost any one of which could have been fatal on its own, let alone in conjunction with any one or all of the others: "lifestyle diseases, climate change, the refugee crisis, environmental degradation, completely congested cities, water pollution, air pollution, social unrest and unemployment." It was this or disaster.

I've tried to summarize this extremely strange piece as best I can, but if you want the full effect you really have to read the original for yourself—assuming you haven't already, that is. Summaries of course lose something in the retelling, and in this case the strangeness is what's most obviously diminished. It's not just what's said so much as the way it's said. Social changes that should at the very least alarm if not horrify the reader—quite literally, the destruction of more or less everything we know today—are described in this utterly flat, robotic tone, almost like procedurally generated text. It's extremely jarring. So strange in fact, that my initial reaction to the piece was to think it must be some kind of parody. But that was before I knew what I now know about the World Economic Forum and the Great Reset agenda.

Maybe it's just that the author is a Dane (she is) and an extremely liberal one at that. A flat-pack person, with flat-packed views and a flat-packed personality—maybe though that flat-pack tone is quite apt. Isn't it precisely what we'd expect from the inhabitant of a world where so much, perhaps even everything, of what it means to be human has been stripped away and labeled retrograde? For what could possibly animate, excite, or challenge a person living in that nameless city? Parody or no, I thought it certainly wasn't the kind of world I would want to live in. And I wasn't the only one who felt this way—far from it. The backlash against the article, mainly through social media and alternative-media reporting, came thick and fast. Initially, this drew a "clarification" from the author herself, which was added at the end of the piece as a note:

*Some people have read this blog as my utopia or dream of the future. It is not. It is a scenario showing where we could be heading—for better and for worse. I wrote this piece to start a discussion about some of the pros and cons of the current technological development. When we are dealing with the future, it is not enough to work with reports. We should start discussions in many new ways. This is the intention with this piece.*

As a piece of fire-fighting, this "clarification" was an utter failure. The World Economic Forum soon had a raging inferno of public criticism and speculation to deal with—and the time for wet towels was long past. So, at some point—I don't know exactly when—the piece was quietly removed from the Forum's website. Since it was published elsewhere, though, you don't need to read screengrabs or go to the Wayback Machine to read it. It remains up on *Forbes*, for instance.

Although "Welcome to 2030" covers more or less every theme of the Great Reset, from the abolition of private property to the key role of AI and robots, it's worth noting that the phrase "Great Reset" doesn't actually feature in the piece at all. Another essential aspect of the Great Reset that doesn't feature, apart from in passing, is food. Remember that "pasta machine" and "crepe maker"? Our nameless guide appears to subsist solely on carbs, which is actually more telling than you might think, since an integral part of the Great Reset is a transition to diets that are entirely, or almost entirely, plant-based. If you know anything about the Great Reset already, I'd wager that phrases like "You vill eat ze bugs!" and the clapback "I will not eat the bugs!" are likely to be among the first to jump into your head, apart from the ominous "you will own nothing and have no privacy." The truth is, though, that eating bugs is just one small part of what the Great Reset will mean for the way we, as a species, consume food. Alternative protein sources like cockroach milk—four times more nutritious than cow's milk![2] —and new ersatz plant-based meat alternatives are actually just one aspect of a much larger plan for food transformation that turns on two stated needs: to reduce the environmental, especially greenhouse-gas, effects of traditional agriculture and to produce enough food to feed a global population that is projected to reach ten billion by 2050. Be in no doubt: these measures are not incidental to the new planetary tyranny the globalists are fast-building. Control of the food supply has been

---

[2] London, "Cockroach milk is being hailed."

the foundation of the tyrant's fortress since the dawn of agriculture, as we shall see, and in this respect the Great Reset will be no different.

This book, and the eponymous Eggs Benedict Option, are my response to the Great Reset and in particular its vision of a revolution in the way we eat. In place of a globalist model of food production and consumption that will only further sicken us and make us into the compliant slaves the globalists want us to be, I will propose a new, nationalist model to produce and eat food that has the potential to destroy the globalists, at the same time as revitalizing and freeing us—indeed, by doing those very things. But before I lay out my vision, we must examine the Great Reset in more detail.

Just to be clear, what we are dealing with is not a conspiracy theory. In this respect, the Great Reset is nothing like theories about the death of JFK or the moon landings or Nazi bases in Antarctica. I will not be directing you, at any point, to look for boxes of documents hidden in a warehouse somewhere, nor to take my word about missing evidence or witness testimony that came into my possession in shadowy circumstances, nor will I be referencing cryptic tweets by former astronauts about ancient evils lurking under the ice. I won't even be asking you to read between the lines—or, at least, not very much. The policies of the Great Reset and its official slogan, "Build Back Better," are on the lips of prime ministers and presidents, members of royalty, business leaders, celebrity activists and so-called thought-leaders, more or less everywhere you care to turn (with a few important exceptions). The global elites are convinced it will happen, as they now keep telling us, and just this once I think we should take them at their word. No, the Great Reset is not a conspiracy theory. The only thing that's up for debate is whether it's a good or a bad thing. Either this is a plan to change our world for the better by radically transforming the way we live, or it is a plan to enslave the nations to a new form of global corporate government. It can't be both.

## The Great Reset in Depth

Despite the very public nature of the Great Reset plan, until recently the focus of the mainstream media was on debunking it, pure and simple. "The baseless 'Great Reset' conspiracy theory rises again," wrote Davey Alba in *The New York Times*, on November 17th, 2020. "'The Great Reset' Conspiracy Flourishes Amid Continued Pandemic," cried the Anti-Defamation League a month later.

But outright denials have now given way to official recognitions that, yes, the Great Reset is in fact a real thing. In its classic, shameless way, the mainstream media got to change the story once again. The Great Reset itself is no longer a conspiracy theory. Rather, the truth about it is simply being misrepresented. Yes, there really was a World Economic Forum summit called "The Great Reset" in June of 2020; yes, it really was all about ways to transform the world economically and socially; and yes, some of the world's most powerful people really were in attendance (albeit virtually, due to the pandemic), including the Prince of Wales, who gave the opening address— but this was actually a totally benign gathering that has just been "hijacked by conspiracy theories," as the BBC put it in June 2021. "Like many popular conspiracy theories, this one starts with a grain of fact." Thanks, BBC, very cool!

Attempts to gaslight the public about the Great Reset now focus on the pandemic and the claim that it was planned as a means to implement the globalists' "build back better" agenda. I don't have anything much to say here about the origins of the pandemic. What I will say, though, is that the World Economic Forum certainly has a knack for unfortunate timing, hosting a pandemic planning exercise ("Event 201") in October 2019 that managed to predict almost every major aspect of the coronavirus pandemic, from the type of disease down to the social restrictions governments would enact.[3] And it certainly didn't

---

[3] Center for Health Security, "Event 201."

help dispel any dangerous conspiracies when its founder, Klaus Schwab—more on him shortly—then released a three-hundred-page book called *COVID-19: The Great Reset* just months after the pandemic was first declared. Even in those early months, Schwab seems strangely confident of the course the pandemic is going to take.

> *At the time of writing [June 2020], the pandemic continues to worsen globally. Many of us are pondering when things will return to normal. The short response is: never. Nothing will ever return to the "broken" sense of normalcy that prevailed prior to the crisis because the coronavirus pandemic marks a fundamental inflection point in our global trajectory. . . . Radical changes of such consequence are coming that some pundits have referred to a "before coronavirus" (BC) and "after coronavirus" (AC) era.*[4]

The pandemic is not simply a terrible event, Schwab explains: it is also a golden opportunity for the Great Reset. Things cannot—will not—continue as they were: the crisis has laid bare just how broken the system is and how desperately we need a fundamental change. We need an economic reset, a societal reset, a geopolitical reset, an environmental reset, a technological reset, an industry reset, and an individual reset—each of which has its own chapter or sub-chapter in the book. Everything must go!

The book closely follows the agenda that was laid down a month before at the World Economic Forum's 50th Annual Meeting in Davos. As mentioned above, it opened with a speech from the Prince of Wales, in which he outlined a five-point plan for restarting the global economy on a new, sustainable footing. "We have a unique but rapidly shrinking window of opportunity to learn lessons and reset ourselves on a more sustainable path," the Prince said. His five points were as follows:

---

[4] Schwab and Malleret, *COVID-19: The Great Reset*, 12.

## Who (or What) Is Klaus Schwab?

It's not a surprise that much of the resistance to the Great Reset currently focuses on the founder of the World Economic Forum himself, Klaus Schwab. It's an understandable tendency: when we see a plot, especially a grand plot, we seek a mastermind. And there, at the center of an intricate web that spans the globe sits . . . a strange little kraut with glasses, a bald head, and a turkey neck. I've referred to Klaus Schwab as a "thrift-store Palpatine" elsewhere, and truth is, I still don't quite know what to make of him. Evil genius? Figurehead? Distraction?

Space alien?

A lot of interest has been directed towards Schwab's supposed ties to the Rothschild family, something the WEF has been keen to debunk.[5] Other details about his history are less subject to uncertainty, but again I'm not sure what to make of them. A recent article on *Unlimited Hangout* dug deep into the Schwab family history and turned up connections to the atomic-weapons programs of Nazi Germany and Apartheid South Africa.[6] Here's what the article has to say, in brief.

Before and then during the Second World War, Klaus' father Eugen managed a factory at Ravensburg for the Swiss firm Escher-Wyss, which was intimately involved with the Nazi war effort. This involvement included the production of heavy water, a key ingredient for atomic bombs. At the factory in Ravensburg, under Eugen Schwab's management, forced labor was used throughout the war, and a special camp was maintained on the premises for the workers, who included civilians and POWs. After the war, Eugen continued to work for Escher-Wyss and to ascend the world of German manufacturing, apparently without any repercussions.

---

[5] Hudnall, "FACT CHECK: IS KLAUS SCHWAB."
[6] Vedmore, "Schwab Family Values."

In 1967, Klaus completed his studies at Harvard, where he was taught by Henry Kissinger, and went to work for his father's old company, which soon after became Sulzer-Escher-Wyss. Under the younger Schwab, the newly reorganized company began to move away from its roots in manufacturing to become a technology corporation. This included nuclear power, and it would appear that during Klaus' tenure at the firm, he was involved in early attempts by the South African government to develop its own nuclear weapons. Escher-Wyss' involvement in the Nazi atomic-weapons program may have been one reason the South African government sought the company out.

Klaus Schwab's tenure at Escher-Wyss lasted only three years, and in 1971 he founded the European Management Symposium, which would later become the World Economic Forum. One of the key influences in his decision to found the Symposium was the Club of Rome, an early and highly influential think-tank made up of members of the global scientific and financial elite, much like the World Economic Forum today. As is well known, one of the Club's main preoccupations was global population reduction; see for instance its 1972 book *The Limits of Growth*, which warns that "if the world's consumption patterns and population growth continued at the same high rates of the time, the earth would strike its limits within a century." One of the authors of the book, Aurelio Peccei, delivered a speech about it at the third meeting of the European Management Symposium, in 1973.

What does all this mean, though? Johnny Vedmore, the author of the *Unlimited Hangout* piece, believes that we are clearly dealing with a longstanding eugenic dream handed down from father to son. In my opinion, we should be careful not to let such speculation become a distraction. Why do the ultimate motivations of Klaus Schwab matter? What difference does it make whether the World Economic Forum is doing what it's doing to fulfil some ancient conspiracy, or simply to make as much money and have as much power as possible? The things that we can easily verify about the World Economic Forum and its partners—the things that they're actually demonstrably doing—are bad enough on their own terms that we don't need to make them any worse. We have all the reason in the world to oppose the globalists on the basis of what we can readily know at this very moment. I'm not saying, however, that the deeper moral and intellectual roots of the Great Reset aren't important, because they clearly are, as Alexander Dugin shows. I just think there are better, i.e. more urgent, things to be doing than trying to get to the bottom of who—or what—Klaus Schwab is.

1) *To capture the imagination and will of humanity—change will only happen if people really want it.*
2) *The economic recovery must put the world on the path to sustainable employment, livelihoods and growth. Longstanding incentive structures that have had perverse effects on our planetary environment and nature herself must be reinvented*
3) *Systems and pathways must be redesigned to advance net zero transitions globally. Carbon pricing can provide a critical pathway to a sustainable market.*
4) *Science, technology and innovation need re-invigorating. Humanity is on the verge of catalytic breakthroughs that will alter our view of what it possible and profitable in the framework of a sustainable future.*
5) *Investment must be rebalanced. Accelerating green investments can offer job opportunities in green energy, the circular and bio-economy, eco-tourism and green public infrastructure.*[7]

---

[7] Quoted in Dugin, *The Great Awakening*, 1–2. See also Inman, "Pandemic is chance to reset."

There can be little doubt that the pandemic, and especially the lockdown measures, has accomplished many of the things that the World Economic Forum wants to happen as part of the Great Reset, or at the very least laid the necessary groundwork for them. In order to understand these things properly, it is essential that we understand the term "stakeholder capitalism." In 1971, the same year the World Economic Forum was founded by Klaus Schwab, he introduced the term "stakeholder capitalism" in a book entitled *Modern Enterprise Management in Mechanical Engineering*, which drew on his academic background in engineering and economics. The Forum's website describes the term on Schwab's "About" page by means of a maxim: "that the management of a modern enterprise must serve not only shareholders but all stakeholders to achieve long-term growth and prosperity." But what does the system actually entail? In basic terms, it means that corporations should modify their activities to benefit their stakeholders as well as their shareholders. Stakeholders are basically any and all groups that are in a position to lose or gain from a corporation's decision-making—apart from its competitors, of course.

Stakeholder capitalism, in the World Economic Forum's own thinking, is opposed to "neoliberalism," a doctrine which Schwab, in his book *The Great Reset*, claims favors "competition over solidarity, creative destruction over government intervention and economic growth over social welfare."[8] Instead of the exploitation of the neoliberal free market, what we get with stakeholder capitalism is greater cooperation among governments, NGOs and corporations, and also increased governmental intervention in the economy. This is "the return of big government," as Schwab puts it, and it is an inevitability as a result of the global pandemic. Indeed, this is "one of the great lessons of the past five centuries in Europe and America . . . [that] acute crises contribute to boosting the power of the state."[9] In situations like a pandemic, only governments are

---

8 Schwab and Malleret, *Great Reset*, 78.
9 Ibid., 89.

properly placed to make the decisions that need to be made, says Schwab.

"Stakeholder capitalism" is not the only name that has been given to the system advocated by the World Economic Forum. It has been called "corporate socialism" and "capitalism with Chinese characteristics" by Michael Rectenwald,[10] and "communist capitalism" by the Italian philosopher Giorgio Agamben, for instance. The stakeholder capitalist model has been criticized for its obvious tendencies towards monopoly and, as the alternative names given to it above suggest, its tendency to introduce a socialist political system by the back door. And it's precisely for that reason that even some "proper" socialists are now advocating it.[11] It's worth noting, though, that this vision of corporate socialism is not a new one, as the historian Anthony Sutton notes:

*Old John D. Rockefeller and his 19th century fellow capitalists were convinced of one absolute truth: that no great monetary wealth could be accumulated under the impartial rules of a competitive laissez-faire society. The only sure road to the acquisition of massive wealth was monopoly: drive out your competitors, reduce competition, eliminate laissez-faire, and above all get state protection for your industry through compliant politicians and government regulation. This last avenue yields a legal monopoly, and a legal monopoly always leads to wealth.*

*This robber baron schema is also . . . the socialist plan. The difference between a corporate state monopoly and a socialist state monopoly is essentially only the identity of the group controlling the power structure. . . . We call this phenomenon of corporate legal monopoly—market control acquired by using political influence—by the name of corporate socialism.[12]*

[10] Rectenwald, *Google Archipelago*, 54–65 and 123–24.
[11] Campbell, "Towards a Less Irrelevant Socialism."
[12] Sutton, *Wall Street and FDR*, 72.

The pandemic has produced one of the greatest wealth trans-
fers in history. The destruction of working people and small
businesses has made the wealthiest people in the world even
wealthier, beyond even their wildest dreams, and is a giant
leap in the direction of corporate monopoly. A study out of Harvard and Brown, for instance, showed that employment for the
lowest wage earners in the US declined nearly 25 percent during the period between January 2020 and March 31st, 2021.[13]
Millions of small businesses were forced to close due to the lockdowns, and as much as 60 percent of those closures have been
permanent.[14] At the same time, the world's biggest companies—Amazon, Facebook, Apple, Google, Microsoft—were post-
ing eye-watering record profits. Amazon founder and CEO Jeff
Bezos, for instance, added $75 billion to his net worth in 2020
alone, and billionaires as a class in the US increased their net
worth by over a $1 trillion as of January 2021.[15]

Accelerating the tendency towards corporate monopoly is
not the only way that the pandemic has helped tilt the world
in the direction of the Great Reset. In the words of Michael
Rectenwald:

> *Developments advancing the Great Reset agenda include
> unfettered immigration, travel restrictions for otherwise
> legal border crossing, the Federal Reserve's unrestrained
> printing of money, the subsequent inflation, increasing
> taxation, the increased dependence on the state, the sup-
> ply-chain crisis, the restrictions and job losses due to vac-
> cine mandates, and the prospect of personal carbon
> allowances.[16]*

The incredibly close cooperation we've seen among governments, Big Tech, Big Pharma, the legacy media, international

---

[13] The data are available at tracktherecovery.org
[14] Sundaram, "Yelp data shows 60%."
[15] Sainato, "Billionaires add $1tn."
[16] Rectenwald, "What Is the Great Reset?"

and national health organizations, and NGOs is also directly out of the World Economic Forum's playbook. We should consider this a real foretaste of the integrated governance of the Great Reset future. The reach and power of Big Tech, in particular, which Rectenwald has dubbed "the Google Archipelago" in his book of the same name, has grown incredibly in the past two years, as demonstrated by its ability not only to help determine the outcome of the US presidential election through direct and indirect interventions, but also in its newfound confidence to act as the very arbiter of truth on a global scale.

All of the World Economic Forum's efforts have focused, then, on building networks among the most influential persons and organizations in the world, in the private and public sectors. Its copious political and social entanglements are illustrated nicely if we go back and look, for a moment, at the author of "Welcome to 2030," Ida Auken. Auken was a member of the Danish Social Liberal Party, having defected from the Socialist People's Party two years earlier. She is now a serving member of the Social Democrats. While a member of the Social Liberal Party government, she was minister for the environment, just like her uncle, Svend Auken, a famed environmentalist and man often referred to as "the best Prime Minister Denmark never had." The niece has deep ties to the World Economic Forum. She is one of its "Young Global Leaders," described on the group's website as "a community of innovators from diverse backgrounds and experiences" which aims to "inform and influence decision-making and mobilize transformation." Among her fellow "innovators" are Jacinda Ardern (prime minister of New Zealand), Emmanuel Macron (president of France), two Scandinavian crown princes and a crown princess, Leonardo DiCaprio, Mark Zuckerberg (founder of Facebook), Larry Page (founder of Google), and a whole host of other royals, politicians, leaders, activists and titans of business from around the world. Shortly after writing the 2030 piece, Ida became a member of the Forum's Europe Policy Group, and she's now a member of its Global Future Council on the Future of Cities and

Urbanization too. She's also active in the world of business, working as an advisor for various environmentally friendly brands, including one that produces organic children's clothing that can be rented and reused, and for a Danish consultancy that specializes in so-called "corporate social responsibility." Apart from her political and commercial work, she has been a priest in the Church of Denmark, like her mother, and wrote at least three books on religious topics before becoming a member of the Danish parliament in 2007.

While it would be tedious to note all the organizations with which the World Economic Forum has partnered—in 2014, *The Economist* noted that, of 2,622 attendees at that year's annual meeting in Davos, 1,595 were from businesses, 364 from governments, 246 from NGOs, 234 from the press, and 183 from academia—its partnership with the UN is worth mentioning. In June 2019, the two organizations signed a memorandum of understanding that the World Economic Forum would help with the advancement of Agenda 2030, a series of sustainability goals for 2030 that were adopted by all UN member states in 2015. Agenda 2030 is made up of seventeen goals, such as "end poverty in all its forms everywhere" (Goal One), "achieve gender equality and empower all women and girls" (Goal Five), and "take urgent action to combat climate change and its impacts" (Goal Thirteen). Each goal is broken down into further targets, with a total of 169 targets overall. The World Economic Forum has promised to provide funding for the UN's climate-change work as well as providing other assets expertise for "digital governance" to help the UN "meet the needs of the Fourth Industrial Revolution."[17]

Although the coronavirus pandemic is now providing the main justification for accelerating the Great Reset, the term itself has been around for at least a decade. The name had already been coined when the "Welcome to 2030" article was written, in 2016, although it commanded nowhere near as

---

[17] Ibid.

much attention as it does now. Exactly when the name was first minted, and by whom, is unclear, however. One of the themes that I'll explore in this book, with the help of the Russian thinker Alexander Dugin, is how the aims of the Great Reset are a continuation of a much older tradition of globalism. While the "Great Reset" is certainly not a phrase earlier generations of globalists like Bertrand Russell or Julian Huxley would have used, the "hypothetical" situation described in, say, Russell's *The Impact of Science on Society*—namely, the emergence of a scientifically enlightened world government in response to the threat of nuclear war—could easily be described as a Great Reset. It would be hard to see Lord Russell objecting to the use of that epithet, I think. I've even called the vision of a eugenic society outlined in Plato's *Republic* a Great Reset, in my cookbook, *Raw Egg Nationalism*.

We can be certain, at least, that there was explicit talk of the need for a "reset" by the mid-noughties. This was Klaus Schwab at Davos in 2007:

*One thing is for sure: we have to reset our societies, our policies, our selves, if I use computer-networking language. I think it's very important that, in doing this resetting process, we are aware of the latest developments in terms of tools which we use to address these issues.*[18]

That was one year before the Financial Crisis. The economic crash resulted in many things, one of which was an intellectual re-evaluation of the idea of "creative destruction." A 2009 *Atlantic* interview with Richard Florida entitled "The Great Reset" was followed, a year later, by the book *The Great Reset: How New Ways of Living and Working Drive Post-Crash Prosperity*. Florida's argument in the book, like that of the World Economic Forum with regard to the pandemic, is that "great crises . . . represent opportunities to remake our economy and

---

[18] World Economic Forum. "Klaus Schwab."

society and to generate whole new eras of economic growth and prosperity." According to Florida, the Financial Crisis was just one of these Great Resets and would "transform virtually every aspect of our lives":

> *Great Resets are broad and fundamental transformations of the economic and social order and involve much more than strictly economic or financial events. A true Reset transforms not simply the way we innovate and produce but also ushers in a whole new economic landscape. . . . Eventually, it ushers in a whole new way of life—defined by new wants and needs and new models of consumption that spur the economy, enabling industry to expand and productivity to improve, while creating new jobs for work- ers.[19]*

It's unclear what Florida's ties to the World Economic Forum were at the time of writing *The Great Reset*, but he's contrib- uted a number of articles to the Forum's website since 2017, mainly focused on cities and urbanization—his specialization as a university academic. Since 2010 and Florida's book, the number of references to the Great Reset has increased greatly, from *CNN* and *Forbes* articles—such as "Brace Yourself for the Great Reset" in 2017—to the World Economic Forum's annual meetings at Davos, with themes such as "The Reshaping of the World" (2014) and "How To Reboot the Global Economy" (2016).

Public interest in the Great Reset does not appear to have become truly widespread until the summer of 2020, according to Google Trends, with hotspots of interest in the Netherlands, Canada, Austria, Germany and Switzerland. This is probably no coincidence, since June 2020 was when Klaus Schwab's book *COVID-19: The Great Reset* was published; nor is it a coinci-

---

[19] Florida, *The Great Reset*, 5.

dence that these hotspot countries were ones that labored particularly hard under the "emergency" measures brought in to fight the pandemic.

## Understanding the Great Reset in Order to Fight It: Alexander Dugin

Alexander Dugin is one of the most perceptive analysts of the Great Reset, and his short book *The Great Awakening vs the Great Reset* lays out a very useful framework for understanding the plan for global government.

He considers there to be three main points behind the Great Reset:

*Control over public consciousness on a global scale, which is at the heart of "cancel culture"—the introduction of censorship on networks controlled by the globalists;*

*Transition to an ecological economy and a rejection of modern industrial structures;*

*Humanity's entry into the 4th economic order (to which the previous Davos meeting was devoted), i.e. the gradual replacement of the workforce by cyborgs and implementation of advanced artificial intelligence on a global scale.*[20]

Dugin is clear that the Biden presidency represents the real beginning of the implementation of the Great Reset: "The Great Reset begins with Biden's Victory."[21] Under Biden, almost all of Trump's decisions are being reversed, which means a return to policies that push the world away from being multipolar (i.e. having multiple centers of power) back towards a single, unified center of power. The COVID-19 crisis is merely an excuse for the introduction of new technologies and forms of

---

[20] Dugin, *The Great Awakening*, 2.
[21] Ibid., 3.

influence ("mind control") that will help make this possible, by which Dugin clearly means things like health passes and forms of digital identification. American policy is returning to the pre-Trump era, with a renewed emphasis on global interests over national interests, the strengthening of the structures of world government and institutions like NATO, and attempts to weaken and spread instability among the opponents of globalization, whether through so-called "color revolutions" abroad or the use of enhanced surveillance and digital censorship against "domestic extremists."[22]

Although the COVID-19 pandemic is being used as a launch event, if you will, for the Great Reset, this plan for global transformation has a long history, which Dugin thinks is essential to understand it.[23] Dugin sees globalism and the Great Reset not as a break with history, but rather the culmination of liberal ideology, whose roots go back to medieval debates about the nature of ultimate reality. As Dugin puts it:

> *Biden and the forces behind him embody the culmination of a historical process that began in the Middle Ages, reached its maturity in modernity with the emergence of capitalist society, and which today is reaching its final stage . . .*[24]

What did this historical process look like? It began with a debate about the existence of universals (bear with me). To put it in simple terms, medieval theologians split into two camps over the question of whether there are 1) common entities ("universals") or 2) only individual, concrete entities. While those in the former camp drew on the tradition of Aristotle and Plato to argue for the reality of meaningful universal categories and came to be known as "realists," their opponents, "the nominalists," argued that generalizing names of any kind (*nomina*, in Latin)

---

[22] Ibid., 3–5.
[23] Ibid., 7–16.
[24] Ibid., 7.

are just arbitrary conventions and thus have no genuine existence. Although the realists were in the ascendant initially, and the Church actually outlawed nominalism for a time, in the end it was the nominalists and their view of nature that would triumph.

I'm sure the relevance of this debate might not seem immediately obvious to you, but it should become clearer when I spell out, as Dugin does, the stunning implications of the nominalist worldview and its eventually victory over medieval realism. What the nominalist split and final victory amounted to, in Dugin's scheme, was a radical separation—a total separation— of the individual from any form of collective identity. Whether we mean religion, ethnic or racial grouping, or class, all are rendered meaningless, stripped of any force they previously had over the individual. Although the full effects of this separation would take centuries to be felt, we can clearly see, in this ancient debate, the laying of the ideological and the economic foundations of liberalism. Humans are individuals and nothing more, and things, too, are absolute and separate, making it possible for them to be allocated as property to individual owners.

But there was still a long way to go from medieval theologians like William of Occam to the globalists of Davos. Dugin divides the intervening period into three phases, beginning with the emergence of the capitalist order. The bourgeois capitalist order could not have emerged without the destruction of the collective identity and unity of the medieval Church. Nominalism played an essential role in the great schism known as the Reformation, which undermined the authority of tradition and the papacy to interpret scripture and produced numerous Protestant sects each claiming individual authority over religion. This great event was also a fracturing of the political unity of the medieval Church—otherwise known as "Christendom"—and in due course led to a Europe of sovereign nation-states, each of which could be considered as a sort of "political individual." At the same time, the old order of medieval estates (priests, nobles, peasants) began to disintegrate into a single class called the bourgeoisie (a term which originally meant "townspeople"). By the middle of the seventeenth century, then, a new bourgeois order had emerged in Western Europe that was totally at odds with the old. Philosophers like Hobbes, Locke, Hume, Adam Smith, and Kant provided this new order with a developed moral and economic philosophy comprised of capitalism and a historical mission—progress—"to liberate the individual from all forms of collective identity."

The second phase Dugin calls "the triumph of globalisation," as capitalism, through the colonial enterprises of Western European nations, became a global system. And its reigning cast of thought was nominalism, which sat at the center of science, culture, politics and the economy.

In the twentieth century, however, liberal nominalism faced a serious challenge to its global dominance from the left and groups like socialists and communists who sought to overthrow the bourgeois order. From the other wing of the chamber, extreme nationalists also took power in European nations, opposing the bourgeois individualism of liberalism with collective forms of consciousness such as the "nation" and "race." Although these anti-liberal movements were in fact products of Western modernism, they both nonetheless rejected modernity's individualism and the nominalism at its foundation. This shared rejection was well understood by liberal philosopher Karl Popper, who saw these threats to liberalism as two sides of the same coin. Both sides were lumped together as "enemies of the open society."

As we know, neither the communists nor the fascists were able to defeat liberalism in the twentieth century. The capitalist regimes were able to use communism to defeat fascism in the Second World War, before eventually defeating communism in the long Cold War that followed. The ensuing "end of history," as the grand victory of liberalism was famously described by Francis Fukuyama, heralded the real beginning of globalism, according to Dugin, as the world entered a true "unipolar moment" for the first time.

Although it might appear that with the defeat of fascism and then communism in the twentieth century, the liberal nominalist agenda had ultimately come to be fulfilled—"individualism, the market, the ideology of human rights, democracy and Western values had won on a global scale"[25]—in fact, there were still other enemies that remained to be defeated. Thus began the third phase in Dugin's historical process: "gender and posthumanism." Like other forms of collective identity, gender now requires dismantling from a category that is objective, fixed, and meaningful, into a label that represents nothing more than an individual's choice of self-expression—an arbitrary display of the individual's will that can be reversed in an instant. The main enemies, with regard to gender, have become conservative groups and nations that defend the traditional view of the sexes: they have to be beaten into submission and forced to accept the nominalist view of gender, at all costs. In this endeavor the liberals have found powerful allies in the fragmented and confused post-1991 left, which has enthusiastically redirected its efforts from anti-capitalism to gender and identity politics, as well as causes like mass immigration.

The final frontier, if you will, after the dissolution of gender—which is now proceeding apace—can be nothing but the dissolution of personhood itself. This is what is meant by "posthumanism" or "transhumanism": the replacement of human beings as we understand them with hybrid or cyborg entities, artificial intelligence, and genetically engineered beings. Posthumanists and so-called accelerationists are already eagerly looking to the "Singularity," the moment when artificial intelligence assumes the same computational parameters as human beings, as the next stage in history.

This, then, is the moment we have reached in 2022, when, after the long march of nominalism through Western and then global civilization, the Great Reset agenda is being readied for launch. Since the final defeat of communism in 1991, there

---

[25] Ibid., 12.

have been no coherent ideologies to challenge the now-global form of liberalism. By no means, though, is victory assured. As Dugin notes, the globalist plan has now "stalled on several fronts." Putin's Russia, drawing on the nation's ancient traditions and its more recent, communist history of opposition to liberalism, has emerged as a bastion of resistance. Likewise Xi Jinping's China, which has refused political liberalization despite massively growing prosperity and an increasingly global outlook. The Islamic world, too, has continued to struggle to preserve its traditions against Western influence. This has been manifested not just in movements like Al-Qaeda and ISIS, and the continuing rebellion of the Islamic Republic of Iran, but also in the growing independence of nations like Turkey, Afghanistan, and Pakistan from Western regimes. Finally, a wave of populism in Europe and the US has presented a serious threat to the globalists' plans. While the importance of movements like the Yellow Vests in France and Salvini's Lega Nord should not be underestimated, it's clear that the most important, and threatening, event in this populist wave was the election of Donald Trump as US president in 2016. The election of an America First populist as leader of the world's most powerful nation was always going to be a serious problem for the globalists, but even many of those who understood this were shocked by the depth and the desperation of the response from his opponents. The attempts to undermine, neuter, gag and, ultimately, remove Trump started well before he ever entered the Oval Office, continued throughout his presidency, and finally reached their apotheosis in the events of the 2020 election, in which the opposition was forced to throw caution—and their legitimacy—to the wind in order to prevent a second Trump term. And while they succeeded, and a Democrat now sits, albeit in diapers, in the White House, the panic and hysteria have only intensified, because the possibility of a return to America First remains. This is why the Biden administration is doing its best to criminalize America First and its supporters, in addition to ramping up the policy of demographic replacement and other forms of social and cultural disintegration.

This genealogy of the Great Reset, to use a modish term, recommends itself on a number of levels. Not least of all, it's probably the best attempt to place the Great Reset within a broader historical context and to see it not as some kind of aberration from the general course of Western or global history, but as a fulfilment of many of its most prominent tendencies. There is a philosophy underlying globalism: it has its own metaphysics. Only by understanding this can we fully comprehend what is at stake and the depth of the forces arrayed against us. Just as importantly, it gives us a much better idea of how to fight them.

Dugin's own proposed solution to the Great Reset is what he calls "the Great Awakening."[26] "Proposed" may be the wrong word, though, since he sees this as a largely spontaneous phenomenon arising out of grassroots resistance to globalism, particularly in the US. The Great Awakening began in the US—"that civilization where the twilight of liberalism is thickest"—and Dugin sees it exemplified in people like Alex Jones and movements like QAnon, although we might doubt how truly grassroots the QAnon movement is. In its early stages, this movement has been largely one of intuition and instinct rather than doctrine. As Dugin says:

*Unencumbered by serious ideological and philosophical baggage, anti-globalists have been able to grasp the essence of the most important processes unfolding in the modern world. . . . The Great Awakening is spontaneous, largely unconscious, intuitive and blind. It is by no means an outlet for awareness, for conclusion, for deep historical analysis.[27]*

---

[26] Ibid., 27–43.
[27] Ibid., 27–8.

Despite what Dugin sees as the shallowness of much of this opposition, and its tendency to fall into conspiratorial thinking, he believes it is the beginning of a "fundamental historical process."

What's next, then? According to Dugin, the next stage is a broader revolt, as a plurality of different civilizations join together to offer an international front against globalism. Around the world, from Europe to China, from the Islamic world to Russia, there are popular movements and traditions that are intrinsically opposed to the Western liberal worldview. China, for instance, "is a traditional society with thousands of years of history and a stable identity." Its distinct collectivist identity is the source of its resistance to further integration into the liberal world order, despite the fact that it has "taken advantage of the opportunities offered by globalisation to strengthen the economy of its society." While Xi Jinping is "ready to make tactical compromises with the West.... he is strict about ensuring that China's sovereignty and independence only grow and strengthen."[28] What Dugin envisages is a return to a truly multipolar world, where different civilizations are free to pursue their own futures.

This next stage will also necessarily involve active theorization, which has been missing from the early stages of the Great Awakening. In the case of the West, Dugin believes we must look back, beyond liberalism, to older native traditions untainted by nominalism, and also beyond our own cultural and historical boundaries to Eastern traditions. It is as part of this theoretical turn in the Great Awakening that I humbly wish *The Eggs Benedict Option* to serve. This book is not simply a description of the globalists' terrible plan for life in the near future, or of its probable effects, but also a serious attempt to imagine an alternative vision that can guide our action today and in the coming weeks, months and years.

---

[28] Ibid., 36.

## The Eggs Benedict Option

As the WEF acknowledges, to meet the stated needs mentioned earlier (reducing the environmental impact of food production at the same time as producing enough food for ten billion people) will require a massive intensification of industrial agriculture, including the use of a wide array of new technologies and genetically modified organisms, so that everybody can be fed an almost entirely plant-based diet. What the WEF places less emphasis on acknowledging, although it is no less important to the plan, is that this will involve a more or less total consolidation of corporate control over the world's food supply. This is a trend that is already well advanced in places like the US, where a handful of mega-companies, by pursuing vertical integration, dominate the market for meat and other foods. Tyson Foods is one of those companies. Every stage of the process of, say, producing chickens for food is controlled by one company or another that is a subsidiary of Tyson. The breeding stock on the pullet farm—raised by a Tyson company. The raising of the chicks till they reach the right age for culling and processing—done by a Tyson company. The culling and processing—again, a Tyson company. And so on, right to the end consumer. This model allows companies like Tyson not only to gain control over the raw materials needed for their business, but also to maximize their profits and share of the total market.

What I want to do in this book is explore the potential implications of this globalist plan for food transformation, especially with regard to human freedom and human health. The question of freedom is the less complicated of the two. With regard to freedom of choice—just one aspect of the freedom question—it's quite obvious that the globalists will not seek a democratic consensus on a global transition to plant-based diets and corporate control of the food system. Of course, there must be a pretense of consent—a velvet glove—but the fist inside it will be iron all the same. This change to eating habits is

## *What Is Raw Egg Nationalism?*

Good question! It's in the name: raw eggs + nationalism = raw egg nationalism. But maybe that needs just a little more unpacking. Here goes.

Raw egg nationalism blends a focus on individual health and vitality, as exemplified by the consumption ("slonking") of large quantities of raw eggs, with an anti-globalist political stance. This is not some absurdist union, chosen at random. Quite the opposite, in fact. For it is the same forces that tell you not to eat raw eggs—one of the most perfect natural foods in existence—that are leading the anti-human political crusade that seeks to crush the human spirit and destroy the nations, all in the name of profit and global political control. The enemies of human freedom want you to be fat, sick, depressed, and isolated, the better to control you and to milk you of as much economic value as possible, from cradle to grave. We, the raw egg nationalists, want you to be fit, healthy, and free, because the nation needs you. And a nation is only as strong as the people it is composed of.

Only strong nations, confident and united in their own self-interest, can resist the global game of divide and rule. Just look at Donald Trump, for all his faults and failures. Look at the visceral fear, the desperate scrambling, the all-or-nothing sabotage he forced his opponents to engage in, who are the architects and profiteers of ceaseless global war, unrestricted immigration, corporate greed, and mass censorship. Their hatred of Trump is the best evidence that his policy of America First is the antidote to their poison, or at least an essential ingredient of it.

For raw egg nationalists, the egg is not just a potent source of nutrition: it is a symbol of a new world waiting to be born, as well as the means to deliver it.

one that *must* happen, and it must happen *fast*. 2030, the globalists' D-Day, is less than eight years away, although it's possible that the globalists won't be able to move as fast as they'd like to.

The truth is that a great many people simply do not want to give up eating animal products, even if they are offered plant-based alternatives that are supposed to be indistinguishable from them. Can you blame them? Studies have already made it quite clear that the most effective way to get people to eat plant-based foods is not to give them a free choice, but to limit their options, and to make use of social pressure, rather than trying to make claims about the superior taste or health benefits of plant-based foods, which consumers generally don't seem to buy. One study, conducted by researchers at the University of Westminster and published in December 2021, reports that meat-eaters are more likely to eat vegetarian food in a restaurant setting if more than three-quarters of the menu choices are vegetarian.[29] Another study shows that clobbering people over the head with the comparative "social and health costs" of eating meat and plant-based foods before they eat is by far the best way to get them to choose the latter rather than the former.[30] Manufacturers of plant-based alternative foods are waking up to the fact that to beat the real things, they must avoid competing directly with them on their traditional merits as foods. Oatly, for instance, is one brand to watch if you really want to see this new style of marketing taking shape. As part of its "Help Dad" campaign, the oat-milk manufacturer ran a series of adverts in which woke teenagers ambush their bewildered, hopelessly unhip fathers and berate them for daring to want a glass of cow's milk. The simple desire for a glass of milk becomes a humiliation ritual for the older generation. The effect is repellent—I must say—with an unmistakable reek of the

---

[29] Parkin and Atwood, "Menu design approaches."
[30] Ye and Mattila, "The Effect of ad appeals."

Stasi about it. But, more and more, this will be the way of the future.

There is also a far deeper story to be told about the relationship between human freedom and control of the food supply. Elsewhere I've talked about the Neolithic Revolution, when the first settled agricultural states emerged in the Near East, as the very first Great Reset, and I want to explore this idea in greater detail here, by providing an account of the changes of the Neolithic Revolution that's informed by some of the latest scholarship on the subject. I'll use this account to set up some provocative comparisons with the Great Reset today, both in terms of the Neolithic Revolution's consequences for human freedom and in terms of its consequences for human health. Contrary to the popular narrative of historical progress, the hunter-gatherers of the Near East were not desperate to abandon their roving lifestyles in order to be settled agriculturalists. In fact, they did everything they could to resist this change which, like the Great Reset, heralded a total transformation of their way of life. Once this deep context has been established, I'll then consider the agricultural system of the Great Reset in detail, with a particular focus on the work of the EAT foundation, a WEF-partner organization that has produced what it calls the "Planetary Health Diet." Together, these two chapters will form Part One of the book, "Great Resets Old and New."

In Part Two, I'll lay out my own alternative to the Great Reset, the eponymous Eggs Benedict Option. This will be my first attempt to elaborate on the philosophy of raw egg nationalism at length, and will see me drawing on a detailed example from a surprising location. In contrast to the globalist system at the heart of the Great Reset, I'll outline what I consider to be a truly nationalist system of food production, one that places local communities and their needs first. The system I outline could have massive social, physical, and political benefits for the nation. Because, as I've said before, the nation is only as strong as the individuals who make it up. The globalist enemies of the nations know this, which is why they aim, in more or less everything they do, to sicken, isolate, and depress us. The Eggs Benedict Option is, I believe, the antidote not only to the Great Reset, but also to the current system, which has already done so much to destroy the health and vitality of the individual. Indeed, it's important to understand that the current system, at its worst, is not all that different from the Great Reset. In fact, as Alexander Dugin's important analysis of the Great Reset reveals, the liberal world order is actually just one stop on the road to that final goal, one that leads from a bitter theological difference of opinion in the Middle Ages directly to the deracinated hell-world of "Welcome to 2030." This is just as true of the way we produce food as it is of our worldview.

When I lay out the Eggs Benedict Option, I'm going to focus on America, for a number of reasons. First, because I think it has a special role to play in defeating the Great Reset. This was amply demonstrated by the Trump presidency, for all its failures, and the prospect of a return to America First in the Land of the Free is clearly a terrifying one for the globalists—hence the desperate scrambling of the Biden presidency, with its attempts to criminalize true patriotism and to accelerate the "American carnage" Trump promised to end in his inauguration speech. Second, because the industrial farming system is at its most developed—and therefore its worst—in the US. If anywhere is ripe for root-and-branch reform of the way its food is produced and consumed, it's the US. And third—let me be quite honest with you, reader—because that's where my main audience is! Even so, there's no reason why the vision of a new nationalist agriculture couldn't be applied elsewhere, either in North America or Europe. Of course, the specific context would be different, but the essential principles, especially the emphasis on locally produced and distributed food, would remain the same. Raw egg nationalism is not the exclusive property of one nation in particular, but of all people who wish to live lives of great health and happiness. It's that simple.

Since I've started laying down a few ground rules here, I might as well continue for a moment. One of the things I think we need to avoid, at all costs, is playing the enemy's game on the enemy's ground. This is something traditionalists seem to have a very hard time not doing. How many times have we seen some prominent conservative figure waste an entire interview in denying that they're racist or sexist or transphobic, and never actually get to speak on their own terms? The entire policy manifestos and decision-making of "conservative" parties take shape within a totally hostile landscape, and so inevitably assume a defensive character that's greatly disabling. The left has understood, and still understands even now, much better than the right the need to determine the terrain of political warfare. This is why the long march through the institutions was recognized as being so crucial so early on, and why it has been such a catastrophic success. Anyway, in the present case, what I mean is that in trying to fight the Great Reset, we shouldn't accept the premises that lie at the heart of it and are being used to justify all of its sweeping changes. Yes, I believe we should be better stewards of the environment—much better stewards in fact—and should work on local, national, and international levels to reduce the terrible damage that's being done to it. But this is not the same as accepting the increasingly shrill demands of the climate-change crowd, including the World Economic Forum. *Yes, but what are we going to do about rising sea levels? We're literally going to be drowning and boiling to death in twelve years, sweaty!*

The problem is that environmentalism has become synonymous with "climate change," leaving little space for discussion of anything else. In terms of environmentalism, my priorities would be very different. I would focus on the impact of pesticides and herbicides, soil erosion, monoculture and the loss of biodiversity, and the threat of genetically modified organisms, for starters. Many of these problems are part and parcel of the present industrial system of agriculture, which the Great Reset aims to intensify in its quest to feed ten billion people by 2050. I would also focus on the massive contamination of our environment by estrogenic substances, otherwise known as xenoes-trogens, many of which are used in the production of plastics. These substances, which mimic the effects of the hormone es-trogen in human and animal bodies, are wreaking havoc on the health of creatures at almost every level of the food chain, caus-ing weight gain, behavioral changes, and serious reproductive defects that threaten the continuity of many species—includ-ing us. A "spermageddon" scenario, in which all men become actually or functionally infertile, is a very real possibility in the coming decades, and is the focus of a new book, *Count Down*, by Professor Shanna Swan, a reproductive health expert at Mount Sinai University, New York. Following projections of current trends, Professor Swan argues that by 2045 the sperm count of the median man will have reached zero. In basic terms, one half of all men will have no sperm at all, and the other half will have so few that they might as well have none. Although Professor Swan and her work are having a media moment, in-cluding an appearance on Joe Rogan, this is an issue the public is still largely unaware of.

Equally, I don't agree with the claim that we must trans-form the agricultural system to feed ten billion people in the coming decades. Quite simply, I view global population growth as a strategic, but not a moral, concern for the West. All the projections show that the population of Europe, at least, will barely grow and may even shrink in coming decades. The vast majority of population growth will be outside the West, espe-cially in Africa, whose population is projected to increase five-fold by the end of the century, reaching 5 billion. How, then, is this growth our problem? Why should we surrender our way of life because of changes beyond our borders? I've yet to see a convincing moral argument put forward, and doubt there ever will be one. But, in any case, what good are moral arguments in a survival situation? And, be in no doubt, the coming popu-lation explosion is a survival situation for the West, perhaps—surely—the gravest it has ever faced. In the coming decades, if even the same proportion of the African population chooses to migrate out of Africa as does now, Europe will be swamped. What's more likely, though, is that as conditions worsen due to population increase, an ever greater proportion of the African population will make the journey north. Choosing to help African nations with their food supplies may be one part of a determined effort to prevent mass migration, but my feeling is that harder measures, which treat the invasion as the hostile act that it is, will be necessary if Western nations wish to survive. That's a big if, though.

The one premise of the Great Reset that I think we can accept, however, is that now genuinely is a perfect opportunity for us to think about the path we're on and decide to make a meaningful change. Klaus Schwab is right: the pandemic has revealed how broken our current system is, as well as who it ultimately benefits and who it doesn't. This really is a once-in-a-lifetime opportunity—just not for the kind of change that the globalists want.

In order to see fully what the future might hold for us if the globalists get their way, so that we can formulate our own counter-plan, we must first go back in time, to 2030 BC and what I've called "the original Great Reset."

# Part One

## GREAT RESETS OLD AND NEW

# CHAPTER 1
# WELCOME TO 2030 BC:
# THE ORIGINAL GREAT RESET?

*Hard is the life when naked and unhouzed*
*And wasted by the long day's fruitless pains,*
*The hungry savage, 'mid deep forests, rouzed*
*By storms, lies down at night on unknown plains*
*And lifts his head in fear, while famished trains*
*Of boars along the crashing forests prowl,*
*And heard in darkness, as the rushing rains*
*Put out his watch-fire, bears contending growl*
*And round his fenceless bed gaunt wolves in armies howl.*

*Yet is he strong to suffer, and his mind*
*Encounters all his evils unsubdued;*
*For happier days since at the breast he pined*
*He never knew, and when by foes pursued*
*With life he scarce has reached the fortress rude,*
*While with the war-song's peal the valleys shake,*
*What in those wild assemblies has he viewed*
*But men who all of his hard lot partake,*
*Repose in the same fear, to the same toil awake?*

– William Wordsworth, *Salisbury Plain* (1793–94)

There's a story about the birth of agriculture and it goes something like this. Before there was proper agriculture—the regular sowing of annual grain harvests—life was hard for man. Of course, life would go on being hard for man after the establishment of proper agriculture, but before that Archimedean moment, before man started cultivating grains, life was *really* hard. Without agriculture, primitive man was totally dependent on his ability to hunt and kill game, fish, and fowl, and to gather berries, nuts, wild honey, and tubers. All of this involved not only a high degree of fitness and skill, but a significant measure of danger too, and the best foods, meaning the most calorie- and nutrition-dense foods, came at the highest potential cost. So while a Plains Indian (a latter-day Stone Age man) might have subsisted on insects and moss if driven to it by circumstance, he would much rather have eaten fresh liver and still-beating heart and drunk warm blood—and that meant hunting buffalo on the plains or game in the forest, activities that could just as easily be fatal as unsuccessful.[31] Thomas Hobbes said that in the state of nature—before man was subject to sovereign power (i.e. states)—man's life was "nasty, brutish and short," and the poet of *Salisbury Plain*, nor untold other poets, artists, philosophers, and thinkers, didn't disagree either.

By contrast, grain agriculture brought abundance and regularity, and with abundance and regularity, safety. Man could predict and master nature, and therefore his own destiny, in a way that simply had never been possible before that moment. With enough seeds and a proper understanding of the seasons, man could produce a regular harvest of nutritious food that didn't require great physical prowess or bravery—just a certain amount of drudgery—to produce and gather. And who wouldn't prefer a little drudgery over a hunting wound that, if not immediately fatal, would likely fester and still prove a death sentence all the same? A predictable food supply, barring the

---

[31] On their diets and those of the Mountain Men: Holston, "The Diet of the Mountain Men."

occasional crop failure, meant larger populations could be sustained. It meant other things too. It meant that man could get to thinking about and doing the things that really matter: like building towns and cities, for instance; like developing new technology and engaging in commerce, scholarly pursuits, and education; civilization; progress; man's inexorable destiny. In short, man was—and is—much better off as a cereal-cultivating, sedentary creature than he had been as a fully or semi-nomadic hunter-gatherer.

Societies tell themselves stories that justify their institutions and history, whatever they may be, and we are products of the great agricultural revolution as much as Thomas Hobbes, William Wordsworth, or the first farmers of the Near East. No healthy society willingly portrays itself as being on the wrong side of history (which is why the new origin stories Americans tell themselves, like the 1619 Project, are so revealing). And, to some extent, such stories must be true. Ideologies have to be, for people to believe them, at least in the long run. Dispute its benefits all you will, but there's no disputing that grain agriculture radically changed the world. How different the world would be without it, we can scarcely imagine. If you want to try, though, imagine sustaining large urban centers or cities in any other manner. How would it be done? A history of civilization without cities is, for many, an oxymoron.

But it's also equally clear, as recent scholarship is revealing in greater detail, that such an account of the transition to sedentary agriculture is far from complete. The triumphalist tone appears more and more misplaced, at least if the process is being considered from the perspective of those undertaking it. Actually, a better phrase would be "subjected to it." Because instead of there being overwhelming evidence for a strong "social will to sedentism"—in simple terms, a clear desire among hunter-gatherers to leave behind the difficulties and dangers of their lifestyle for the "obvious" benefits of the new agriculture—again and again we see that the first farmers were forced to settle and were then held in place. Forced and then held? By whom? Initially, the answer appears to be by broader environmental conditions, but hot on the heels of changing climate and dwindling natural resources come predatory elites and a totally new phenomenon in the history of man: the first states. Coercion and unfree labor were an essential part of the transition to agriculture, without which it would probably never have been successful. Without force and the threat of violence, the early agricultural states would simply have collapsed, and even with those things on their side, many still did. The archaeological and written record tells us—screams at us—why the people were desperate to leave. Early agricultural man was malnourished, suffering physical stunting and new forms of ill health like rampant tooth decay. He was also prey to new epidemic diseases caused by crowding of not just his fellow humans but also freshly domesticated animals like pigs, sheep, and fowl. Life became a nightmare.

The more we get to know what being an ancient hunter-gatherer was *really* like, the more we understand why early man might have resisted a change to this way of life. The hunter-gatherer's life was one of abundant wild harvesting of animal and plant life, and could even involve a very lazy kind of proto-farming of wild grains. A 23,000 year-old site from the Rift Valley, for example, shows a diet spanning four food webs: twenty large and small animals, sixteen families of birds, and 140 kinds of fruits, nuts, seeds and pulses, as well as a myriad of plants for medicinal and craft purposes.[32] Unlike the standard version of the story of the agricultural revolution, it's not irrigation that plays a key role in the emergence of the first agricultural settlements, but what James Scott calls "wetland abundance"—the sheer cornucopia of resources available to people living on or near rivers, marshes, floodplains, estuaries, and the sea. For this reason, the bountiful area between the Tigris and Euphrates rivers, which will also be referred to as

---

[32] Scott, *Against the Grain.* 41.

the "Southern Alluvium," was ground zero of the first agricultural revolution, and it's here that our attention will be focused. The evidence suggests that hunter-gatherers chose to settle in and close to the wetlands simply because they had ready access there to such a wide range of resources, from food to medicine to building materials, that it would have been stupid not to. Why look a gift horse in the mouth? Over time, though, as these people became permanent agriculturalists under the power of the early states, their horizons would narrow to just a few plants and a few animals, whose tending required a total change to their way of life. The domestication of crops, as well as animals like pigs and cattle, entailed the domestication of man himself. Viewed in its full aspect, it's no wonder that man had to be forced to accept this new life—often multiple times, in fetters and at the business end of a spear.

This new version of an old story is worth telling for a number of reasons. Not least of all, because it's the truth, and more people deserve to know it. But in the context of this book in particular, I want the true story of early agriculture to serve a very particular aim. What I want is to provide a "deep context" for the Great Reset, because I believe there are a number of very close parallels—continuities, even—that can be drawn out and will prove illuminating. The emergence of agriculture is often referred to as "the first agricultural revolution" or the "Neolithic Revolution," and the advocates of the Great Reset, including Klaus Schwab himself, refer to their pet project as requiring a "new agricultural revolution." But this doesn't just mean that the Great Reset will require a revolutionary intensification of agricultural practices, which it will. The Great Reset, like the Neolithic Revolution, will be a total revolution, bringing very similar political, social, and even physical—yes, physical—changes in its wake. As I'll lay out in the next chapter, the transition to a WEF-endorsed plant-based diet, although it may benefit millions of starving and obese in the short term, will not be a boon for our health, but will instead make us prey to many of the ill effects suffered by the first farmers of the first states. For all these reasons, I'm suggesting, and have suggested in the past, that the Neolithic Revolution was, in fact, *the original Great Reset*. Above all, this chapter is a story about the co-emergence of new diets and new forms of social control. It is the most vivid dramatization we have—a real example—of how a totally new social and economic structure emerges from, and is necessarily built upon, a fundamental transformation to the production and consumption of food. We should believe it, because it happened. And that means, among other things, that such a thing can happen again.

A quick note. The account that follows will draw heavily on James C. Scott's book, *Against the Grain: A Deep History of the Earliest States*. This is a fantastic book that everybody should read, and the first place you should go if you want a fuller account of the process I describe below. Another essential book is Steven Mithen's *After the Ice*, especially for the information on Abu Hureyra and Çatalhöyük. It's also worth noting that, while an unavoidable part of the development of fixed agriculture involved the domestication of certain animals, the focus in this telling will be on the cultivation of grains, except when I come to talk about the development of novel pathogens—one of many stings in the tail of this new way of life.

## The Dawn of Agriculture in the Wetlands[33]

The first evidence for plant cultivation and sedentary communities dates back about 12,000 years. Modern *Homo sapiens* is believed to have emerged as a separate sub-species 200,000 years ago, and appears to have spread outside Africa and the Levant within the last 60,000 years. So for 95 percent of modern man's total history, and 80 percent of his history outside Africa, man was not a cultivator who lived in fixed settlements, but a hunter-gatherer who lived in small bands, separate from

---

[33] This section draws on Scott, *Against the Grain*, 43–115, unless otherwise noted.

one another, moving across the landscape. What's more, it's not until around 3000 BC, many thousand years after the emergence of cultivation and sedentism, that we finally see the emergence of the first early states, like Uruk, around the Tigris and Euphrates rivers—which is quite some lag. Providing an explanation why will get right to the heart of the matter of what was at stake in the Neolithic Revolution. So let's do that now.

At a place called Abu Hureyra, in what is now north-western Syria, on the banks of the Euphrates, we can see the beginnings of sedentism and agriculture develop.[34] If you were to travel back in time and visit Abu Hureyra about 14,000 years ago, what you would see would hardly resemble a village as we know it today. Like at 'Ain Mallaha, a woodland site in the hills overlooking the Sea of Galilee, the dwellings at Abu Hureyra seem to be a part of the very landscape itself: cut from the soft rock, with reed-covered roofs at waist height, supported by wooden poles. Much of the work takes place outside the home, in the open, where the people grind and prepare plants they have collected from the surrounding wetlands and the steppe and also prepare animals that have been caught by the hunters. For the hunters, one of the main quarries was wild gazelle, which migrated through the area in vast numbers at particular times of the year. The summer migration would have been a particularly frantic time, as the hunters rushed to catch as many gazelle as possible and then the villagers prepared and preserved them as best they could for the rest of the year. When the gazelle weren't around, the hunters would have caught pigs and wild asses in the surrounding valleys.

The village, if we can call it that, at Abu Hureyra appears to have been a good spot. There is evidence that it was more or less continually occupied for about a thousand years, according to the accumulation of debris, during which time the people continued to hunt the gazelle and gather their plants and

[34] See Mithen, *After the Ice*, 40–45 for a detailed discussion of Abu Hureyra.

started to build dwellings that stood totally above ground. But the good times were about to come to an end. The Younger Dryas, an 800-year period of glacial cooling beginning about 13,000 years ago, would cause serious climatic disruption, altering the movements of the gazelle and making the steppe surrounding Abu Hureyra a far less productive environment. As a result, Abu Hureyra was abandoned, and for all we know its inhabitants reverted to their former lives as nomadic hunter-gatherers.

In about 9000 BC, the site would be inhabited again. This time, though, it was by farmers who built houses out of mud bricks and grew wheat and barley on the surrounding river plain. They continued to hunt the gazelle for another thousand years as well as farming, before suddenly switching to herding sheep and goats.

The story of Abu Hureyra is instructive for the history of early agriculture because it illustrates the importance of positioning, and in particular what Scott calls "wetland abundance." Unlike previous versions of the story of the transition to farming, it appears that it wasn't irrigation that was central to the development of sedentism and farming in the Near East, but the pre-existing natural bounty of wetland regions. (In fact, if early sedentary people were likely to engage in any kind of water-management, it was drainage, rather than irrigation.) Modern historians and archaeologists have had difficulty grasping this, in part, because the region between the Tigris and Euphrates rivers, the Southern Alluvium, has changed considerably between then and now. While today it is mostly an arid zone between the two rivers, once upon a time it would have looked much more like the Mississippi Delta, an enormous wetland system crisscrossed by hundreds of smaller channels whose paths were constantly subject to change. The whole area acted like a huge sponge, sucking up water during the high-flow season and then gradually discharging it in the dry season. The human inhabitants of these marshes would reside on "turtlebacks," patches of ground just above the level of the water, rather like the *chenier* plain of the Mississippi. From these islands, the inhabitants had access to the whole range of resources, both edible and inedible, that the wetlands had to offer:

*[R]eeds and sedges for building and food, a great variety of edible plants (club rush, cattails, water lily, bulrush), tortoises, fish, mollusks, crustaceans, birds, waterfowl, small mammals and migrating gazelles . . .*[35]

At the same time, the wetlands allowed movement by reed boats, which made resource collection much easier and facilitated trade. It's also worth noting that these wetlands were situated at the overlap of different ecological zones, such as steppe, estuarine, and marine zones, meaning that a well-placed settlement would allow access to the resources of some or all of them without the inhabitants ever needing to relocate.

It's clear then, that although sedentism brought with it its own problems, such as crowding and the accumulation of waste—all of which the first sedentary peoples would have been well aware of—the benefits of living permanently or semi-permanently in these watery environments may simply have been so great as to outweigh them. Why constantly move when you have everything you need in the surrounding environment? And what's a little extra trash if your main sources of food, like the gazelles that fed Abu Hureyra, arrive on your doorstep via a kind of primitive DoorDash each year?

There's good evidence that some of these communities, as well as harvesting wild grains, also began to experiment by cultivating them too. Given the pre-existing abundance that surrounded them, it's natural to ask why they would do this. After all, pre-industrial agriculture, especially plough agriculture, is extremely labor-intensive. Wouldn't this just be extra work?

---

[35] Scott, *Against the Grain*, 50.

Again, the wetlands provide the answer. These early experiments with farming are likely to have involved a form of "flood-retreat farming." This means, basically, that you let the water do most of the work for you: you simply wait for the annual floodwaters to recede, and then plant seeds in the soft layer of silt that remains. The land is effectively harrowed and fertilized with zero human input. This form of agriculture is still practiced today around the world, including on the banks of the River Nile, and is seen as the least labor-intensive of all types, whatever the crop may be.

So this, in somewhat condensed form, is the story of how sedentism and grain agriculture came to be, long—millennia, in fact—before what we would recognize as agricultural states ever existed, and it all comes down to the richness of the wetland environments. The question remains, then, of how sedentary farming went on to become not just the dominant mode of production in the region, but how it also came to support a totally new kind of political entity: the state.

Given what's already been said about the place of natural abundance and the ease with which people could live in wetland environments, something must have changed. It's hard to see why these sedentary hunter-gatherers, who might occasionally throw some cereal seeds into the mud if they felt like it, would want to become full-time farmers if they didn't have to. Indeed, it's worth looking ahead, for a moment, to dwell on what it actually meant to make the transition from one form of life to the other. It might be best to begin by thinking of this change in terms of the "tempo" of life. Whereas hunter-gatherers had to be attuned to a multitude of different natural rhythms—of birds, of large mammals like gazelles, of fish and marine life, of a huge variety of wild plants—the early grain-agriculturalists had to attune themselves primarily to the rhythms of often just a single plant, as well as a certain small number of domestic animals. So while at one moment the hunter-gatherer might be preparing for a great migration and the next getting ready to gather a harvest of nuts or acorns, the agriculturalist would be strapped in to a year-long routine that relied more or less entirely on the needs of the grain or grains he hoped to bring to harvest: field clearing, sowing, weeding, watering, guarding the crops, harvesting, not to mention the daily tasks involved in preparing grains for consumption, like pounding, grinding, and making bread. There was little the early agriculturalist did that did not in some way have to do with a vital single plant or plants. In a very real sense, the move to agriculture represents not just the imposition of a new rigidity and uniformity to life, but also a form of alienation from nature—something that can be seen dramatized in frightening, lurid detail at the ancient site of Çatalhöyük.

There is a broader, and more provocative, thesis to be made about domestication of grains and animals, namely, that this process also entailed a domestication of man himself. Despite the fact that it is ultimately man who eats the wheat or pig, the questions does remain of who or what was really serving whom or what. At the very least, it's clear that domestication was not a one-way street. Early agriculturalists can consistently be identified from their skeletons alone. The bones of women from grain-growing communities bear tell-tale marks of the labor they had to perform, such as bent-under toes and deformed knees as a result of all the time they spent kneeling to grind grain. But there are broader morphological changes too that suggest closer analogies with the processes of domestication in plants and especially animals. Just like domesticated animals, agricultural man also suffered a process of physical shrinkage. Skeletal remains show that agriculturalists were smaller than their hunter-gatherer counterparts, and their bones and teeth often show signs of nutritional deficiencies and stress. And while it's true that human shrinkage—smaller tooth size, facial shortening, a decline in stature and robustness, and less sexual dimorphism (differences in size and shape between males and females)—actually appears to have taken place over a longer time period than just the Neolithic Revolution, the transition to agriculture nevertheless left a distinctive imprint on the human form. Anthropologist Helen Leach has even suggested that there is a "distinctive syndrome" of domestication associated with the changes of the Neolithic Revolution. Whether such physical changes also led to changes in behavior, as in domesticated animals, is hard to say on the basis of skeletal remains alone. It isn't beyond the realm of possibility, though, to imagine that settled agriculturalists also experienced the same reduction in "emotional reactivity" as domesticated animals display due to changes in the brain's limbic system, which controls fear, aggression, and flight response, among other forms of behavior.

There were also physical changes of another kind, with equally wide-ranging and yet more dire consequences. The changes of the Neolithic Revolution created a "perfect storm" of pathogens, due to the novel crowding of people and animals that agriculture necessitated. Under such conditions, new strains of pathogens, specifically adapted to humans, were able to emerge and wreak havoc. Although there is little evidence in the archaeological record, since few diseases leave tell-tale marks on human bones, once written records became available, the evidence for epidemic disease in the first states was plentiful. The Epic of Gilgamesh may provide the first description of death by epidemic in its description of bodies floating in the Euphrates, and other early texts are believed to refer to tuberculosis, typhus, bubonic plague, and smallpox. The threat and fear of such diseases is perhaps best attested in the fact that the Akkadian word for "epidemic disease" translates, literally, to "certain death."

Sedentism, even before the full adoption of agriculture, brought about immense new concentrations of people. The earliest permanent settlements would have had population densities ten or twenty times higher than anything man had experienced before this point—perhaps between one and two thousand people living in close contact. This number, in turn, was dwarfed by the early states, such as Uruk, where between twenty-five and fifty thousand people lived—another ten or twentyfold increase. And this is before we take account of the huge numbers of domestic animals, scavengers, and pests that would also have shared the space with them. Scott goes so far as to describe these settlements as "feedlots" for pathogens, and he's not exaggerating. Almost all of the infectious diseases caused by microorganisms that are specifically adapted to humans came into existence in the last ten thousand years, and many of them in the last five thousand. Until recently, these diseases represented the major share of human mortality. This isn't to say that hunter-gatherers didn't suffer from diseases or parasitic infections, just that they suffered from different kinds, which weren't due to overcrowding.

The effects of these new diseases, which were bad enough on their own, were compounded by nutritional deficiencies brought on by the new grain-based diets. A symposium on the health effects of the Neolithic Revolution noted that nutritional stress is not something that's widely observed until the advent of grain agriculture. From then on, various kinds of nutritional stress are evident in the skeletal record, including forms of bone malformation associated with iron deficiency, rickets, and tooth decay. These were almost certainly due to early farmers having a diet rich in carbohydrates but lacking in protein and high-quality fats. Evidence for anemia is particularly strong in the case of agricultural women, owing to blood loss through menstruation. Although evidence of soft-tissue conditions is not forthcoming from the skeletal record, there is some written evidence to suggest, along with our own modern dietary knowledge, that beriberi, pellagra, riboflavin deficiency, and kwashiorkor would have been common among early farmers.

The full effects of these revolutionary transformations were still some way ahead for the early sedentarists of the Southern Alluvium. Nonetheless, scholars are clear that only a "gun-to-the-head" theory can explain the transition to full dependence on agriculture. In the beginning, at least, long before the establishment of the early states, it looks like it was something, rather than someone, that had its finger on the trigger, so to speak. It may be the case that human population increase simply put too much pressure on ecosystems, especially more prized sources of food like large game, with the result that more and more people were forced, as Scott puts it, "to exploit resources that, while abundant, required more labor and were perhaps less desirable and/or nutritious."[36] The archaeological evidence definitely shows, as time passes, a decline in consumption of large wild animals and an increase in consumption of starchy plants, shellfish, and smaller birds and mammals. The long-term role of the climate is unclear, at least after the passing of the Younger Dryas period of cooling, as described in the case of Abu Hureyra. As we move closer to the first states (i.e. closer to around 3000 BC), though, population pressure and the decline of larger game become much more clearly evident as the most probable causes of the growing movement towards grain agriculture.

In truth, it's not actually necessary to know the exact causes so much as to be able to demonstrate that the move to a primary reliance on agriculture was clearly not some process that followed inexorably from adopting sedentism and cultivating grains. Yes, hunter-gatherers could remain in one place and they knew how to cultivate grains, but that didn't meant they had to. And when they had a free choice and were surrounded by the greatest abundance, they appear to have chosen not to rely on grain farming very much, if at all. By the time we get to the first grain-based states, though, the dynamic has radically changed, because for the first time we have not circumstances but people forcing other people into the position of being cereal-cultivating sedentary farmers. This, and in particular the frequent resort to actual slavery, serves to throw into the starkest relief the cost of the Neolithic Revolution for those who would be its principal laborers.

---

[36] Scott, *Against the Grain*, 94.

## Çatalhöyük: A Neolithic Nightmare

The UNESCO World Heritage site of Çatalhöyük in southern Anatolia (modern-day Turkey) is one of the most important sites for understanding the transition from hunting and gathering to settled agriculture. The site, first discovered in 1958, is unusual for its preservation, size, and length of occupation. Situated around two hills, Çatalhöyük comprises thirty-seven hectares and shows evidence of occupation from about 7400 BC to 5200 BC. As well as providing an array of wall paintings, reliefs, sculptures, and artistic features that allow us entry into the spiritual and mental world of its inhabitants, the well-preserved habitations—a dense, streetless row of houses placed back to back—give further insight into life in one of the earliest proper urban centers in the Near East. Let's just say it wasn't pretty.

In his book *After the Ice*, Steven Mithen dedicates an entire chapter to describing just how unpleasant life must have been at Çatalhöyük.[37] As the time-traveling guide of the book ("Lubbock") approaches the settlement, having previously only visited small proto-urban settlements in the area, he realizes he is now somewhere "unlike any place that [he] has seen."

*It appears to have a continuous perimeter wall, one that has no entrance and no desire to welcome uninvited guests. Looking more closely, Lubbock realizes that it is not a single wall at all, but the outcome of many abutting walls from individual buildings that cling tightly together as if in fear of what lies beyond. A dirty, rubbish-strewn river stagnates along one side, leading to stinking swamps and marshes beyond the town. On the other is a muddy pond around which goats are settled for the night.[38]*

[37] Mithen, *After the Ice*, 88–96.
[38] Ibid., 92.

Once Lubbock manages to access one of the houses via a trapdoor on the roof, he finds a familiar Neolithic domestic scene. Familiar, that is, until he turns and is confronted by a "monstrous scene of bulls bursting from the wall." Such twisted sculptures have some precedents at Neval Cori, for instance, an earlier site that featured a large bird, probably a vulture, with a woman's head in its talons, and bizarre half-human half-animal hybrids, but the figures at Çatalhöyük are much more numerous and much more alarming.[39] The walls around the bulls are decorated with geometric designs and handprints, but unlike the famous handprints found in Ice Age caves, these ones seem to be "more of a warning or a plea for help" than a welcome from the inhabitants.

As Lubbock journeys through the rest of Çatalhöyük—"a nightmare vision of the world that farming has brought to these particular members of humankind"—he encounters strange figurines, including a woman sitting on a throne with a leopard on each side of her, their tails wrapping around her body, and everywhere those bulls, varying in pose from room to room, but "always shocking." In one room a pair of breasts project out from the wall, but the nipples are split apart and vulture, fox, and weasel skulls peer out from inside. "Motherhood itself is violently defiled."

Archaeologists have emphasized the order of the spatial arrangements throughout the settlement, which has no precedent in earlier sites, and the "remarkable uniformity in artifact design," again without precedent. The houses were all built to a fixed template, with the same designated areas for different activities.

*To me, it seems as if every aspect of [the inhabitants'] lives had become ritualized, any independence of thought and behavior crushed out of them by an oppressive ideology manifest in the bulls, breasts, skulls and vultures.*[40]

---

[39] Ibid., 89.
[40] Ibid., 95.

While earlier settlements were the products of people who seemed to trust the natural world and felt themselves to be a part of it, Lubbock finds it hard to resist the conclusion that "the people of Çatalhöyük . . . seemed to fear and despise the wild."

I think this account of life at Çatalhöyük fits nicely with what James Scott has to say about the kind of changes the Neolithic Revolution brought to ordinary people's lives, in particular, that the transition to settled agriculture was essentially a form of "de-skilling," a disengagement from a wider nature into a much narrower form of life governed by the rigid biological schedules of just a few grain plants. And of course this new relationship to nature—we might call it "alienation"—would have been reflected in the mental world of early farmers too.

The origins of this new mental world are likely to be illuminated further through cutting-edge genetic analysis. In the main text, I talk briefly about potential changes to the limbic system of humans due to their "domestication" as farmers. The limbic system is a very ancient part of the brain that deals with emotion, behavior, and memory, among other things. At the time when James Scott was writing *Against the Grain*, the study of ancient genetics was less well established than it is now, so his conclusions about domestication of the brain were very impressionistic and based on analogy with domesticated animals. But now a new paper, "Population Genomics of Stone Age Eurasia," has revealed a variety of telling genetic traits associated particularly with the first farmers of the Near East. The paper notes: "Loci [genes] associated with mood-related disorders, like increased anxiety, guilty feelings, and irritability are over represented in Anatolian farmer ancestry."

Did these genetic changes produce Çatalhöyük, in all its frightening aspects, or were they a product of living there? Maybe it was both? Whatever the case may be, it's no wonder so many early agriculturalists fled places like Çatalhöyük, and the grain-state cities that would replace them, as soon as they could.

## The First States[41]

By the fifth millennium BC, there were many settled populations living in small towns of perhaps a thousand or so inhabitants growing crops of domesticated grains. Although such settlements existed outside the Southern Alluvium, the most durable, long-lasting, and stable examples were to be found within the Alluvium, exploiting the continuing abundance of the wetland environment.

As we've already seen, these early settlements represented a novel concentration of manpower and food production in the history of mankind. Never before had so many people lived together in a single place and produced harvests of food in such a manner. These settlements were not, however, states in any real sense of the word. They lacked the necessary forms of social stratification including kings, administration including tax officials, institutions like armies, monumental structures like palaces, and, most importantly of all perhaps, city walls. Rather, these novel urban centers provided the necessary conditions for states to emerge. While there might be settled grain-farming populations in the Alluvium that had no state, there could be no early states without settled farming populations. This doesn't mean that there was no central authority in these non-state settlements, though. As Steven Mithen points out:

> As soon as farming had begun, the surpluses arising from the new, high-yielding genetic variants [i.e. domesticated grains] had come under centralized control, as is evident from the buildings at Jerf el Ahmar in 9300 BC, Beidha in 8200 BC and Kom K in 5000 BC. From the very start of farming, food had become a commodity, a source of wealth and power for those who controlled its distribution.[42]

---

[41] This section is drawn from Scott, *Against the Grain*, 116–82.
[42] Mithen, *After the Ice*, 509.

What states essentially did, in Scott's terms, was to "harness" the grain-producing power of these early settlements for their own purposes. "Parasitize" or "capture" might actually be more fitting terms, since it's abundantly clear that coercion and unfree labor, up to and including slavery, were essential to their efforts, as we'll see. The city-state of Uruk looms largest in the historical record of the earliest states, because of its size and development, and because it pioneered the form that would later be seen at Nippur, Kish, Isin, Lagash, Eridu and Ur. Uruk's city walls enclosed an area twice the size of classical Athens, nearly three thousand years later, and were probably home to between twenty-five and fifty thousand subjects.

It's worth reflecting, for a moment, on how grains actually enabled these early states to emerge and function. In short, we're talking about taxation. Grains are the only kind of crop that can produce a suitable surplus to form the basis of taxation. No grains, no taxation. It's that simple. But why? Because, in Scott's words, grains are "visible, divisible, accessible, storable, transportable and 'rationale.'"[43] Although other starchy plants may have some of these desirable characteristics, none has all of them. Tubers like potatoes can be hidden (i.e. they're invisible and thus inaccessible) and dug up when needed—often lasting as long as a year or even two underground—whereas a grain harvest ripens above ground and more or less simultaneously, making the tax collector's job a real breeze. If a tax official, or indeed an army, turns up at the right time, they can simply cut, thresh, and take as much of the harvest as they choose. (In the Middle Ages, when the tithe ("tenth") was in force, that was precisely how things worked: the cut grain would be assembled in the fields and the collector would come and take a tenth of it.) Non-grain peoples, by contrast, particularly hunter-gatherers, live in ways that make taxation all but impossible. If you're a state official, finding these people, especially if they're mobile, will be a problem in

---

[43] Scott, *Against the Grain*, 129.

itself, even before you decide what exactly it is they're supposed to give you and in what quantities. Fish? Gazelle? Nuts and berries? There's no way to guarantee they'll even have any of these things when you decide to turn up, let alone in the amounts you might want to ask of them. Neither of these problems arises, though, if you have a sedentary population producing grains.

Why and precisely how early states emerged are questions that are difficult to answer. The time around 3000 BC appears to have been one of severe climate change, with a marked decline in sea levels and the water volume in the rivers, forcing settled populations in the Southern Alluvium to concentrate more and more around what water remained. Still, this doesn't provide a why or how. Did state organization emerge organically from within these increasingly dense settlements, whether by popular or minority decision? Or were these settlements captured, quite literally, by forces from outside? The second possibility is at least as likely as the first, given how common throughout later history it was for sedentary agricultural populations to be captured by non-settled peoples, who then became the social elite in charge. The Mongol conquests are by far the most spectacular instance of this second possibility.

What matters, ultimately, is that we are in the age of the early state, and things are now very different. The central principle of early statecraft was the acquisition and control of populations for the production of agricultural surpluses, and it is for this reason that Scott has called the early states "population machines." As the Russian economist Chayanov proved decisively, however, peasants do not produce surpluses—at least, not willingly. Under ordinary circumstances, they will simply back off from work once they have produced enough to meet their needs. If you want to get peasants to produce surpluses, then, you must compel them, and this is precisely what the early states did. Coerced labor, in various forms up to and including full slavery, was absolutely essential to the existence and ongoing survival of all early states, especially since the worst aspects of the transition to agriculture were now in massive effect. The most terrible social and physical effects—the drudgery, alienation from nature, reduced physical health, and increased susceptibility to epidemic disease—all manifested themselves at once, making these early states extremely fragile things, always inches from collapse. Only a massively increased reproduction rate and constant influxes of new people could prevent this. As a result, one of the principal means to produce a sizeable surplus was war. For early states, war was less a matter of slaughtering your enemies and conquering their territory, than capturing as many of them, and their families, as you could and putting them to work in your fields and granaries. Early states rarely boasted about taking territory, because that wasn't what they really wanted or needed.

Although slavery, like agriculture, was not in any sense "invented" by these early states, they were responsible for employing it on a previously unseen scale. Human bondage has been widely practiced throughout history and is well documented in non-state peoples on more or less every continent. Under the new agricultural states, though, slavery became an essential tool to maximize the extraction of surplus produce—the purpose of the state. Just how central slavery was to the development of more or less all states, in all places, is attested by the fact that, until as late as AD 1800, perhaps three-quarters of the world's population existed under some form of servitude.

This is another very clear sense in which the agricultural revolution represented a domestication of man. Scott cautions us to take seriously Aristotle's claim that a slave is a tool in the same sense as an ox. Although it might offend modern sensibilities, Aristotle was not joking. Slaves became as integral a part of the early state's means of production and reproduction as livestock and grain fields. A society like classical Athens was composed of a majority of slaves, as much as two-thirds of the population, according to Moses Finlay. In such a society, slavery was considered a natural institution and the question of abolition never arose. The same too was true of Sparta, the only difference being that the Athenian slaves were largely captives taken in war, while the Spartan "helots" were indigenous agriculturalists who were conquered by the Spartan elite and made to work for them.

The domestication analogy can be pushed yet further. "At the very center of domestication is the assertion of human control over the plant's or animal's reproduction, which entails confinement and a concern for selective breeding and rates of reproduction."[44] What to make, then, of the strong preference for capturing women of reproductive age? Clearly, early states were not just interested in the physical labor these women could perform. This preference is something that was also evident among, for example, the fearsome Comanche, when they raided European settlements on the frontier. Men, old women, and male children would usually be killed outright, while young girls and fertile women would be captured and spirited away back to Comancheria.[45] Given the challenges to human health presented by life as an agriculturalist in the early states, it's probable that constant influxes of captured women may have been necessary to ensure a stable reproduction rate. I'll have more to say about the effects of malnutrition on fertility in the next chapter. Other aspects of custom and law, such as the institution of land in property and the division of labor within the household would also have had the practical effect of domesticating women's reproduction.

It's no wonder that the early states were extremely fragile things, prone to collapse as much due to internal—epidemic disease, revolt, exhaustion of natural resources—as external pressures like war. It's also not hard to imagine that such collapses, seen from the perspective of ordinary workers, were in fact positive things to be welcomed. Scott actually talks of a "Golden Age of Barbarians," when it was still possible to escape the reach of the agricultural state and live a totally different

---

[44] Scott, *Against the Grain*, 181.
[45] See Gwynne, *Empire of the Summer Moon*.

form of life as a so-called "barbarian." This Golden Age, which I'll return to at the beginning of the final chapter of the book, would last for millennia, until perhaps at least AD 1600, when the state at last became the dominant mode of political organization across the length and breadth of the globe. "Until then a large share of the world's population had never seen a (routine) tax collector or, if they had seen one, still had the option of making themselves fiscally invisible."[46]

Be these things as they may, the die was cast nonetheless: once the Neolithic Revolution was consummated, the state form, based on the control of a grain-based agricultural surplus and the settled population that produced it, was here to stay. Life would never be the same again.

### Dairying and the Bronze Age Steppe Expansions

Owing to a series of revolutionary studies of ancient DNA, we now know that the genetic character of more or less all Europeans was fixed through a series of migrations from two main sources in the last 10,000 years. The first source was a migration of Neolithic farmers from what is now modern-day Turkey (c. 9,000 years ago) and the second, steppe pastoralists (c. 5,000 years ago) from the Pontic-Caspian steppe in southern Ukraine and Russia. The Yamnaya, the principal steppe people in question, have been dubbed "the most murderous people of all time" (*New Scientist*) and "the most violent group of people who ever lived" (*Daily Mail*). These monikers are not sensationalist. The genetic studies reveal that while the Neolithic farmers who made the earlier journey into Europe brought their families with them, only Yamnaya men made the journey into Europe from the steppe, replacing the male Early European Farmers they found. The Yamnaya migration, then, looks like one big mounted warband that either killed or enslaved the Neolithic

---

[46] Scott, *Against the Grain*, 252.

men of Europe and took their women as wives. Although many of the academics who have been instrumental in these revolutionary studies are now doing their best to walk back the full implications of the genetic data they have revealed—mainly because they fear such an account too closely resembles ideas about European and Aryan history promoted by the Nazis—the data speaks for itself. The horse has bolted.

One aspect of the Yamnaya culture that's receiving increasing amounts of attention is their lifestyle and diet, since we already know, for instance from the case of the Mongols, that pastoralists are generally healthier and more robust than neighboring agricultural peoples. As a result, pastoralists have also enjoyed military advantages over their settled neighbors.[47] Was this so for the Yamnaya vis-à-vis the Early European Farmers? It certainly looks that way. A new paper, published in the summer of 2021, shows that the emergence of dairying—keeping livestock for milk—allowed the Yamnaya people to expand rapidly across the steppe and may have driven their "invasion" of Europe.[48] Using protein analysis of teeth samples, the authors of the new paper show that the Yamnaya consumed milk and various forms of milk product from cows, sheep, goats, and horses. They also consumed fish and meat from livestock and gathered a variety of local plants. By comparison with the early agriculturalists, the Yamnaya would have been incredibly well fed, and notably larger and stronger. The ability to produce nutritious milk products "on the hoof," combined with the newfound mobility conferred by horse domestication, allowed the Yamnaya to increase their range massively, from the Altai Mountains in the East, to Europe in the West (nearly 4,000 miles). History would never be the same. Got milk?

[47] See for instance, Weatherford, *Genghis Khan*, 87, 92.
[48] Wilkin et al., "Dairying enabled Early Bronze."

## The Original Great Reset

*"Great Resets are broad and fundamental transformations of the economic and social order and involve much more than strictly economic or financial events. A true Reset transforms not simply the way we innovate and produce but also ushers in a whole new economic landscape... Eventually, it ushers in a whole new way of life—defined by new wants and needs and new models of consumption that spur the economy, enabling industry to expand and productivity to improve, while creating new jobs for workers."*
— Richard Florida, *The Great Reset,* pg. 5

It should be clear now, I hope, that my talk of the Neolithic Revolution as the first Great Reset has something to it. A broad and fundamental transformation of the economic and social order? Check. Transformation of the way we innovate and produce? Check. A whole new economic landscape? Check. New wants, needs and models of consumption? Check. Expanded industry? Check. New jobs for workers? Check. Of course it seems incongruous to describe events in the Stone Age in such wonkish terms—I can't picture Gilgamesh launching his latest slaving raid in the name of "spurring the economy" or "increasing productivity"—but, regardless, the point stands. All of these things resulted almost immediately from the adoption of settled grain agriculture under the aegis of the very first states. The further forward in time we go, as the ramifications of the Neolithic Revolution multiply, and the ripples spread outward, the more obviously is the definition fulfilled.

The only aspect of the definition that might be stretched by the Neolithic Revolution is the timeframe. As I said when I rounded out the last section, it took millennia for the form of the state to become dominant the world over, but dominant it did become. Although it might have taken longer for the Neolithic Revolution to make its effects known than the economic resets of America in the 1870s or during the Great Depression (the two main examples Richard Florida uses in his book), the birth of agriculture was nonetheless a totalizing event. For this reason, I think, it thoroughly deserves the moniker "Great," as well as "Reset." (It's worth remembering that things in the distant past tended to happen a good deal slower than they do today. Just look at a map of travel times before railways, for instance, to see how much slower life was even two hundred years ago.)

Making this comparison has been essential for my purposes here, because I want readers to be in no doubt how intertwined dietary and social transformation can be. We might even ask whether one could happen without the other. Whatever the answer to that question, a revolution in food production and consumption is certainly what will underpin the World Economic Forum's vision of the Great Reset—a "broad and fundamental transformation of the economic and social order" that will take not thousands of years to come to full fruition, but perhaps less than a decade. Knowing this, and everything else I've said about the Neolithic Revolution and its effects, we can now turn to the writings of the WEF and its partner organizations on this looming food revolution, and in particular to the idea of a "Planetary Health Diet."

# CHAPTER 2
# THE PLANETARY HEALTH DIET:
# A NEW GLOBAL DIET FOR AD 2030

*"As the world's premier forum for international economic cooperation, the G20 carries responsibility for leading the resilient recovery of the global economy from the coronavirus crisis. Resilient recovery is not possible without transforming food production and consumption. Food has emerged as a macro critical risk to global economic stability."*

– EAT Advisory Board, Open Letter to the G20

In the summer of 2020, the EAT Foundation sent an open letter to the leaders of the G20, the world's twenty most powerful nations, on the subject of global food production and consumption. The letter's opening words are quoted above. According to the letter's authors, the first twelve weeks of the pandemic had already revealed that "resilient recovery from Covid-19 [*sic*] can only be achieved by radically transforming our food systems." Food, in their words, is "at the heart of the global risk landscape." While this was just as much the case before 2020, we didn't realize it—at least not enough. It has taken the emergence of a new respiratory virus and its rapid spread across the world to reveal just how broken the existing system is.

COVID-19, the authors say, is both a "cause" and an "impact" of this state of affairs. Dismissing the even-then very credible possibility that the virus was a lab release, the authors state quite baldly that it is instead a "virus spill-over from wildlife associated with human incursion into intact ecosystems for food, and food trade"—a cause of global risk. On the other hand, it is an "impact" of global risk, because its spread has exposed and amplified existing inequalities. Among the listed inequalities are "obesity and diseases associated with unhealthy food," which have increased mortality from COVID-19, as well as food shortages, displacement of workers, and disruption of supply chains. In short, COVID-19 was a disaster waiting to happen.

And yet, despite all the efforts of governments around the world, "not one of the measures in our current field of focus— vaccine development, social distancing, testing, the wearing of masks, economic shutdown—can address the root causes behind zoonotic pandemics," i.e. of diseases transmissible from animals to humans. And this before you even factor in the "far more dangerous climate disruptions or the accelerating extinction crisis already underway." Eliminating the potential for another zoonotic pandemic like COVID-19 is only the beginning of the work that must be done.

Modern food production and consumption, in their entirety, must be rethought. They are "undermining the main shields protecting humanity from harm." Having cited various authorities to prove their point about this need for radical transformation, and in particular the EAT Foundation's own "authoritative" commission with *The Lancet* into "Food, Planet, Health," the letter's authors then lay out their proposal. They implore the G20 to institute a new global agenda, "grounded in the best available science and economic analysis, and guided by established universal norms." This agenda must address at least seven key elements, which are, in brief: the protection of remaining natural ecosystems, on land and sea, from further encroachment by farming; the production of nutritious carbon-neutral food; policies to improve access to such food; a reduction of food waste by at least half; economic policies that put sustainability and equity at the center of the global recovery; a focus on sustainable, healthy, ethical investment by corporations, at the expense of "narrow, short-sighted profit"; and, last of all, the creation of a new system of information to allow people to lobby in favor of the necessary changes and make better food choices, both in terms of sustainability and health.

So far, so familiar—or at least it should feel that way. As I've already explained in the Introduction, the EAT Foundation is a partner with the World Economic Forum, but if you missed that—or if you forgot—you wouldn't have a hard time guessing some kind of connection between the two organizations just from reading the open letter. The rhetoric is near-identical with that of Klaus Schwab in his book *COVID-19: The Great Reset.* As they say, *COVID-19 as a one-in-a-lifetime opportunity to transform the world for the better—we just can't go on as we were before, etc.* And of course the dreary "Build Back Better" slogan features at least once too, near the end of the letter. As well as the message, there's also the timing, which hardly seems coincidental: both the book and the open letter were released in the summer of 2020, when most people were struggling to make sense of what the pandemic actually meant. Not the World Economic Forum, though, or the EAT Foundation either. Funny, that.

The letter is a great illustration of what the EAT Foundation, and behind it the World Economic Forum, does with the stakeholder capitalism model, not only in terms of the ideas put forward but also the means by which they are spread and adopted. The letter is addressed directly to the G20, which, in the authors' own words, accounts for "85 percent of the world economy and three quarters of world trade," and the letter's signatories—the EAT Advisory Board—are a who's who of corporate, academic, governmental, and non-governmental figures, including members of Google, Greenpeace, the Harvard

T.H. Chan School of Public Health, the Wellcome Trust, and the government of Pakistan.

The EAT Foundation will be a particular focus in this chapter, because it is one of the main ways the World Economic Forum advances its Great Reset agenda in the world of food, and because it has produced the most sustained attempts to define exactly what people's eating habits are going to look like in the world of the Great Reset. I'll also supplement the EAT Foundation's work with other material from the World Economic Forum's website, which regularly features articles on the subject of the future of food. In particular, I'll be looking at the so-called "Planetary Health Diet," which was developed out of the EAT-*Lancet* Commission on Food, Planet, Health mentioned in the open letter. The Planetary Health Diet is, as the EAT Foundation proudly trumpets, the first truly global diet: a set of dietary guidelines that are intended to apply to everybody on earth, regardless of who they are or where they live—or almost everyone, I should say. There's no reason to believe that our globalist overlords will be changing their dietary habits any time soon; after all, their counterparts in the Neolithic, the predatory elites of Ur, Uruk, Lagash, et al. didn't. But the point remains that this new diet is intended to be part of a uniform, truly global revolution in the way food is produced and consumed—the first such in human history. It hardly needs saying that it will not—indeed, could not—be a voluntary change.

What I want to do in this chapter, besides outlining the Planetary Health Diet, is to try to make sense of what it would really mean for the world if it were implemented. The impacts of the diet can be split into two broad categories: environmental-social and physical. By "environmental-social," I simply mean how the proposed changes to agricultural practices and food distribution would affect the environment and the people involved in those activities, especially the farmers. We've already established that the Great Reset is a process that will involve, among other things, the abolition of probably all forms of private property and new total forms of tracking and surveillance. There is no question that we are talking about a massive restriction of individual freedom with the adoption of this diet, so I won't labor this aspect of the social effects. As far as the environmental impacts are concerned, I want to reiterate what I said in the introduction about not making the mistake of fighting the battle on the enemy's terrain. The Planetary Health Diet is framed, above all, as a means of drastically reducing the carbon footprint of agriculture. Although I'll have something to say about whether or not the proposed changes to agricultural practices would actually benefit the environment—and proper stewardship of the environment is an integral part of the Eggs Benedict Option—I won't be evaluating the Planetary Health Diet's potential to mitigate the harmful effects of global warming. I just don't accept the premises and neither should you. The fact that some of the practices that are central to the Great Reset vision of transformed global agriculture, especially the production of lab-grown meat, may actually turn out to release more carbon than traditional agriculture is an amusing but largely incidental one; nevertheless, it does deserve mention.

Probable physical changes to health as a result of adopting the diet will be a more significant focus of this chapter. I take it as a given that a diet based around the kind of whole foods our ancestors ate is vastly superior to any alternative, and especially to an almost totally plant-based diet—which virtually no societies, certainly not ones we might wish to emulate, have ever adopted—but, even so, I think the reasons why deserve some explanation. I'll discuss the pioneering work of Dr. Weston A. Price, who charted in real time the degenerative effects of changing from an ancestral to a modern, carbohydrate-heavy diet, and I'll also consider the negative effects of some of the main constituents of the Planetary Health Diet, which include phytoestrogenic foods like soy, vegetable and seed oils, and predominantly plant-based sources of protein. This will also be where I consider the potential ill effects of consuming genetically modified food, which is a key component of the World Economic Forum's plan. While the negative environmental effects of cultivating genetically modified crops are bad enough, the danger to human health and longevity by consuming them, and other forms of genetically modified food, is no less clear and present. We are meddling with forces we don't fully understand, and the long-term health effects are anybody's guess. Previous incidents, perhaps most notably the Showa Denko incident, when thousands were injured or killed by a food supplement created by genetically modified bacteria, illustrate the potentially tragic risk of simply assuming that genetically modified products are safe for consumption until proven otherwise. If a plan to feed the world, or indeed any community, can be built only on the consumption of such foods, well, I say it is no plan at all.

This is also where I get to make some more provocative comparisons with the physical effects of the Neolithic Revolution. In the previous chapter, I talked about the abundant physical record that shows the terrible price man paid as he transitioned from the rich plenty of hunter-gathering to settled agricultural lifestyles. Like today's Great Reset, this involved a massive narrowing of his food choices. It is my contention that the Great Reset could similarly result in very obvious forms of physical decline for the majority of the world's population. Could we even end up with a literal two-tiered society, as was the case in earlier periods like the Middle Ages, when the nobles towered over most of the peasantry? Perhaps we won't arrive at the tiered society of the Eloi and Morlocks from *The Time Machine*, the famous H.G. Wells novella—at least not by 2030—but it's a possibility that deserves consideration. And funnily enough, the notion that man might have to be shrunk to reduce his carbon footprint has actually been put forward by a prominent "bioethicist" affiliated with who else but—no prizes if you guess—the World Economic Forum. Among his many bizarre and sinister claims, S. Matthew Liao, a professor at NYU, has also suggested genetically modifying people to make them allergic to meat, in the manner of the alpha-gal syndrome brought on by a lone star tick bite, so that they couldn't eat meat even if they wanted to. Yes, you read that right. I'll talk some more about him and his insane ideas in a separate section within this chapter.

Before I examine the Planetary Health Diet in detail, it's worth spending a little more time looking at the EAT Foundation itself. What is this organization and what does it do? The EAT Foundation is, in its own words from its website, "a global non-profit startup dedicated to transforming our global food system through sound science, impatient disruption and novel partnerships." EAT began in 2013 as an initiative within the Stordalen Foundation, a private charitable foundation established by Norwegian billionaire Petter Stordalen and his wife Gunhild, to promote "sustainable business." The Stordalen Foundation is committed to a vision of pushy philanthropy, in which charitable donations are matched by pressure on key institutions and decision-makers—or "necessary nudges," as the Foundation's website puts it. Gunhild Stordalen, who sits on the board of trustees of EAT Foundation as its president, alongside representatives chosen by each of the partners, is heavily enmeshed in the food-NGO scene. As well as being part of the World Economic Forum Stewardship Board on Food Systems, she advises the UNICEF Advisory Group and the UN's Scaling Up Nutrition Movement Lead Group. In 2021, she played a key role in the UN's Food Systems Summit.

Two more partners joined the Stordalen Foundation when the original EAT initiative became the EAT Foundation, in 2016. These were 1) the Stockholm Resilience Center, a joint governance and management initiative between Stockholm University and the Royal Swedish Academy of Sciences, and 2) the Wellcome Trust, the fourth wealthiest charitable foundation in the world. The Wellcome Trust was founded in 1936 with a legacy from Henry Wellcome, the British founder of one of the precursors to pharmaceutical giant GlaxoSmithKline, with which the Trust still maintains a number of strategic partnerships. The Trust's main focus is on research into improving human and animal health, including heavy involvement in disease research, such as the Ebola Emergency Initiative. The Trust has also been heavily involved in research into treatments for COVID-19. This resulted in sharp criticism when its financial interests in many of the pharmaceutical companies involved was revealed. In 2021, a report in *The BMJ* showed that the Trust had a £275 million stake in Novartis, which manufactures therapeutics including dexamethasone, and a £252 million stake in Roche, which makes monoclonal antibodies.[49] It's worth noting that the trust's portfolio of investment goes well beyond biomedical companies. It also owns Farmcare, for instance, Britain's largest lowland farming organization, which it bought from the Co-Operative Group in 2014, for £249 million.

The EAT Foundation has a number of different initiatives and partnerships to promote its vision of sustainable and healthy eating. One particular focus is cities. The Food Systems Network, for instance, comprising fifty member cities across five continents, aims to support "city efforts to create and implement integrated food policies that reduce greenhouse gas emissions, increase resiliency and deliver improved health and nutrition outcomes."[50] Another initiative, known as CHEW ("Children Eating Well"), involves a partnership with UNICEF to "create thriving and equitable cities for children." Other focuses include: the Good Finance Initiative, in partnership with the global investor network FAIRR Initiative, which encourages governments and corporations to foster healthy and sustainable food-production practices; FOLU, the Food and Land-Use Coalition, a private-sector initiative launched at the UN to "transform the global food and land-use systems," with initial efforts focusing on Colombia, Indonesia, and Ethiopia; and the

---

[49] Schwab, "Covid-19, trust, and Wellcome."
[50] Quoted from the EAT Foundation's website, available as at the time of this publication

Plant-Forward Global 50 Ranking, a list of fifty chefs and restaurants "who are advancing plant-forward food choices" and "providing inspiration for change." EAT'S biggest initiative, though, is FReSH ("Food Reform for Sustainability and Health"), which it describes as "an effort to drive the transformation of the food system and to create a set of business solutions for industry change." When the initiative launched in 2017, twenty-five corporations were involved, and the number has now grown to over thirty, among which are Bayer, Cargill, Danone, Deloitte, DuPont, Google, Ikea, Kellogg's, Nestlé, PepsiCo, Syngenta, and Unilever. FReSH involves a total re-evaluation of the food system at every level, from consumption, through retail, packaging, and distribution, to production, "to determine what levers business can pull to contribute to food system reform in order to create healthy and enjoyable food for all, produced responsibly, within planetary boundaries by 2030." (You'll notice that I've been quoting the EAT Foundation's words quite liberally. As unpleasant as it might have made the previous few paragraphs to read, this was a deliberate choice on my part. I think it's important to understand the way this hideous flat language is used to disguise what's really going on. The fact that a scheme like the Great Reset can be more or less encapsulated in slang like "Own nothing, eat bugs, live in the pod" is powerful testament to this deception, and part of the reason why such slogans are so infuriating to the globalists.)

As diverse as these initiatives might seem, they are almost all united by drawing on the findings of the EAT-*Lancet* commission on Food, Planet, Health, to which we'll now turn. It's here that the notion of a "Planetary Health Diet" is developed and explained.

## The Strange Case of S. Matthew Liao

In mid-2021, footage resurfaced of a bioethicist proposing a series of bizarre solutions to the threat of man-made climate change. Speaking at the 2016 World Science Festival ("the Davos of Science"), S. Matthew Liao, who has held appointments at Oxford, Johns Hopkins, Georgetown, and Princeton and is now a professor at NYU, suggested that the "problem" of people eating too much meat could be solved simply, by making people allergic to it.[51]

*I, for example, have a milk intolerance, and some people are intolerant to crayfish, and so possibly we could use human engineering to make it so that we're intolerant to certain kinds of meat, to certain kinds of bovine proteins.*

He then notes, with apparent approval, that such an intolerance to red meat already exists in nature, in the form of alpha-gal syndrome, which is caused by a bite from the lone star tick. It's estimated that as many as ten million Americans may now have red meat allergies as a result of tick bites.[52]

Liao goes on in the video to suggest that another way to reduce man's carbon footprint would be to shrink him. Seriously.

*It turns out that the larger you are—think of the lifetime energy that's required to transport larger people rather than smaller people. But if we're smaller, just by 15 centimeters, I did the math, and it's a mass reduction of 25 percent, which is huge. And a hundred years ago we were all on the average smaller, about 15 centimeters smaller. So think of the lifetime greenhouse gas emissions if we all had smaller children.*

---

[51] Video at World Science Festival, "Could We Make Humans?"
[52] Andrews, "Up to TEN MILLION Americans."

This apparently was too much for the other panelists, who all begin to laugh. "How small?" one panelist asks. "We shouldn't be so small that we get eaten by cats," Liao replies.

Liao has been pushing such bonkers solutions to climate change, which he calls "biohacking," since at least 2012, when a paper he and a colleague published caught the eye of the editors at *The Atlantic*.[53] The paper's three main suggestions are: reducing human height through IVF screening (i.e. removing embryos for taller offspring) or the administration of hormones to stunt childhood growth; using skin patches to stimulate meat intolerances; and enhancing the cognitive abilities of women using "smart drugs" so that they choose to have fewer children (since that's what smart women do, right?). Other biohacking proposals in the 2012 paper include genetically engineering humans to have "cat's eyes" so they can see in the dark, thereby reducing energy usage, and the prescription of pro-social hormones like oxytocin to ensure people cooperate with tackling climate change. (Wait . . . isn't that last idea basically the plot of a Christian Bale film!?)

The notion of "biohacking"—genetically engineering organisms to produce desirable traits—has become a central part of the World Economic Forum's vision for the Fourth Industrial Revolution, and not just in plants; see, for instance, the WEF-sponsored academic paper "Bioengineering Horizon Scan 2020," or Klaus Schwab's book *Shaping the Future of the Fourth Industrial Revolution* for details of some fairly current proposals on hacking the human genome.[54] It's not surprising, then, to discover that Liao is closely affiliated with Klaus Schwab and his organization. NYU, where Liao now works, appears to be a nexus for WEF interests. Larry Fink, CEO of BlackRock, is on the board of trustees of both NYU and the WEF, and Liao has hosted WEF members at his NYU Center

---

[53] Anderson, "How Engineering the Human Body." And Liao, et al., "Human Engineering and Climate Change."
[54] Kemp et al., "Point of View." and Schwab and Davis. *Shaping the Future*, 155–76.

for Bioethics, including Francesca Rossi, a member of the WEF's Council on AI and Robotics. At the time of writing, information about Liao's affiliation with the WEF appears to have been removed from the internet, probably because of all of the negative coverage he and his insane ideas have had since the 2016 clip re-emerged last year.

## The EAT-*Lancet* Commission on Food, Planet, Health: The Great Reset in Food

*"Food is the single strongest lever to optimize human health and environmental sustainability on earth. However, food is currently threatening both people and planet. An immense challenge facing humanity is to provide a growing world population with healthy diets from sustainable food systems.... Unhealthy diets now pose a greater risk to morbidity and mortality than unsafe sex, alcohol, drug and tobacco use combined. Global food production threatens climate stability and economic resilience and constitutes the single largest driver of environmental degradation and transgression of planetary boundaries. Taken together the outcome is dire."*

– Summary Report of the EAT-*Lancet* Commission

So begins the report of the EAT-*Lancet* Commission on Food, Planet, Health, a collaboration between the EAT Foundation and *The Lancet*, one of the world's oldest medical journals, which brought together thirty-seven "scientific experts" in the fields of nutrition, health, sustainability, and policymaking to answer a single question: "Can we feed a future population of 10 billion people a healthy diet within planetary boundaries?"[55] The commission produced its findings in 2019

---

[55] From the EAT Foundation website page on the Commission

in a detailed report, which can be read on the EAT Foundation's website.[56] I will be quoting from it below, unless otherwise stated.

According to an early footnote in the report, the notion of "planetary health" that will be applied to global food systems was first put forward in 2015 in a joint commission between *The Lancet* and the Rockefeller Foundation. The focus of that commission was on bringing environmental concerns into focus in the field of public health, "which has traditionally focused on the health of human populations without considering natural systems." The notion of a "Planetary Health Diet" is intended to do exactly the same for food.

The Commission proceeds from twin assumptions: 1) that by 2050 the world will have a population of ten billion people, all of whom will have to be not just fed, but fed a healthy diet; and 2) that this will have to be done in a way that allows the UN Sustainable Development Goals and the Paris Agreement on climate change (i.e. the "planetary boundaries") to be respected as well. Both of these assumptions are set in stone; they cannot be changed. So what is needed, the report states, is nothing less than "a radical transformation of the global food system . . . urgently."

One of the main hindrances to the achievement of this "radical transformation" thus far has been "the absence of globally agreed scientific targets for healthy diets and sustainable food production." Although it is clear that "a diet rich in plant-based foods and with fewer animal source foods confers both improved health and environmental benefits . . . there is still no global consensus on what constitutes healthy diets and sustainable production" or how these can be scaled to meet the needs of ten billion people. This is precisely what the Commission must produce: "universal scientific targets for the food system that will apply to all people and the planet."

---

[56] Also cited as Willett et al., "Summary Report of the EAT-*Lancet* Commission."

The report outlines two targets and five strategies to achieve them. The first target is "Healthy Diets" and focuses on the precise macronutrients and food sources people should be eating. The report summarizes its vision of a healthy diet in the following way:

*Healthy diets have an optimal calorie intake and consist largely of a diversity of plant-based foods, low amounts of animal source foods, contain unsaturated rather than saturated fats, and limited amounts of refined grain, highly processed foods and added sugars.*

The adoption of the diet will have "major health benefits," we are told. The Commission claims it will prevent around eleven million deaths a year, or between 19 and 24 percent of total deaths among adults worldwide.

The report uses an image of a plate divided among various food sources to represent how the diet would actually look in terms of volumes of food—note "volumes," which don't necessarily equate to calories, as we'll see. One half of the plate is taken up by vegetables and fruits. Of the other half, more than two-thirds is taken up by whole grains, plant-sourced protein (divided roughly in half between legumes and nuts) and unsaturated plant oils, with the remainder being divided among starchy vegetables, dairy foods, animal protein, and added sugars.

In terms of calories, the division looks somewhat different. The report gives a reference intake of 2,500 calories a day. The largest food group, by calories, is whole grains, with an intake of 811 calories, followed by unsaturated plant oils, with 354 calories, then nuts, with 291 calories, and legumes, with 284 calories. Fruits, dairy foods, and added sugars are each allocated somewhere around 100 calories a day. The smallest daily intakes are reserved for chicken and other poultry (62 calories), fish (40 calories), starchy vegetables (39 calories), beef, lamb, and pork (30 calories), and eggs (19 calories).

To give you an idea of just how small some of these figures actually are, let's take eggs as an example, since this is a foodstuff whose future I have something of an interest in. If a large egg weighs 50 grams, it will contain about 80 calories, with the majority of calories (about 60 percent) coming from fats, and almost all of the remaining 40 percent coming from protein. No doubt you've already done the math yourself, but I'll say it anyway: on the Planetary Health Diet you'll get to eat a quarter of a large egg a day. Eat your heart out, Rocky! The other animal-based protein targets are similarly miniscule. The 30 calories you'd be allowed from beef, lamb, and pork could be as little as 15 grams of meat—the thinnest of thin slices.

Just how much consumption patterns will have to change to meet the targets of the Planetary Health Diet is represented in a set of infographics illustrating the "diet gap" in particular regions of the world. In North America, for instance, the diet gaps are at their widest. Consumption of red meat is 638 percent of what it should be according to the new guidelines. Consumption of eggs is 238 percent, consumption of poultry 234 percent, and consumption of dairy 145 percent of what it should be. Elsewhere, such as in Asia, the gaps are much smaller.

Interestingly, the Food, Planet, Health report contains a statement, albeit it in a footnote, that, because the healthy diet targets allow for a range of food intakes, the Planetary Health Diet is somehow respectful of geographical and cultural differences around the world: "it does not imply the global population should eat exactly the same food." But there's no hiding the fact that whatever choice is offered is drastically limited. Adding in some extra legumes here and taking away some nuts there, or perhaps drinking a bit more milk and not having that extra-thin wafer of beef, hardly represents variation in any sense we'd understand or appreciate now. The broad outline of the diet is clear—largely plant-based with little to no animal sources of protein and fat—and this will be the same the world over.

The second target is "Sustainable Food Production," which simply means that production of food to meet the guidelines of the Planetary Health Diet must be achieved "within planetary boundaries."

These planetary boundaries are measured by six key metrics: climate change, land-system change, freshwater use, nitrogen cycling, phosphorus cycling, and biodiversity loss. Besides the beneficial effects of the adoption of the Planetary Health Diet itself, significant reductions in food waste (up to half) and improvements to production processes are the main ways the Commission believes food production can be made sustainable. In the most optimistic scenario, a number of options are successfully implemented, including:

> *Closing yield gaps to 90%; a 30% increase in nitrogen use efficiency, and 50% recycling rates of phosphorus; phaseout of first-generation biofuels, and implementation of all available bottom-up options for mitigating food-related GHG [greenhouse gas] emissions. . . . [L]and use is optimized across regions such that it minimizes impacts on biodiversity.*

The report then outlines five strategies for achieving the two targets. The first strategy is to "seek international and national commitment to shift toward healthy diets," which is precisely what the EAT Foundation was attempting to do with its open letter to the G20. Such commitments would involve, for instance, "making healthy foods more available, accessible and affordable," improving the way food is marketed, running information campaigns about healthy diets and sustainability, and implementing the EAT Foundation's guidelines. The other strategies are basically those mentioned in the open letter to the G20 and focus on changing agriculture and land management, including reorienting agriculture from producing large quantities of grain for livestock to consume and introducing

new methods of crop management, to establishing international mechanisms for governing land use and optimizing every
stage of the food supply chain to reduce waste as much as possible.

Some crucial aspects of the Planetary Health Diet remain
vague or non-existent. Most notably, there is no mention of
whether there will be different recommended daily allowances
for different people (could a handsome bodybuilder get a few
extra calories?), or of how adherence will be enforced. Given
that one of the principal justifications of the Planetary Health
Diet is to reduce carbon emissions, a personal carbon allowance
seems the most obvious mechanism for enforcement, but some
other kind of social-credit-based system is clearly also possible.
As a recent article in the British newspaper *The Independent*
explains:

> *Each month, [personal carbon allowances] would see
> every person or household in the country given a limited
> emissions quota to spend on heating, energy, travel, food
> and possibly consumer goods.*[57]

The idea has been floating around for some time, since at least
the late 1990s, and in 2006 and 2007 the British Environment
Secretary, David Miliband, commissioned two reports on how
such allowances might actually work. At that time, users would
have had a "credit card" with their personal allowance stored
on it, but now a phone-based app seems the most obvious
method of delivery.

Despite these elements being unclear at present, the EAT-
*Lancet* Commission represents the most detailed statement we
have of how people will eat after the Great Reset. Supplemented with other writings that have appeared on the World
Economic Forum's website, the Commission provides more
than enough information for us to think in detail about the

---

[57] Drury, Colin. "Should everyone have their own personal carbon quota?"

probable social-environmental and physical effects of the adoption of such a diet. Let's start with the social-environmental effects.

### Social-environmental Effects of the Planetary Health Diet

Since we're talking about the Great Reset and stakeholder capitalism, the dominant theme is, of course, corporate control. It should already be clear, from what I've said, how closely implicated a great many of the world's most powerful corporations are in the planning and implementation of the Great Reset's food agenda. Just cast your mind back to the EAT Foundation's FReSH initiative, for instance, a partnership with such behemoths as Bayer, Cargill, Danone, Deloitte, DuPont, Google, Ikea, Kellogg's, Nestlé, PepsiCo, Syngenta and Unilever. These are precisely the companies that are poised to benefit the most from the Great Reset and the changes it will bring to the world of food.

In truth, we don't need to think hard to imagine what a world of total corporate control in food will look like, since it exists to a large extent now, in the present. With the Great Reset we are simply looking at a change, not of kind, but of degree. A 2021 op-ed on *Civil Eats*, "Giant Meat and Dairy Companies Are Dominating the Plant-Based and Cellular Meat Market," shows the extent to which the biggest players in meat and dairy in the US have already captured the traditional meat and dairy markets and are now positioning themselves to capture the ersatz and plant-based markets as well. I will be quoting directly from it.

*Civil Eats* reported on how the big players have been ruthlessly consolidating their control of the meat and dairy markets in the US, while at the same time "presenting an illusion that there are numerous, competing alternatives." Most consumers look no further than the brand name on this or that product, ignoring the small print and missing the fact that ultimately the brand is merely a veil, hiding the product's true identity and ownership, which reside with one of just a handful of enormously powerful companies. And make no mistake, this "illusion" of consumer choice is deliberately cultivated, in part because it helps to obscure the fact that companies that might be seen as harming the environment through industrial agriculture are also manufacturing alternatives, such as plant-based protein, which claim to be the solution to that harm.

All of these companies pursue a broad policy of breaking "ownership envelopes" to out-compete their peers. Strategies to increase the size of the firm go beyond simply dominating one aspect of the market, such as processing meat, and spill over into more or less every aspect of the food production and distribution process. This is the vertical integration I talked about in the Introduction. And now that many of these companies have "nowhere else to go," as it were—now that they dominate the traditional animal-product markets to such an extent that they can scarcely acquire further share without exercising a total monopoly—they are turning to other emerging markets, and that means plant-based protein and lab-grown meat. In the process, they are seeking to rebrand themselves not as purveyors of foodstuffs—meat or dairy—but instead as purveyors of that all-important and most desirable of macronutrients: protein. Tyson Foods has already trademarked the term "The Protein Company," and all manner of big hitters are acquiring salmon aquaculture farms, or pea-protein and insect-protein firms—or all three, and more besides. Nestlé now owns Sweet Earth, a plant-based meat brand, and Unilever owns The Vegetarian Butcher, for instance.

While this industry consolidation has of course benefited the big corporations, the effects for the little man have been almost uniformly bad: "higher prices for consumers, lower incomes for factory workers, farmers, and ranchers, and decreasing agricultural diversity, among other impacts."

In recent years, a number of the big meat-processing firms, including JBS, Tyson, WH Group/Smithfield, and Perdue, have been forced to pay hundreds of millions in government fines and to settle class-action lawsuits. It was alleged that they had used a specially created firm to coordinate as a cartel and fix prices in their favor. In 2017, JBS—a Brazilian meat-processing firm that has grown not only to dominate the traditional meat market but now also has multiple brands that focus on areas like organic meat, grass-fed meat, and plant-based protein—was fined $3.16 billion after it admitted that it had bribed nearly two thousand politicians in Brazil. The goodwill and favorable treatment these bribes bought allowed JBS to make new acquisitions across the globe.

Despite this clear evidence of corruption, regulators have been happy for these companies to continue behaving in the same predatory manner, greenlighting further acquisitions and allowing them to use sharp practices to put smaller competitors out of business. JBS, for instance, was allowed by US regulators to acquire a lamb-processing facility in Colorado from Mountain States Rosen at a bankruptcy auction, which it then announced it would convert into a beef-processing facility. Since this facility was one of the few remaining facilities of its type in the state, many of Colorado's sheep producers were expected to go out of business.

As a 2021 *New York Times* article on the ongoing travails of America's small beef ranchers puts it, "the distress of American cattle ranchers represents the underside of the staggering winnings harvested by the conglomerates that dominate the meat-packing industry." Despite record beef prices during the pandemic, in part due to the significant disruption to supply chains, the small ranchers who supply much of the beef that Americans are paying more and more for scarcely benefit at all. "You're feeding America and going broke doing it," said one farmer from Missouri. "It doesn't pencil out to raise cattle in this country anymore." But while the disruption to supply chains is in part to blame for the difficulties of small farmers, it's clear, as one senior White House economist wrote in a blog post, that it is "also the result of corporate decisions to take advantage of their market power in an uncompetitive market, to the detriment of consumers, farmers and ranchers, and our economy." The big companies can simply dictate prices to farmers, usually far below the prices they would reasonably be willing to accept, and the farmers can take them or leave them. In reality, though, the choice for these small ranches is one between a lingering death and a more immediate suicide, with most choosing the former. "I wanted to tell him to go to hell," another farmer said, recalling the price offered to him for his cattle by a JBS representative. "But what choice did I have?" So it goes.[58]

It's clear, then, that agriculture, especially in the US, is already well on the path towards the corporate capture envisaged by the World Economic Forum. How far this will ultimately lead is, of course, still a matter for speculation. It's entirely possible that, under the Great Reset, there will be no small farmers or food producers at all, that all agricultural concerns will be owned by corporations like Cargill and JBS. The extent to which humans will even participate in agriculture is also unclear. As we've already seen, the Fourth Industrial Revolution is centered on the notion that the vast majority of all work will be automated, and we can assume that agriculture will be no different. It should be no surprise that the World Economic Forum is an enthusiastic advocate of applying AI and robots to revolutionize the productivity of farming. In March 2021, for example, it released a "community paper" on "Artificial Intelligence for Agriculture Innovation," as part of a broader initiative under the same name, led by the Forum's Center for the Fourth Industrial Revolution in India. The report examines the potential for AI and robotics to transform the "agriculture ecosystem" from top to bottom, by such means as AI models that improve crop planning by linking data from

---

[58] Goodman, "Record Beef Prices."

weather forecasts, soil monitors, warehousing and logistics infrastructure, and markets, or through AI-enhanced pest control and drone-based field mapping.

It's worth looking in more detail at some of the types of foods that are going to be produced by the farmers of the future under the Great Reset plan—whoever (or whatever) they may be. For one thing, this helps to reveal yet further the extent and nature of the corporate control the globalists want to bring to the food supply. We've just seen that the meat and dairy kings are now rebranding themselves as "protein companies," investing in alternative forms of plant-based, insect-based, and lab-grown protein. This is a smart move. Because these new foods are proprietary technologies, they can be patented. And what does that mean if not more control and more profit? Although globocorp can rip off small farmers and make them accept a pittance for their cattle, it can't patent a cow, which we might consider as the essential "building block" of a beef business. But what about steak grown in a cell-line culture? Everything about this technology, down to the cellular level, can be patented and owned, allowing the corporation with the patent to own, quite literally, every stage of the process from production to distribution. And so yet another, perhaps even the final, "ownership envelope" is broken. This makes it easier to understand why, actually, many of these corporations may not resist the demise of traditional agriculture in the manner we might expect, or even at all. If traditional, animal-based agriculture is abolished and the only forms of "animal" meat people can eat are produced in a lab, the corporations that produce them will have an incredibly powerful monopoly—one that is likely never to be broken.

Lab-grown meat doesn't feature in the EAT-*Lancet* Commission's report, but it's something the World Economic Forum has been pushing for some time. A Forum article from October 2020 asks, for instance, "How soon will we be eating lab-grown meat?" and suggests that it is a sustainable and ethical alternative to traditionally produced meat. "Although it sounds complicated, cultured meat takes much less time to grow, uses fewer of the planet's resources, and no animals are slaughtered."

This happy assessment of lab-grown meat—all pros and virtually no cons—collapses under scrutiny. While it's true that you can grow a steak more quickly than a whole cow, the actual environmental costs vis-à-vis traditional methods aren't obviously better, and may in fact be much worse. A 2015 paper, "Anticipatory Life Cycle Analysis of In Vitro Biomass Cultivation for Cultured Meat Production in the United States" (phew!), compared the use of land and other resources between lab-grown meat and the real stuff. One thing that becomes obvious very quickly from this paper is that the production of lab-grown meat requires surprisingly large inputs of resources like soybeans and corn, energy, and massive amounts of water. These are ingredients most people would never know are essential to the production of lab-grown meat. After all, if you're not grazing any cows or feeding them in a grain lot, why would you need soy and corn? The answer is, you need them to provide peptides and starch for the growing process. Vitamins and minerals must also be mined, isolated, and processed. Special growth factors, which are expensive and also notable because they're extremely unpalatable to vegetarians and vegans (see below), must also be added. Energy is needed to maintain the correct temperature and aeration in the bioreactor, as well as to provide lighting. The cultured tissue is also at high risk of contamination; stringent cleaning methods must therefore be followed, which use lots—and I mean lots—of water. The authors estimate that the process requires just under 75,000 liters of water to produce 555 kilograms of biomass.

Clearly, a naive approach to the resource-use of "sustainable" lab-based alternatives to meat will not do—unless, of course, your intention is to pull the proverbial wool over people's eyes. The authors of the "Life Cycle Analysis" study found that the land use required for the necessary inputs in their model was twenty times that of a previous study. As a result, they conclude that the "global warming potential" (GWP) of lab-grown meat significantly exceeds that of pork or poultry. Although they claim that the GWP of lab-grown meat is better than beef, the model of environmental impact they use for cattle production doesn't take into account the fact that the biological emissions of cows, including those dreaded burps and farts, are part of a cycle and not suitable for a direct comparison with the greenhouse emissions from fossil-fuel use.[59]

That's not the only problem for those who proclaim lab-grown meat's impeccable credentials. In actual fact, it's not the case that "no animals are slaughtered" during the production of artificial beef, the lab-grown movement's jewel in the crown. At present, the blood of unborn cow fetuses—otherwise known as fetal bovine serum (FBS)—is an essential ingredient in the production of lab-grown beef, and this must be harvested from their mothers after slaughter. Without FBS, it appears to be very difficult, if not impossible, to make artificial cells work properly, because only FBS has the correct mix of hormones to encourage growth. FBS also happens to be expensive, often more than $1,000 a liter, and this is one major part of the reason why cultured meat has cost as much as $200,000 per pound. Although lab-grown meat companies have announced the creation of new growth mediums—a bargain at around $400 a liter!—as long as FBS continues to be involved in the production of lab-grown meat, vegetarians and vegans are liable to give it a wide berth, assuming they're in possession of the full facts about its production, of course.[60]

There are plenty of reasons to doubt, then, whether lab-grown meat will ever truly be economically or ethically viable. But this still hasn't stopped the rich and powerful from tripping over one another to invest their cash in startups, including Bill Gates, Richard Branson, Sergey Brin, Peter Thiel, Kimbal Musk, and John Mackey. In February of 2022, a new startup called Wildtype, focusing on producing cell-cultured

---

[59] This issue is discussed in detail in Rodgers and Wolf, *Sacred Cow*, 131–47.
[60] Philpott, "The Bloody Secret Behind Lab-Grown Meat."

salmon, received $100 million of investment funding, which included donations from Robert Downey, Jr. and Leonardo DiCaprio. The World Economic Forum also clearly buys the hype. As far as it's concerned, reducing the product's marginal costs—especially the cell-culture media, which are estimated to account for between 55 and 95 percent of these costs—is the most pressing concern for those who wish to turn a profit in the lab, but it will happen. The WEF discusses the progress of lab-grown meat in detail in a 2019 white paper on Alternative Proteins, as part of its Meat: the Future series. According to the white paper's own calculations, costs have been reduced from hundreds of thousands of dollars a kilogram to as little as $25. And as for any problems with the perception of lab-grown meats—the white paper doesn't mention the use of FBS—there are already "not-for-profits" like the Gates-funded Good Food Institute and the Institute for the Future working to change that. A recent study in the journal *PLOS One* found that "information content"—that is, what people were told about lab-grown meat—had a clear effect on whether or not they would eat it and, just as importantly, whether they would be prepared to pay above the cost of normal meat for it.[61] Frame lab-grown meat as a product with social and environmental benefits that make it superior to normal meat, and people are much more likely to do both of those things. In short, the World Economic Forum is confident cultured meat will be feeding people "at scale" in the future.

Genetically-modified organisms (GMOs) are another essential part of the future of food under the Great Reset. Again, as with lab-grown meat, it's worth noting that the use of GMOs isn't mentioned explicitly in the EAT-*Lancet* Commission's report, only heavily implied. It is, however, something the World Economic Forum enthusiastically promotes in numerous publications on its website. For instance, a December 2018 article on the website, "This Is How to Sustainably Feed 10 Billion

---

[61] Rolland et al., "The effect of information content."

People by 2050," provides a list of twenty-or-so action points to improve food production and includes a discussion of how genetic modification will be used to improve crop breeding:

*New advances in molecular biology offer great promise for additional yield gains by making it cheaper and faster to map genetic codes of plants, test for desired DNA traits, purify crop strains, and turn genes on and off.*

Another thinkpiece from the website, this time guest-written by a Stanford professor, Henry Greely, asks "Are we ready for genetically modified animals?" and touts the potential of the CRISPR technology to "open the entire living world to human manipulation." Greely notes that "crops and fuel are the 'big ticket' items for DNA modification," but he also strikes a cautious note in his assessment that the technology needs serious regulation to prevent unwanted spread of genetic material and potentially dangerous uses "whether run by well-intentioned biohackers or bioterrorists."

A third piece, whose primary author is Tanzanian academic Ramadhani Noor, focuses on the potential of GMOs to "tackle world hunger." Like the professor from Stanford, Noor et al. note that GMO crops "could be our best hope to feed an increasingly hungry planet," but their assessment of the risks is much more severe. They anticipate situations in which "biotech companies may develop experimental gene-edited crops for testing in developing countries where the need for food is greater than the political will to protect the masses." They then point to the experience of India, where a massive spate of suicides by poor farmers has accompanied the poorly regulated adoption of GMO crops in the country. The causes of these suicides? "Indebtedness" (i.e. from buying the seeds, which are more expensive than regular varieties and must be re-purchased each season) and "crop failure" (because the seeds don't work as well as they're supposed to)—two very negative effects of the "corporate model of industrial agriculture introduced in India."

It's interesting to note, in light of what Noor et al. say about these potential dangers, not just of GMOs but also, seemingly, of the stakeholder capitalism model itself, that their article features a rare disclaimer at the end: "Publication does not imply endorsement of views by the World Economic Forum." Perhaps the article's inclusion was just a rare gesture at the notion of editorial balance from Klaus Schwab? Because the World Economic Forum definitely doesn't endorse Noor et al.'s views on GMOs, at least not the negative views anyway. And it's not difficult to see why. A heavy reliance on GMOs to feed the global population would further empower corporations and afford them an even tighter control over the food supply. Once again, it comes down to the fundamental issue of ownership. Like lab-grown meat, genetically modified organisms can be patented and therefore fully owned by the corporations that produce them. That means, among other things, that if you use GMO seeds, you have to agree to use them in the manner the corporation chooses. This is true already today. If, for instance, you buy Monsanto's special Roundup Ready seeds, you have to sign an agreement not to save the seed produced after harvesting for re-planting the next season. You can't sell seeds to other farmers either. In short, you must return to Monsanto—and no-one else—each season for more seeds. And if you don't? Get ready to meet the so-called "Monsanto mafia," the corporation's secret police force that spies on farmers by photographing and filming them at work and at community meetings, sending agents to pretend to be surveyors, and pressuring farmers to allow the corporation access to their private records.[62] Monsanto's bully-boy tactics have received coverage in mainstream outlets including *Vanity Fair*, as well as spawning dedicated websites like monsantomafia.com to document the outrageous lengths to which the corporation will go to protect its precious GMO seeds.[63] Monsanto has even been known to sue non-GMO

---

[62] Mercola, "Seeds of Evil."
[63] Barlett and Steele, "Monsanto's Harvest of Fear."

farmers whose fields have been contaminated with its GMO seed if they then refuse to pay, despite the contamination being absolutely no fault of their own. The corporation misled the US Supreme Court when it claimed it would never do this.[64] Just five companies—Monsanto, Syngenta, Bayer, Dow and DuPont —now dominate the world of seeds, as a result of hundreds of acquisitions of smaller companies in a fifteen-year period. Again, don't be fooled into thinking the world of the Great Reset is that far away. We're already half-way there.

Let's move now from the social effects to the environmental. Beside the fact that these genetically-modified crops are commodities that suit the purposes of corporations more or less perfectly, there are a whole slew of environmental risks associated with them. Not least of all, we must contend with the obvious and very real risk of genetic transfer between organisms, which could have potentially devastating effects on broader ecosystems. Scientists have already shown that, in the case of canola, GMO varieties of which are widely used especially in North America, genetic transfer between GMO and non-GMO varieties takes place regularly in the wild and leads to novel forms of hybridization.[65] These hybrid plants have also been shown to be persistent, meaning that they can reproduce freely in the wild without cultivation. In truth, though, it's difficult to know exactly what to expect, since genetic modification is a relatively new practice and there are no real long-term data. Genetic transfer to animals, including humans (which I'll talk about later), is also a possibility, again with as-yet unknown effects. The simple fact we have to grasp is that if we are going to proceed with planet-wide genetic engineering before long-term safety tests have been carried out, as the architects of the Great Reset would have us do, we may have to reckon with unintended consequences of a type and on a scale we have never witnessed before. This is a truly existential Pandora's box-type

---

[64] Engdahl, "Monsanto is 'like a mafia.'"
[65] Schafer et al., "The Establishment of Genetically Engineered."

situation, and anybody who presents the issue simply as a technical one—in which all that is required is for gene-editing technology to be perfected in a lab—is either frighteningly naive or deliberately attempting to mislead. It's that simple. Whereas we might have to wait a little longer for some of the worst effects of GMOs to make themselves known, others are already abundantly clear, like the problem of "superweeds" associated with the ever-increasing use of herbicides like Roundup and dicamba. Many GMO crops are created to be herbicide-resistant—usually for the seed company's own signature brand—but this herbicide-resistance has a paradoxical effect. A kind of arms race develops between the farmers, with their herbicides, and the weeds they're trying to destroy. Whether through genetic transfer from the GMO crops or by other means, the weeds gain ever-greater levels of resistance to the herbicides, so more and more must be used with diminishing effect. Finally, the old herbicides become largely or totally ineffective, at which point new ones must be made and then the whole process begins again.

The herbicide dicamba, for instance, was developed by Monsanto as an alternative to Roundup.[66] Roundup has been marketed as the perfect accompaniment to Monsanto's own Roundup Ready GMO seeds, which are engineered to be resistant to Roundup, unlike weeds. Or, rather, that was once the case, because now many weeds have developed resistance to Roundup and become "superweeds," meaning that a new herbicide had to be developed to kill them. Monsanto chose dicamba, a chemical that had originally been developed in the 1960s. (A 2018 review indicates that at least thirty-eight weed species have now evolved resistance to glyphosate, the active ingredient in Roundup, across thirty-seven different countries and in thirty-four different crop and six non-crop situations.)[67] From 2015, Monsanto began producing new seeds branded as

[66] Elmore, "The herbicide dicamba."
[67] Heap and Duke, "Overview of glyphosate-resistant weeds worldwide."

"Roundup Ready Xtend," which could tolerate heavy spraying of both Roundup and dicamba. It wasn't long, however, before farmers were reporting that weeds were also becoming resistant to dicamba as well. So it goes.

One response to the problem of superweeds has been for farmers to return to tradition by diversifying the crops they grow and using time-honored agricultural methods like cover-cropping.[68] Many of these methods are central to a new—or should I say, old—way of farming that has come to be dubbed "regenerative agriculture." I'll discuss regenerative agriculture later, at some length, when I lay out the Eggs Benedict Option. Another response, though, is to continue the arms race, producing ever-new cocktails of toxic chemicals, and ever-new varieties of crops that are resistant to them, in a desperate—but also very lucrative—attempt to outrun the weeds. Witness, for instance, how Bayer recently sought approval for a new type of seed that would produce crops resistant to five different kinds of herbicides.[69] Could we see the day when Bayer markets seeds that are resistant to ten, twenty, fifty different chemicals? In a future where agriculture is totally controlled by big business, where all food crops are genetically engineered to increase yields and ensure resistance to herbicides—which is to say, if the Great Reset comes to pass—there's every reason to suppose we could.

Of course, this isn't the only thing that's wrong with massive use of herbicides; rather, it's just the beginning. Use of chemical herbicides has all sorts of horrible effects that go well beyond encouraging the growth of superweeds. Glyphosate, the active ingredient in Roundup, has received the most attention in this regard. It is the most widely used herbicide in history, and, in keeping with this fact, there is now a veritable mountain of evidence to substantiate the damage it does. Hundreds of studies have been published on the various harms glyphosate causes, whether to animal, insect, plant, or human. In

---

[68] Creech, "Discover the Cover."
[69] Held, "Bayer Forges Ahead."

2015, the sheer weight of evidence led the World Health Organization to declare that glyphosate is carcinogenic in animals and probably in humans too. Given the commercial interests at risk, not just from lost sales but also lawsuits, this classification was sharply contested and soon became something of a political football.[70] Still, new studies keep being added to the pile to corroborate these and other aspects of the herbicide's effects, as well as adding new ones. Just this last year, studies have shown, variously, that glyphosate exposure: causes gut-flora disruptions in humans that are associated with neurological and psychiatric diseases[71]; results in increased DNA methylation in post-menopausal women, a molecular change that can cause cancer and increase cellular aging[72]; destroys the gut flora of bees, weakening their immune systems and making them more susceptible to disease[73]; reduces the presence of beneficial microbes in the soil and wider environment[74]; and alters the production of phytohormones in non-target crops, reducing their yields and weakening their natural defenses.[75]

Glyphosate is only the most prominent example of an herbicide wrecking more or less everything it touches. Dicamba, which we saw has been marketed as a complement to Roundup, is also known to have unpleasant effects. These are made worse by its very high volatility, which means that it quickly changes from liquid to vapor, especially if it's warm. In 2021, thousands of farmers in the US reported to the EPA that dicamba sprayed by other farmers, sometimes as far as a mile and a half away, had damaged crops in their fields.[76] The range of different plants affected was wide: trees, including sycamore, elm, and oak; azaleas and roses; tomatoes; peppers; and peas. In 2017,

---

[70] Kelland, "In glyphosate review."
[71] Barnett et al., "Is the Use of Glyphosate?"
[72] Lucia et al., "Association of Glyphosate Exposure."
[73] Motta et al., "Glyphosate induces immune dysregulation."
[74] Daisley et al., "Deteriorating microbiomes in agriculture."
[75] Fuchs et al., "A Glyphosate-Based Herbicide."
[76] Elmore, "The herbicide dicamba."

"dicamba incidents" affected nearly four million acres of land across the US, in almost three thousand recorded incidents. The number has only increased in subsequent years, along with spraying.

Chlorpyrifos, one of the most common pesticides in the world, is now the subject of a huge class-action lawsuit in California, after the plaintiffs alleged that decades of spraying in four counties in the Central Valley agricultural area caused serious neurological damage, including in children.[77] Almost 61 million pounds of the pesticide were applied to the area in question between 1974 and 2017. It's reckoned that as many as one hundred thousand people may have to dispose of all their personal belongings due to contamination. "We have found it in the houses, we have found it in carpet, in upholstered furniture, we found it in a teddy bear and we found it on the walls and surfaces," the lead attorney for the case said. Studies have linked chlorpyrifos to developmental abnormalities in the brains of babies, lowered IQ and cognitive development, autism, stunting, lung cancer, and Parkinson's disease.[78] A new study released in 2022 suggests that exposure to the pesticide may also have some role to play in the global obesity crisis.[79] Researchers observed that the pesticide reduces the metabolic rate of the brown fat tissue of mice, causing it to burn fewer calories. This promotes fat storage and, in the long run, could trigger significant weight gain. A reduction of just 40 calories a day, if calorie intake remained stable, would lead to an extra 5 pounds of weight gain over the course of a year.

It's not a mistake that the architects of the Great Reset have very little to say about the negative effects of copious use of industrial chemicals in agriculture. In truth, just as these chemicals are an essential part of the current system, without which it couldn't function, so too will they be an essential part

---

[77] Associated Press, "Pesticide caused kids' brain damage."
[78] A list of studies linking chlorpyrifos to these negative effects, and more, can be found at Malkan, "Chlorpyrifos."
[79] Wang et al., "The pesticide chlorpyrifos."

of the new, because really it's nothing more than an intensification of the way we already do industrial agriculture today. Although the food transformation envisaged by the Planetary Health Diet would see the production of grain for livestock more or less totally eliminated—something that, in the context of regenerative agriculture, is actually desirable, as we'll see— this simply means that the grain produced will be put to other uses, i.e. helping to feed ten billion humans instead. So perhaps this isn't really much of a change at all: from cattle to the new cattle class of humans. But, in all seriousness, we shouldn't let the "meat-free" marquee distract us from the essential truth that the Great Reset, certainly in the world of agriculture, is more of the same, but in many ways worse. It's just today's agriculture cranked up to eleven.

To give the devil his due, the EAT Foundation's aim to halve the obscenity that is food waste today is no bad thing, nor is the aim to protect biodiversity by preventing the expansion of farmland into pristine habitats, whether that be the encroachment of soy growers into the Amazon rainforest or of palm-oil plantations into the homes of our orangutan friends in Indonesia. Industrial farming of livestock, especially pigs and poultry, is an abomination that cries to the heavens for redress and should be brought to an end as swiftly as possible: nothing more needs to be said. I'd be the first to admit that these aims, on paper at least, are admirable. But the actual reality of the Great Reset plan is something very different entirely. With regard to industrially farmed animals, there's serious deception involved, since we must accept the premise that there's no other way to raise livestock on a large scale than in industrial concentration camps, producing toxic concentrations of waste and greenhouse gases, when in fact there is, as we'll see when I lay out the Eggs Benedict Option in the next chapter. According to the architects and advocates of the Great Reset, the only way to eliminate the terrible ills of factory farming of livestock is to eliminate the farming of livestock altogether. This just isn't true.

But let's focus for a moment on what the aim not to expand existing farmland really means, since it leads us to what is almost certainly the greatest flaw in the Great Reset plan for transforming global food production. In simple terms, not expanding existing farmland means that this land will have to be pushed harder and harder in order to produce the necessary yields to feed a massively expanded world population. What's more, a significant amount of farmland that is currently used for pasturing animals will have to be abandoned, since it's unsuitable for raising crops. According to Diana Rogers and Robb Wolf, perhaps as much as 60 percent of all agricultural land globally is unsuitable for anything other than grazing animals.[80] It's also the case that large swaths of land that are suitable for growing crops are, in fact, only suitable for growing certain crops, and sometimes even only a single crop. Large parts of North Africa, for instance, are only suitable for growing olive trees, yet this land is often blithely labeled "arable land" as if it's no different from the wheat fields of Ukraine. According to the Food and Agricultural Organization, of the 36 percent of the earth's total land surface that is considered arable, just 3 percent is considered prime crop land. And yet the EAT Foundation and the World Economic Forum are confident that, even if the amount of land used for all forms of farming actually decreases, ten billion people can still be fed the Planetary Health Diet through technological innovation, which basically means GMOs, more chemicals, and "smarter" techniques for managing planting, the application of fertilizer, pest control, and harvesting.

What this fails to take into account, on a fundamental level, is that the soil is not some never-ending resource from which limitless quantities of food can be brought forth, so long as the right technical procedures are followed. Critics of the current global system of industrial agriculture often refer to the system as "extractive" agriculture, and with good reason: this method

---

[80] Rodgers and Wolf, *Sacred Cow*, 160–161.

of farming takes from the soil and gives little to nothing back. Instead, it exhausts the precious organic matter that makes the soil fertile, as well as reducing the microorganisms and invertebrates that help recycle nutrients from dead plant matter—all of which together make up the thing we call topsoil:

> *One tablespoon of soil contains more than one million living organisms, and, yes, every one of them is eating. Soil isn't just dirt. A square meter of topsoil can contain a thousand different species of animals. These might include 120 million nematodes, 100,000 mites, 45,000 springtails, 20,000 enchytraeid worms, and 10,000 molluscs.*[81]

Topsoil is, quite simply, a living system whose complexity boggles the mind:

> *[Topsoil] is a filter and a container, a mass of integrated micro and macro matter, and a living substance that cannot be understood by reduction. Its final form contains so many members and symbiotic relationships that it constitutes, in the words of the soil scientist Nyle Brady, the "genesis of a natural body distinct from the parent materials from which the body was formed."*[82]

Topsoil depletion is the classic problem of monoculture—planting and harvesting large areas with just a single crop—and the Great Reset offers no real solutions to it, just further, more intensive extraction. The question is, then: how much more of this is tenable?

Exactly how bad the situation is for the world's agricultural topsoil is a matter of some debate. On what was once the North American prairie, which has been reduced to just two percent

---

[81] Keith, *The Vegetarian Myth*, 18.
[82] Stoll, *Larding the Lean Earth*, 14.

of its original size, the topsoil can now be measured in inches, where once it was 12 feet deep.[83] One estimate, made in 2014 by an economist at the Food and Agriculture Organization, suggests that at current rates of topsoil degradation, there might be no more than sixty years of farming left in the world before the soil is simply unable to produce food.[84] Whether you believe this estimate or not, which we might take as the worst-case scenario for grain agriculture, the basic premise of the "extractive" criticism of modern industrial farming—that we're heading for serious trouble if we take from the earth and never give back—is unassailable. With regard to the natural regeneration of topsoil, Steven Stoll offers a sobering picture of the pace at which this wondrous substance can recover:

> *Lost soil is unrecoverable, and the pace of its formation is so slow that the end product must be considered nonrenewable. One survey of a southern district in the 1930s found earthworks abandoned on land not cultivated since 1887. Under the pine crowns, on high ground, the researchers found fifty years of accumulated topsoil one-sixteenth of an inch deep. At that rate of creation the pines would see their first inch in eight hundred years, their first foot in ninety-six hundred years—the age of agriculture itself. In human time it can be lost forever. . . . Subsoils are the bones of the earth. They have no living organisms and no rotting plant food, and they hold little water. All these are lost with topsoils, and people follow.[85]*

So if it took just 150 years to deplete 11 feet and 10 inches of topsoil on the North American plain—and remember that at least half of that period would have been without mechanization and the extensive technical and chemical apparatus of today's Midwestern farmers—it might take over 100,000 years to

[83] Keith, *Vegetarian Myth*, 36.
[84] Rodgers and Wolf, *Sacred Cow*, 122.
[85] Stoll, *Larding the Lean Earth*, 17.

restore what was lost, by allowing nature to take her course unaided . . .

What we need, if we are not to lose the precious topsoil, is a system of agriculture that gives as well as takes from the earth, that doesn't require huge quantities of chemicals to sustain an artificial abundance but instead protects and nurtures the complex biological system without which, ultimately, no food can be grown. That's what regenerative agriculture promises to do, and I'll return to it in due course in the next chapter. But before that, I want to turn to the physical effects we might expect the Planetary Health Diet to have on the ten billion people it is supposed to feed.

### *Grains and Carbohydrates: How Much Is Too Much?*

Let me be totally up-front with you. I don't eat grains at all, and I feel a hell of a lot better for it. Even when I ate expensive organic sourdough bread, I'd still feel bloated. So when I gave up grains for good—not just wheat—I noticed an immediate effect, which went far beyond no longer feeling bloated. My mental processes felt much sharper, and my mood was noticeably heightened. I'm far from alone in reporting such improvements, either.

In the 2016 paper "Bread and Other Edible Agents of Mental Disease," Paola Bressan and Peter Kramer make the argument that grain consumption, by disrupting gut function, is directly implicated in causing various mental diseases. Many of you will have been made aware of this provocatively titled paper by Mike Ma's book *Harassment Architecture*. According to Bressan and Kramer, grains help cause mental disease in two ways: 1) by making the gut more permeable, causing food to leave the gut and travel to areas where it shouldn't go, which makes the immune system attack these particles as well as substances that look like them and are vital to the proper functioning of the brain; and 2) by releasing opioid-like substances that can cause mental dysfunction if they end up reaching the brain (see point 1). The authors point to a variety of different evidence in support of their claims. During World War II, for instance, when wheat shortages were common in many European countries, hospitalization rates for schizophrenia dropped with the shortages, whereas in the US, where consumption rose steadily across the period, hospitalization rates increased. Similarly, in the islands of the South Pacific, where wheat was not traditionally consumed, rates of schizophrenia skyrocketed when Western grain products were introduced. As well as the array of anti-nutrients contained in grains (i.e. seeds), something I talk about in the main text at length, gluten—the elastic protein that makes bread bread—also plays an important role in these negative processes. For example, gluten is known to attack an enzyme used in the production of GABA, a neurotransmitter that is essential for proper brain function. Gluten intolerance is rising fast (the most extreme form is coeliac disease), at a time when the worst form of gluten is becoming more common, and not just in bread and traditional wheat products, but also in a whole variety of other products that make use of it for its binding and thickening properties. One survey of products in Australian supermarkets found gluten in nearly two thousand different food items, from sauces to processed meats, and over one hundred non-food products, including pain relievers and even shampoos.[86] Although some people are especially sensitive to gluten, it appears to trigger "some action" in everybody's gut, regardless of sensitivity. If you want to read more about the possible role of grains in mental and digestive dysfunction, I'd suggest reading *Grain Brain* by David Perlmutter.

A related issue is how many carbohydrates we should be eating. Since I'm a devotee of the great Vince Gironda, the bulk of my calories come from fat. But that doesn't mean I don't eat

---

[86] Atchison et al., "Wheat as food."

carbs at all. In fact, I probably get a decent amount from all the raw milk and milk products I consume, and I do eat local raw honey and home-grown fruits and vegetables when they're in season. One thing that's clear is that excessive carbohydrate consumption is implicated in a wide variety of conditions, from insulin resistance and diabetes, to dementia. Eating too much sugar—which is what all carbohydrates are, at base—disrupts hormonal function, permanently in the end (insulin resistance and diabetes), and also disrupts basic cellular functions through a process called glycation.[87] Just how much is too much, however, isn't immediately obvious. Some, in the keto, paleo, and carnivore camps, argue that we shouldn't really be eating carbohydrates at all, while others suggest we can eat more without risking adverse health effects. It's undeniable, at least, that most people today eat too many carbohydrates, which is why low-carb diets such as ketogenic diets, but also paleo diets that limit carbohydrates to "primitive" sources (i.e. excluding grains), have such tremendous power to transform people's health, even in very short periods of time.[88]

As general advice with regard to grains and carbohydrates, I would say to ensure you are only consuming the highest quality (i.e. organic) produce, so as to minimize your exposure to toxic chemicals used in non-organic agriculture, and to ferment all grains in the traditional manner, so the anti-nutrients are disabled. Both of these points are explained in the main text. Most of all, pay close attention to how your diet makes you feel. The spirit of raw egg nationalism has been one of joyous self-experimentation from the start, and I would urge you to adopt that spirit yourself. If you're curious about the effects of eating fewer carbs or cutting out grains, or both, just do it! If it makes you feel much better, stick with it. If it makes you feel crummy, don't. (But give the diet at least six to eight weeks before you make a decision, if you can.) Finding out what truly works for

[87] See Shanahan, *Deep Nutrition*, 207–34 for an in-depth discussion of why eating too much sugar is bad for you.
[88] See for instance, Frasetto et al., "Metabolic and physiologic improvements."

you is something nobody else but you can do—certainly not a physician whose understanding of nutrition is probably thirty years out of date at best and who is more accustomed to prescribing pills than thinking carefully about the foods their patients eat.

## The Physical Effects of the Planetary Health Diet

So we've seen what the social and environmental effects of this total food transformation are likely to be, and none of them are good—unless, of course, you're an executive at Bayer or Cargill. But what about the physical effects of the adoption of the flagship Planetary Health Diet? After all, we're talking about a significant change to the eating habits of the vast majority of the world's population, ostensibly for the better. But although advocates claim it will make people healthier in addition to reducing the harmful effects of agriculture on the environment, in truth, perhaps with a few exceptions, global adoption of the Planetary Health Diet can be expected to do no such thing. In the same way that the Planetary Health Diet is based on a series of mistakes about how to make agriculture better for society and planet, so too is it based on a series of fundamental errors about human beings, the kind of creatures they are, and the foods they need to thrive. Whether these errors are actually deliberate—by which I really mean chosen with deliberate malice—I'll leave to you to decide.

So what do humans need to eat in order to thrive? To answer this question, there's no better place to look than the work of a very important dentist—maybe the most important dentist in history—a man by the name of Weston A. Price. Born in Ontario, Canada, in the late nineteenth century, Price became a dentist at a pivotal moment in modern history, just as industrial foods began to become the dominant type in the developed world and spread to the rest of the world as well. From his practice in Cleveland, Ohio, over the course of the next thirty years Price saw a worrying decline not just in the mouths but also the overall health of the children he treated. Crowded teeth, foreshortened jaws, and numerous cavities were accompanied by other serious health problems including asthma, allergies, and even behavioral difficulties. In particular, Price noticed that children's dental arches (the roof of the mouth) were narrowing, along with their nasal passages, distorting the entire shape of their faces. He began to form the hypothesis that these changes were caused by the diets these children were eating. To put this theory to the test, together with his wife, Florence, Weston Price traveled the globe in search of people who displayed perfect physical health, so he could see what they ate and how it differed from what the children back in Ohio were eating. At that time, it was still possible to discover cultures that were untouched by modern industrial food, or largely so, and even in places as close to home as the Outer Hebrides, islands off of the north-western coast of Scotland. The book Prince would come to write on his journey of discovery would be called *Nutrition and Physical Degeneration*, and today it surely ranks as one of the greatest pieces of nutritional research that has ever been carried out. Given its focus on physical form and beauty—"eugenic overtones" would probably be the euphemism of choice today—as well as the categorization of racial and tribal groups—by a straight white male, no less—it's a book that won't be remade any time soon, so we must be extremely grateful to have it.

When looking for "perfect physical health," what Price wanted to see was absence of the kind of dental decay and arrested facial development that so marred the children back in the Corn Belt. He also looked for wider markers of good health, especially evidence of freedom from disease in all its forms. His search took him from the Swiss Alps to Scotland, from Indian reservations in North America to New Zealand and the islands of the South Pacific, and across the length and breadth of Africa, where he studied thirty different tribes. Price's interest was in a proper scientific comparison, so he took copious notes on the diets of the various people he encountered, as well as samples of the food they ate. One of the most valuable and memorable things he did was to take pictures of his subjects. Even today, those pictures remain extremely powerful. In particular, his studies of twins—one of whom followed what we might call their ancestral diet, while the other consumed "the displacing foods of our modern civilization"—illustrate his thesis more vividly and immediately than all the words he could write, as fascinating and as worth reading as they are. Where the one twin clearly displays perfect health, with a properly formed dental arch, handsome, regular teeth showing no signs of decay, and a broad, well-developed face, the other shows all the hallmarks of being a victim of the deleterious effects of industrial food. QED—or just about.

One group that displayed perfect physical health was the Torres Strait Islanders, who lived on a group of islands between Australia and Papua New Guinea. In Price's words, the Islanders were part of "a zone that is abundantly supplied with sea animal life, this being the scene of the richest pearl fishing industry in the world."[89] The Islands were under Australian rule, with government representatives and stores that had been established to provide "modern clothing in addition to food, chiefly white flour, polished rice, canned goods, and sugar." Getting the Islanders to accept these foodstuffs, however, was proving no easy task. On Murray Island, for instance, there had been great resistance to these imports, and at the time of Price's visit there was some doubt about whether it would be safe to visit the island, "since on the last visit of the government officials, blood was almost shed because of the opposition of the natives to the government's program."[90] As Price noted:

*Physical characteristics of all these residents of the Torres Straight Islands, regardless of their tribal groups, were,*

---

[89] Price, *Nutrition and Physical Degeneration*, 184.
[90] Ibid., 184–85.

*sturdy development throughout their bodies, broad dental arches, and for all of those who had always lived only on their native food, a close proximity to one hundred per cent immunity to dental caries.[91]*

He marveled at their seamanship and fishing skills, and in particular the way they would jump into the water to spear fish even when sharks were around. The locals maintained that when fish were in abundance, a shark would never attack a human, but Price notes that "we saw one pearl diver who bore enormous scars received from the jaws of a shark."[92]

The contrasts in health between the Islanders eating their traditional foods and the local White population, which included missionaries and officials, as well as their children, were especially striking. The local government-appointed physician, who tended to around four thousand people, said that he had never seen a case of cancer among the Islanders, despite seeing dozens among the much smaller local population of Whites, who were almost all affected by the dental and facial problems caused by eating modern food, nor had any of the Islanders ever required a major medical procedure.[93]

Price was neither the first, nor the last, to note the tremendous good health of hunter-gatherers and pastoralists especially. Medical doctors such as Dr. Edward Howell, a contemporary of Price, reported on the near-complete absence of cancer amongst the indigenous peoples of northern Canada, as well as heart disease and diabetes.[94] Dr. Josef Romig, another doctor among the natives of northern Canada, shared with Price his experiences of native health and vitality, which serve only to confirm Price's own observations. Romig, like Howell, noted the almost complete absence of any of the prevailing diseases of modern civilization among these people.

[91] Ibid., 192.
[92] Ibid., 189–90.
[93] Ibid., 195.
[94] Keith, *Vegetarian Myth*, 190.

Furthermore, he noted that if a native who had become assimilated to modern life became ill with tuberculosis, a condition that would normally prove fatal on modern foods, could often be cured by returning to their native diet. These people ate "whale, caribou, musk ox, Arctic hare, rock ptarmigan, walrus, seal, polar bear, seagulls, geese, ducks, auks and fish, all often (but not always) eaten raw or fermented," as well as a few Arctic plants preserved in seal oil and the fermented stomach-contents of dead caribou.[95]

Although Price studied a variety of different cultures, ranging from hunter-gatherers and pastoralists to full-blown agriculturalists, all of whom ate a wide variety of different foods, he was able to recognize a fundamental pattern among every one of the groups who displayed perfect physical health. One of his clearest conclusions was about the superior value of foods from animal sources. In the words of Dr. Ron Schmid, Price was able to provide clear evidence of "natural laws concerning dietary needs, laws that operate in human beings everywhere to regulate immunity, reproduction and virtually every other aspect of health."[96]

*Tribes eating grains-based natural-food diets had well-formed dental arches and resistance to various diseases, but their physical development, resistance to dental decay, and strength were inferior to tribes eating more animal-source foods. The people strongest physically and often 100 percent resistant to dental diseases were herdsmen-hunter-fisherman. In towns and ports where some groups ate a combination of refined and primitive foods, problems developed, but not to the extent occurring when native foods were abandoned entirely.[97]*

---

[95] Ibid.
[96] Schmid, *Native Nutrition*, 24.
[97] Ibid., 22.

As a general principle, what the healthiest people favored most of all was nutrient-dense animal foods rich in fat. That means organ meats and bone marrow, oily fish and their roe, egg yolks and fats like lard and butter. Liver was especially prized, often eaten raw. Indeed, the favoring of liver often extended to special taboo-like customs surrounding its consumption. Among the Nuer of Sudan, a pastoralist tribe, they believed the liver possessed a special sacred character, being the seat of a person's soul. As a result:

*[A] man's character and physical growth depend upon how well he feeds that soul by eating the livers of animals. The liver is so sacred that it may not be touched by human hands. It is accordingly always handled with their spear or saber, or with specially prepared forked sticks. It is eaten both raw and cooked.* [98]

Dr. Schmid identifies six classes of foods, the consumption of one or more of which was "absolutely essential" to the exemplary health of the tribes Price singled out:

1. *Seafood: fish and shellfish; and fish organs, liver oils and eggs*
2. *Organ meats from wild animals or domestic pastured animals*
3. *Insects*
4. *Fats from birds and monogastric (having a single stomach) animals such as aquatic mammals, Guinea pigs, bears and pigs*
5. *Egg yolks from pastured birds*
6. *Whole milk, cheese and butter from pastured animals.* [99]

---

[98] Price, *Nutrition and Physical Degeneration*, 146.
[99] Schmid, *Native Nutrition*, 25.

One of Price's key insights was into the vitamin content of these foods. When he analyzed the ten thousand samples he had taken while in the field, he discovered that the healthiest groups were consuming well over ten times the amount of vitamins A and D of the average American, as well as four times more minerals and water-soluble vitamins. The fat-soluble vitamins, in particular, which Price referred to as "catalysts" or "activators," are necessary for the assimilation of other crucial nutrients, including protein, minerals, and other vitamins.[100] "In other words," as Sally Fallon puts it, "without the dietary factors found in animal fats, all the other nutrients largely go to waste."[101] The fact that much of the fat these people consumed was raw seems to have been important, since raw fat contains lipases—fat-digesting enzymes—which ensure full digestion of the fat.[102]

Price also drew attention to the importance of fermentation, soaking, and sprouting when any form of seed (grains, nuts, and tubers) was eaten. This could even take the very simple form of only eating plant matter that has been pre-digested by a caribou, as we saw with the Arctic cultures mentioned above. These processes have dual benefits. First, they increase the concentration of enzymes and probiotics, both of which aid digestion, and second, they help to disable the anti-nutrients contained within the seeds, which can otherwise have serious health effects on the eater. Anti-nutrients are aptly named, since they basically prevent you from getting nutrition. It's easiest to think of them as a plant's defense mechanism, or one of them. Since a plant can't get up and go anywhere to avoid being eaten, chemicals are used instead to exact a toll from anything that tries to eat it. One common form of anti-nutrient, found in nuts, legumes, and grains, is phytates. These bind with minerals in the digestive tract once eaten and, as a result, prevent the eater from gaining access to them. Calcium, for instance, is

---

[100] Keith, *Vegetarian Myth*, 190.
[101] Fallon Morell, "Ancient Dietary Wisdom," 90.
[102] Keith, *Vegetarian Myth*, 190.

bound by phytates, and so a diet high in phytate-containing foods can quickly lead to deficiencies, which the body then tries to alleviate by releasing calcium from vital tissues like teeth and bones, weakening them in the process. Cultures without adequate knowledge of these preparation techniques, such as Middle Eastern cultures where flatbreads are made with whole, untreated wheat, see widespread stunting and reduced adult height as a result.[103]

Price is absolutely clear, in no doubt whatsoever, that optimum health cannot be achieved by eating plants alone. "It is significant," he says, "that I have as yet found no group that was building and maintaining good bodies exclusively on plant foods. A number of groups are endeavoring to do so with marked evidence of failure."[104] I'd be tempted, if I weren't determined to do the best possible job of demolishing the claims of the World Economic Forum and its allies, to conclude this section here. Many—I should think most—of you probably didn't need any convincing of the superiority of animal-based diets for health in the first place, so Price's findings may not provide quite the Damascene moment for you that they did for Lierre Keith, a reformed vegan and author of *The Vegetarian Myth*. Here's how she describes her first encounter with Price, after decades of being wracked with pain from a vegan diet:

*And there I was, with my spine coming apart at the seams for no apparent reason, staring at his [Price's] photographs. No one in those cultures had my disease. Perfect teeth, perfect bones. They had no arthritis, no degenerative conditions. Understand the pain level I was living in by then: I couldn't sit for more than thirty minutes or stand for more than ten. . . . And here were these pictures. Fourteen cultures where teeth and bones held through their lives, all the way to the end. It was their food that*

---

[103] Keith, *Vegetarian Myth*, 190.
[104] Price, *Nutrition and Physical Degeneration*, 276.

*carried them through. And I ate precisely the opposite. . . .*
*I had done this to myself.*[105]

Forget latter-day hunter-gatherers and pastoralists: the consumption of plant-based diets is a very clear deviation from a human optimum that was established before there were even modern humans (*Homo sapiens*, I mean), millions of years ago. The evidence for this—from archaeological evidence to the very structure of our skeletons and organs, as well as that of our nearest ancestor species—is so abundant and obvious that it's a wonder anybody even tries to dispute it.[106] But dispute it some do, often with absurd results. It's widely claimed, on the basis of the work of a single author, R.B. Lee, that our ancient ancestors were actually gatherer-hunters rather than hunter-gatherers, gaining 65% of their calories from plants and the rest from animals. When Dr. Loren Cordain tested this theory with a computer model that considered only plant foods our ancestors would have had access to, it turns out they would have to have eaten as much as 12 pounds of vegetation a day![107] But absurdity has never been a bar to belief—something that hardly needs saying after the events of the last two years. Even so, I think it's important to try to explain in further detail what is missing from or wrong with plant-based diets if we want to understand exactly what the negative effects of global adoption of the Planetary Health Diet may be. Although the Planetary Health Diet does include some space for animal products, as we've seen, the amounts are token amounts, nothing more. In heart and soul, this is a plant-based diet, and should be treated as such.

The deficiencies and problems of plant-based diets basically come down to four factors: protein quality; nutrient density and

---

[105] Keith, *Vegetarian Myth*, 193.
[106] See Ibid., 139–46 for a detailed discussion of the evolutionary evidence. A recent Israeli study of the archaic Stone Age, up to two million years ago, suggests that our ancestors were not just carnivores but "hypercarnivores." See Ben-Dor et al., "The evolution of the human trophic level."
[107] Keith, *Vegetarian Myth*, 146–7.

vitamin and mineral deficiencies; fat types; and phytoestro-gens. We'll examine each of these in turn before considering likely population-level effects of adoption of the Planetary Health Diet. I'll also address the added deficits of consuming genetically modified foods and the pesticides and herbicides that are needed to produce them. Although what follows will be a pretty in-depth discussion, it's not totally exhaustive of the downsides of plant-based diets. If you're looking for such an ac-count, I'd suggest reading a book like Lierre Keith's *The Vege-tarian Myth.*

Our first factor, protein quality, is easy to explain. Stated simply, protein is harder for us to absorb from plants than from animals, and as a result it's easier to become protein-deficient on a plant-based diet than a diet that incorporates decent amounts of animal products. Take note: this is one of many ways in which the bald macronutrient listings on the side of food packaging are misleading. Yes, your plant-based burger might contain, say, 20 grams of protein per 100 gram patty, but in reality that 20 grams of protein is very different from the 20 grams you'll get from a 100 gram patty made from the real thing. The plant-based protein will, without fail, be of an infe-rior quality, meaning less of it can be used by the body. This was substantiated nicely in a recent overview study. The au-thors collected sixteen previously published studies that com-pared the muscle-building effects of animal and plant proteins. On the basis of their meta-analysis, they concluded that "ani-mal protein tends to have a more favorable effect on lean mass compared to plant protein, and the benefit appears more pro-nounced in younger adults."[108]

Protein quality can be broken down into two aspects: 1) amino-acid profiles; and 2) digestibility. Let's start with amino-acid profiles. The building blocks of proteins are amino acids. There are twenty that our bodies need, nine of which can only be obtained from our diet, making them "essential"—a term

---

[108] Lim et al., "Animal Protein versus Plant Protein."

which can be misleading, since it suggests, wrongly, that we somehow don't need the other eleven, when we do. The nine essential amino acids are phenylalanine, valine, threonine, tryptophan, methionine, leucine, isoleucine, lysine, and histidine. While all of the non-essential amino acids can be produced within the body in sufficient quantities, the production of some can be limited under certain conditions, including stress. Animal products are "complete" proteins, meaning they contain all the essential amino acids, whereas plant proteins lack one or more of the essential amino acids, especially leucine, which plays a crucial role in muscular protein synthesis and athletic performance.[109]

Digestibility, the second aspect, is self-explanatory. Even if a protein source has a fantastic amino-acid profile, if your body can't actually digest the protein, it's as good as useless. As well as containing fewer essential amino acids, plant proteins are generally less digestible than animal proteins. Indexes of protein quality like the Protein Digestibility-Corrected Amino Acid Score (PDCAAS), which has been adopted by the World Health Organization as its preferred method for measuring protein quality, fudge their scores by failing to take into account the presence of anti-nutrients in plant foods, which can seriously affect digestibility.[110] As we saw mentioned above, fermentation was an important aspect of the diets of traditional cultures that displayed perfect health, precisely because it disables many of the anti-nutrients present in all forms of seed. Compounds like lectins, tannins, and trypsin inhibitors can all affect protein digestion and prevent the body from absorbing those crucial amino acids. So while the PDCAAS might give soy protein a score of 1.0, an equivalent score to the best animal protein sources (eggs and milk), in truth soy protein is far less digestible. The PDCAAS score for peanuts is 0.52, and for wheat gluten—gluten is a protein, if you didn't know—just

---

[109] Mero, "Leucine Supplementation and Intensive Training."
[110] Rodgers and Wolf, *Sacred Cow*, 87. and Sarwar, Ghulam. "The Protein Digestibility–Corrected Amino Acid Score."

0.25. Furthermore, there's now evidence that digestibility of plant proteins also depends upon the age and state of a person's gut.[111]

A direct comparison of two protein sources, one animal and one plant, will illustrate these points nicely.[112] To get the same amount of protein as you would find in 4 ounces of sirloin steak (30 grams of protein and 4.5 grams of fat, totaling 181 calories), you'd need to eat 12 ounces of kidney beans and 1 cup of rice (30 grams of protein, 122 grams of carbohydrates, and 2.4 grams of fat, totaling 638 calories). Not only do you have to eat a lot more food, and consume a lot more carbohydrates, to get the same amount of protein from the beans, but the quality of the protein is worse too. With the kidney beans you would have significantly less methionine, threonine, tyrosine, and histidine, and you would only have more cysteine and phenylalanine.

And this is just a comparison of the protein content of these two foods. When we take into account vitamin and mineral content, it becomes clear just how much more nutrient-dense sirloin steak is than beans, and animal foods than plant-based foods more generally. In particular, the steak contains a whole host of B vitamins that are totally lacking in beans, especially B12. Vitamin B12 is an essential vitamin that simply cannot be found in plant foods. Although there are some analogues for B12 in algae and seaweed, they are much less effective in the body and may actually even increase the body's demand for B12. A B12 deficiency is very bad news indeed. It can cause, among other things, infertility, mental illness, and various forms of neurological damage. As a result, many vegetarians and vegans supplement with vitamin B12 for as long as they remain on the diet—all the while denying that this is a clear sign that a plant-based diet is less ideal than an omnivorous

[111] Dallas et al., "Personalizing protein nourishment."
[112] This comparison, including the discussion of relative vitamin and mineral contents, is drawn from Rodgers and Wolf, *Sacred Cow*, 68–71, 88–91, and 100–104, with some key extra references to studies added.

one—but many don't supplement at all, often because they're simply unaware of what they're missing out on. Sixty percent of adult vegans are estimated to have a B12 deficiency, and 40 percent of adult vegetarians.[113] Animal foods, unlike plants, are a tremendous source of B vitamins all round, which play a variety of essential functions in the body, from energy metabolism to preventing birth defects.

Vitamin D3 is another essential vitamin, like B12, that vegetarians and vegans are often deficient in. Although vitamin D3 can be synthesized by the body through exposure to sunlight, huge numbers of people around the world suffer from a deficiency owing to lack of exposure to sunlight and insufficient amounts of the vitamin in their diet. All the best dietary sources of vitamin D3 are from animal foods, especially fatty fish, liver, and eggs. Vitamin D deficiency affects calcium absorption in the body and was traditionally associated with rickets, a condition involving soft bones and skeletal deformities, but further research has revealed that the vitamin is also important in cognitive function, heart health, and preventing diseases and conditions like asthma, diabetes, multiple sclerosis, and cancer. Vegans have been shown to have high rates of bone turnover as a result of low vitamin D and calcium levels, and fracture rates are 30 percent higher among vegans than those who consume animal products.[114] As well as low levels of calcium in plant-based foods, which also takes less bioavailable forms than in animal foods—you would need to consume as much as 6 cups of spinach to get the same amount of calcium as in a glass of milk, for instance—anti-nutrients are also present in plant foods, with greens like spinach and kale containing compounds that prevent calcium absorption.

Combined B12 and D3 deficiencies are so common among vegetarians and vegans that researchers have recently come

---

[113] Gilsing et al., "Serum concentrations of vitamin B12." and Herrmann, Wolfgang. "Vitamin B 12 Deficiency in Vegetarians."
[114] Hansen et al. "Bone turnover, calcium homeostasis." and Iguacel et al. "Veganism, vegetarianism, bone mineral density."

up with a novel form of supplementation, in the form of gummy candies. Because of the differing solubilities of the two vitamins, it's been difficult to get them both in a single pill, but researchers discovered that the two could be combined in an emulsion-filled gel made of pectin.[115] So the next time you see an adult vegetarian or vegan chewing on gummies, it may not be because they're really just an overgrown child who prefers soft hyper-palatable foods to real nutrition, but instead to prevent the serious effects of a B12 and D3 deficiency. Of course, it could also be both.

Iron is another essential mineral which is best taken from animal foods, especially red meat. Heme iron, the most absorbable form, is only found in animal foods, and studies have shown that it is the optimal form for ensuring proper iron uptake in the body. Up to 20 percent of heme iron in red meat can be absorbed by the body, whereas only between 1.4 percent and 7 percent of iron in plant-based food can be.[116] Again, don't take food labeling at face value when it says plant food X contains plenty of iron: that's only half the story. Anemia caused by iron deficiency is the most common mineral deficiency in the US, affecting at least a quarter of all adults and nearly half of all pre-school children. Iron is necessary for the transport of oxygen in the blood, so a deficiency will have cardiovascular effects including fatigue and breathlessness, as well as impaired immune, mental, and muscular function. Having adequate levels of iron is important for women, especially during menstruation and pregnancy, and for infants and children. In New Zealand, hospitalization for iron deficiency has doubled in the last ten years, as vegetarianism has grown by almost 30 percent and carnivores have abandoned beef and lamb for chicken and pork.[117]

---

[115] Ghiraldi et al. "Emulsion-Filled Pectin Gels."
[116] Scrimshaw, "Iron deficiency."
[117] Nylka, "More spent on low iron hospitalisations."

Other nutrients that people on plant-based diets tend to lack include glycine, iodine, creatine, choline, selenium, methionine, and taurine. Iodine deficiencies are especially serious and can lead to irreversible brain damage. Indeed, ensuring proper thyroid function is a real problem for vegetarians and vegans, especially if they consume soy, as we'll see. Many of these nutrients and minerals are associated with mental function, and so it's no wonder that depression and even lowered IQ appear to be linked to plant-based diets. Zinc, a mineral that is not readily found in plant foods, is generally low in vegetarians and vegans, with serious effects on their mental health. One study showed that zinc supplementation for twelve weeks was enough to improve mood significantly.[118] Creatine, which we tend to associate with weight training and bodybuilders like Mike O'Hearn, is actually an essential nutrient and, again, something vegetarians and vegans tend to lack. Creatine deficiencies have been linked to reduced brain function in vegetarians. The reduction in fluid intelligence and memory may be as much as one standard deviation, or approximately 15 IQ points. Supplementation with creatine has been observed to reverse this, and eating meat would also have the same effect.

*It is possible that, although vegetarianism appeals to people with higher intelligence, becoming vegetarian reduces fluid intelligence and working memory. . . . People may notice a reduction in cognitive functioning when they become vegetarian if fluid but not crystallized intelligence is affected. (That is to say, becoming vegetarian may impair one's ability to solve problems without causing one to forget what one has learned, so the effect may not be noticeable.)[119]*

I think this explains a lot, don't you?

---

[118] Solati et al., "Zinc monotherapy increases serum."
[119] Cofnas, "Is vegetarianism healthy for children?"

Something else vegetarian and vegan diets lack: cholesterol. "But isn't that a good thing?" you say. Yes, I'm sure you've been told that cholesterol is bad, probably more times than you can remember. "Cholesterol causes heart disease, which causes death" might as well be the mantra, or at least one of the mantras, of modern medicine. Lierre Keith describes it as "the bulwark that the nutritional vegetarians [i.e. vegetarians who claim we should all be so on nutritional grounds] will stand behind."[120] But the truth is, you've been lied to. We all have. It's a complicated story, which requires a full book-length exposition. Thankfully, there are books like Dr. Malcolm Kendrick's *The Great Cholesterol Con* to explain precisely why, how, and with what effects this lie has been propagated.[121] Maybe you know that President Eisenhower had a stroke in 1957, but did you know that this was more or less the beginning of the popular demonization of cholesterol and saturated fat—an unprecedented attempt to get us to abandon the animal fats that humans have treasured and consumed since the dawn of time? Probably not.

The story is actually more complicated than a sitting US President just having a stroke and the dietary guidelines changing overnight. The complete story involves: dodgy cholesterol experiments performed on rabbits, which eat cellulose and not fat and animal protein; a rigged seven-country study by a self-appointed "nutrition expert" named Ancel Keys, which identified saturated fat as the cause of raised cholesterol and raised cholesterol as the cause of heart disease; and the 1968 McGovern Commission, chaired by Senator George McGovern, which was tasked with formulating nutrition guidelines to reduce rates of disease affecting Americans, including heart disease. Although the McGovern Commission's recommendations to increase carbohydrate and reduce fat, especially saturated fat, consumption were widely criticized within the scientific

---

[120] Keith, *Vegetarian Myth*, 160.
[121] There's also lots of good information in Shanahan, *Deep Nutrition*, 121–62 and in Keith, *Vegetarian Myth*, 160–86.

community at the time, the writing was already on the wall.[122] From then on, the full weight of government support, including massive subsidies, would be behind those advocating for satu-rated fat consumption to be reduced or eliminated and replaced by polyunsaturated fats from seed, fruit, and vegetable sources. What this means, at base, is that for sixty-something years we've been urged to cut animal foods drastically, and es-pecially red meat and dairy products like butter, and replace them in many cases with new foods that humans have never eaten until the last hundred years. As we might expect, this approach—often called the "Lipid Hypothesis"—underlies the dietary recommendations of the Planetary Health Diet, which note the "health burden" of illness caused by red meat and sat-urated fat consumption and propose "healthy plant oils" as the main source of fat calories.

The first thing that's worth stating, quite baldly, is that there's absolutely no good evidence that consuming cholesterol raises your blood cholesterol, unless you have a disorder.[123] The dodgy experiments on rabbits I mentioned previously, in which the poor little chaps were fed animal protein and cholesterol rather than plants, could not be replicated in animals that ac-tually should be eating animal protein and cholesterol. When you feed those things to a dog or a cat or a fox, their cholesterol does not increase (unless their thyroids were tampered with or removed). A meta-study of 167 cholesterol-feeding experiments shows increasing dietary cholesterol has no or negligible effects on blood cholesterol, and that there is no relationship with heart disease risk. The body regulates cholesterol production very closely, with about 80 percent of the cholesterol in your body being produced by the liver and the remaining 20 percent coming from your diet. If you eat more, the body produces less, and if you eat less, the body produces more. However, although

---

[122] The Commission is discussed at length in Rodgers and Wolf, *Sacred Cow*, 53–56.
[123] The discussion of cholesterol that follows is drawn from Keith, *Vegetarian Myth*, 160–86, except where otherwise stated.

the body produces the majority of your daily need, consumption still appears to be essential to meet it.[124]

In the Lipid Hypothesis, saturated fat consumption is more or less directly equated with raised cholesterol levels, although eggs, for example, contain lots of cholesterol, but not a lot of saturated fat. You may have heard of the French Paradox: the fact that the French consume 4.5 times as much butter as Americans, but have significantly lower rates of heart disease. But have you heard of the Greek Paradox, the East African Paradox, the Swiss Paradox, or even the Pacific Island Paradox? All these different peoples eat high quantities of saturated fat and have low levels of heart disease. The famous Maasai warriors, a group singled out by Weston Price for their tremendous health and vitality, eat up to 300 grams of animal fat a day and have relatively low blood cholesterol levels, as well as being free from heart disease. As a result of his studies of the Maasai, George Mann declared the Lipid Hypothesis to be "the public health diversion of this century . . . the greatest scam in the history of medicine."[125] The simple truth about cholesterol and its relationship with saturated fat is no more complicated than this: cholesterol is generally found in animal foods, and animal foods generally contain saturated fat. That's it. That's where the association begins and ends.

Low cholesterol is a killer, and you need saturated fat, not least of all to produce the cholesterol your liver *has* to produce. Let's take a look at a few studies. Consider the Minnesota Coronary Experiment, for instance, a double-blind randomized controlled trial—i.e. science's gold standard for trials—that took place in seven institutions in Minnesota between 1968 and 1973, with the aim of investigating whether replacing saturated fat with vegetable oil (which contains high levels of polyunsaturated fats) would reduce heart disease by lowering blood

[124] Enig, *Know Your Fats*, 6.
[125] Mann, "Diet-Heart: End of an Era."

cholesterol. And what were the results? For every 30-point decrease in cholesterol observed, the death rate increased by 22 percent.[126] So much for the Lipid Hypothesis! These results have been corroborated time and again. According to a Finnish study of people aged over 75, those with cholesterol levels in the highest third had half the death rates of those who had the lowest.[127] A study of nearly thirteen million Korean adults showed that low total cholesterol was associated with increased all-cause mortality risk (i.e. if you had low cholesterol, you were more likely to die of anything, across the board).[128] A study of six thousand French men over a period of seventeen years showed that the men whose cholesterol levels declined the most had the greatest risk of cancer.[129] I could go on citing more and more studies.

So why is cholesterol essential, so essential that if you don't have enough, you're significantly more likely to die than if you do? Lierre Keith puts it nicely when she says that, without cholesterol, we'd all be puddles. Huh!? What she means is that cholesterol is absolutely vital to maintaining our bodily structure at a cellular level, to keeping all the liquid in, since that's, fundamentally, what we are. We couldn't be the creatures we are without it. Cholesterol doesn't dissolve in water, which is why it's the perfect material for constructing cell membranes. Then there is its role in the nervous system and brain. Cholesterol is essential to the formation of both. Synapses, the junctions between nerve cells, are more or less entirely made out of cholesterol. Twenty-five percent of the body's cholesterol is in the brain, which is made up of over 60 percent saturated fat. Cholesterol is also needed for the manufacture of vitamin D in the body, which takes place by the action of sunlight on the skin. Our various sex hormones, including testosterone, could not be produced without cholesterol either, and we certainly

---

[126] Ramsden et al., "Re-evaluation of the traditional diet-heart hypothesis."
[127] Tuikkala et al., "Serum total cholesterol levels."
[128] Yi et al., "Total cholesterol and all-cause mortality."
[129] Zureik et al., "Decline in serum total cholesterol."

need those, at least if we want to undergo proper sexual differentiation.

The hormonal aspect has been of crucial importance for raw egg nationalists. The anabolic—i.e. muscle-building—power of cholesterol was central to the great Vince Gironda's system of natural bodybuilding and his recommendation that the bodybuilder consume vast quantities of raw eggs when looking to gain muscle. But Gironda didn't just pluck this idea from a chicken's backside—far from it. As well as being a maverick and great self-experimenter, he was also extremely well read in the ethnographic, scientific, and medical literature of his day. With regard to eggs in particular, he seems to have been working on an analogy with the way burn victims used to be treated. In the early decades of the twentieth century, to counter the terrible muscle-wastage that follows serious burns, victims were given a diet of 36 eggs a day in various forms, until this was replaced by treatment with synthetic steroids. Were eggs a kind of natural steroid, then? That conclusion might stand to reason. Although Gironda knew that large quantities of protein, which the eggs would have provided, were essential to developing muscle mass, he seems to have intuited that it was the large quantities of cholesterol that were the magic ingredient. Interestingly enough, new research has substantiated Gironda's ideas about eggs and cholesterol. A study led by the scientist Steven Riechman, for instance, has shown a linear dose-response between cholesterol intake and lean body mass increase (i.e. the more you consume, the greater the muscle increase), and another group of scientists has shown that a high cholesterol diet significantly increases myofibrillar protein synthesis, which is a measure of muscle growth.[130] A slightly different kind of study compared the effects of consuming just egg whites versus whole eggs, with the conclusion that whole

---

[130] Riechman et al., "Statins and Dietary and Serum Cholesterol." and Lee et al., "Dietary Cholesterol Affects Skeletal Muscle."

eggs are better muscle-building food.[131] On the basis of Riech-man's research, this should come as no surprise, since the yolk is where all the cholesterol is found. The precise mechanism behind cholesterol increasing muscle growth isn't totally clear. It may simply be because all the extra cholesterol gets con-verted into testosterone, which then drives muscle growth, or it may be by some other pathway, such as changes to cell-mem-brane viscosity, control of inflammation, or cell signaling.[132] The testosterone route seems most likely, though. Saturated fat is one of the building blocks of cholesterol in the body, and a number of studies show that a high saturated fat diet will increase testosterone. In one study, men who reduced their fat intake from 40 percent of calories with a significant amount of saturated fat to a 25 percent fat diet with low saturated fat saw a decrease in their testosterone levels. When they returned to their original diet, their testosterone levels rose accordingly.[133] Other studies have shown that diets low in saturated fat re-duce testosterone levels.[134] One new study is particularly re-vealing for my purpose here, with this book, since it shows that the worst possible diet for maintaining optimal hormone levels as a man is—wait for it!—a low-fat vegetarian diet. While a low-fat diet will make testosterone levels fall by an average of 10 to 15 percent, a low-fat vegetarian diet will make them plummet by an average of 26 percent.[135] All in all, then, it looks like a big win for eggs, red meat, and Vince Gironda.

So we need saturated fat and cholesterol. Unfortunately, fat and especially saturated fat consumption has plummeted in re-cent decades. At the same time, people have not been getting healthier—quite the opposite, as if that even needs saying. By renouncing saturated fat, we have not entered some new golden age of health. And one of the main reasons for this is

---

[131] van Vliet et al., "Consumption of whole eggs."
[132] Riechman et al., "Cholesterol and Skeletal Muscle Health."
[133] Hämäläinen et al., "Decrease of serum total."
[134] Lambert, "Saturated fat ingestion regulates."
[135] Whittaker and Wu, "Low-fat diets and testosterone in men."

precisely the "healthy" fats that have been recommended as alternatives to animal fats: seed and vegetable oils. More and more research suggests they're responsible for a whole host of serious negative health effects, including the main condition they were supposed to solve: heart disease. Heart disease is now the number one cause of death for both men and women.[136] Talk about dietary gaslighting!

Something of a crusade against seed and vegetable oils has emerged over the past couple of years on the right side of Twitter, so you may already be familiar with the evidence for why these oils are bad news. Much is made of the fact that, until the beginning of the twentieth century, if these oils were used at all, it was not as foodstuffs but industrial lubricants, glue, or paint. But the science is a little more complicated than your—admittedly correct—intuition that you would be better off eating butter than crazy glue. It will be necessary for me to simplify things a little here, since I don't want to turn this into a complete primer on lipid science. If you're looking for a much more in-depth discussion of the various kinds of fat and their properties, I'd suggest reading Catherine Shanahan's *Deep Nutrition*. (I would suggest you pay less attention, though, to her recent, and very disappointing, advocacy for Zero Acre Farms, a tech startup which aims to produce a cell-cultured "healthy" alternative to vegetable oils. Although the production process is a secret at present, it almost certainly involves the use of GMOs. As we already know, that means patents, among other things.)

Basically, it comes down to the fact that vegetable and seed oils mostly contain polyunsaturated fatty acids (which I'll refer to from now on as "PUFAs") rather than monounsaturated or saturated fatty acids. According to Sally Fallon and Mary G. Enig in their book *Nourishing Traditions*:

---

[136] Shanahan, *Deep Nutrition*, 128.

*[Significant consumption of PUFAs] has been shown to contribute to a large number of disease conditions including increased cancer and heart disease, immune system dysfunction, damage to the liver, reproductive organs, and lungs, digestive disorders, depressed learning ability, impaired growth, and weight gain.*[137]

That's quite the list, huh? What makes PUFAs so bad is, among other things, their inherent instability. While saturated fats are chemically stable, because they are "saturated" with hydrogen, monounsaturated and especially polyunsaturated fats are not. This makes them form reactive particles known as free radicals that attack tissues they come into contact with by altering their molecular structure. While free radicals are actually used by the body as part of its own defense system, a diet containing PUFAs can cause uncontrollable cascades of oxidative damage. This damage affects different parts of the body or cell structure differently: DNA might mean cancer; blood vessels might eventually mean heart disease. The production of most seed and vegetable oils—a harsh industrial process that generally involves the application of heat and chemicals through multiple stages—makes the resulting oils even more reactive and thus even worse for you.[138]

PUFAs have also been implicated in a wide variety of autoimmune and inflammatory conditions, including arthritis, Parkinson's, Alzheimer's, and chronic pain. Omega-6 fatty acids, which make up a large part of the fat in most commercially produced seed and vegetable oils, seem to be particularly responsible for these effects. Studies have shown how omega-6 fatty acids cause "inflammation, high blood pressure, irritation of the digestive tract, depressed immune function, sterility, cell proliferation . . . [and] cancer."[139] Again, quite the list. In part,

---

[137] Fallon and Enig, *Nourishing Traditions*, 10.
[138] Shanahan, *Deep Nutrition*, 134–9.
[139] Fallon and Enig, *Nourishing Traditions*, 11.

this appears to be because omega-6 fatty acids prevent the correct formation of prostaglandins, a type of hormone that plays a variety of roles, including blood clotting, pain sensation, inflammation, hormone regulation, and cell growth. Since these hormones are made from fat, it's not hard to see why eating the wrong kind could interfere with them.[140]

As if that weren't enough, PUFAs make you fat too. Omega-6 fatty acids have been shown to stimulate the body's endocannabinoid system, which affects appetite, making us eat more and, crucially, store more fat. Mice consistently gain more weight the more linoleic acid, an omega-6 fatty acid, they are fed.[141] On a related note, the endocrine-disrupting chemical BPA, which is used in the manufacture of plastics, has been shown to have similar effects, also through stimulating the endocannabinoid system. At concentrations that are now common in many waterways in the US, BPA will make zebra fish overeat and become obese.[142] The fish also develop fatty liver syndrome, which is linked to obesity and diabetes.

While vegetable and seed oils contain significant quantities of omega-6 fatty acids, they almost entirely lack omega-3 (DHA and EPA), types that are associated with a variety of protective purposes in the body.[143] Omega-3 deficiencies have been linked with cancer, depression, diabetes, arthritis, auto-immune conditions, and dementia. According to one estimate, 20 percent of all Americans have so little omega-3 in their bodies that it is impossible to detect. The richest sources of omega-3 are fatty fish, eggs, meat, and dairy, but because of the widespread practice of feeding livestock grains, many of these foods now contain less omega-3, and more omega-6, than they once did. Exactly how much of an effect this practice has on the fat quality of

---

[140] Keith, *Vegetarian Myth*, 185.
[141] Mamounis et al., "Linoleic acid causes greater weight gain." See also Naughton et al., "Linoleic acid and the pathogenesis of obesity."
[142] Tian et al., "New insights into bisphenols."
[143] See Keith, *Vegetarian Myth*, 185–86.

animal products is a matter of debate, though, with some saying that it actually causes much less of a change than is often claimed.[144] What really matters is that plant-based diets are almost entirely lacking this important nutrient.

Let's take a closer look, for a moment, at one particular seed oil. Soybean oil is now the most widely consumed oil in the US. Across the twentieth century, consumption of this novel oil increased a thousandfold. Once upon a time, not that long ago, nobody in the US, or anywhere else for that matter, ate soybean oil. Give how much soybean oil is now eaten, you would hope it has some beneficial effects. Unfortunately, evidence suggests that its consumption is intimately tied with some of the worst health problems being experienced in the US today. It is already well-established that soybean oil is obesogenic in mice—i.e. makes them fat—but a worrying study from 2020 shows that it causes serious genetic dysregulation and neurological damage, too.[145] The genes that were dysregulated by soybean oil included genes associated with inflammation, neuroendocrine and neurochemical processes, insulin signaling, and the production of oxytocin. Oxytocin is the famous "love hormone," which is responsible for social bonding, among other things. Other genes that were affected are linked to neurological diseases including Alzheimer's disease, Parkinson's, and autism. The previous research on soybean oil's obesity-causing effects was also substantiated: it increased insulin resistance and the mice consuming it also experienced the greatest amount of weight gain, despite consuming the same number of calories as the other mice in the study, which didn't consume soybean oil. The authors of the study are in no doubt that, although the study was carried out on mice, the results strongly suggest "that the [soybean-oil-rich] American diet may be not only contributing to increased rates of metabolic disease but also affecting neurological function."

---

[144] See Rodgers and Wolf, *Sacred Cow*, 73–80 for a detailed discussion of the relative nutrient profiles of grain-fed and grass-fed beef.
[145] Deol et al., "Dysregulation of hypothalamic gene expression."

Which leads nicely on to our final point in the discussion of why plant-based diets are less than ideal: phytoestrogens. Phytoestrogens are plant compounds that mimic the effects of the animal hormone estrogen in the body, generally referred to as the "female" hormone.[146] They do so in more or less the same manner as xenoestrogens, the industrial compounds I mentioned in the introduction to the book. Because of their estrogenic properties, plants rich in phytoestrogens have long been used in traditional remedies to treat women's problems, especially menopause, which is the result of a massive decline in estrogen production as a woman ages; hops, for instance, were traditionally used to treat night sweats, hot flushes, mood swings, and vaginal dryness. The problem comes, however, when phytoestrogens are consumed in such quantities that they seriously interfere with the body's natural hormonal balance, and that includes for both genders.

While a great many plant-based foods contain phytoestrogens, soy receives the most attention, for a number of reasons. Soy products are probably the main phytoestrogen-containing plant foods that people eat today, largely because soy has been heavily promoted as an "ideal" protein source for vegetarians. We've already seen that its PDCAAS score is—misleadingly— the same as the perfect animal protein sources, eggs and milk, and many believe that it is a simple substitute for these animal products. Almost all of the plant-based meat alternatives, such as the Impossible Burger, are built around soy, on the assumption that it is the closest form of plant protein to meat. Huge amounts of money have been spent to get people to eat soy in recent decades, including, perhaps most amusingly, $34 million spent by the American government to get Afghan farmers to plant soybeans as a food crop. A string of crop failures led

---

[146] It may be somewhat misleading to refer to estrogen simply as the "female" hormone, however. According to some researchers, such as Dr. Ray Peat, it's better to think of estrogen as a kind of stress hormone that is responsible especially for proliferation and growth. This explains the role of estrogen in a number of different cancers, for instance, including forms of breast cancer. See Peat, "Aging, estrogen, and progesterone."

the Afghans to abandon the project after four years.[147] As far as I can tell, the World Economic Forum hasn't had much to say about soy, but legumes—of which soy is an example—and nuts are the main sources of protein on the Planetary Health Diet, so I think it is safe to assume that soy will be a large part of what the nameless citizen is going to eat in 2030.

Although soy has long been consumed in certain cultures, such as Japan, for centuries, it has only entered public consciousness as a "healthy" plant food much more recently.[148] For most of its history of cultivation, soy was a "cover crop" grown in rotation because of its ability to fix nitrogen and restore nutrients to the soil. It was not a significant food crop at all. The highly processed forms of soy that people are eating now bear little resemblance to the carefully treated—usually fermented—forms of soy that were traditionally consumed, such as miso and tempeh. Because of its significant anti-nutrient content—trypsin inhibitors, which disable a particular digestive enzyme and cause gas, bloating, digestive pain, and diarrhea, and phytates, which bind minerals and prevent them from being absorbed by the body—soy was only considered edible in cultures that had found ways to disable those compounds, especially the trypsin inhibitors. Even in such cultures, soy foods were generally used only as condiments, consumed in small quantities, often in a fish broth. About the only groups that ate soy in large quantities were monks, who ate tofu (unfermented soy bean curd) because it helped them to keep their vows of sexual chastity by reducing their libido (more on this in a moment), and starving Chinese peasants. But then again, as Lierre Keith observes, starving Chinese peasants also ate their own children.

One of my favorite studies of soy phytoestrogens and their effects on living creatures involves male monkeys that were fed a diet rich in soy isoflavones. Over a period of fifteen months,

---

[147] Cohen and Arkin. "Afghans Don't Like Soybeans."
[148] The discussion of soy that follows draws especially on Keith, *Vegetarian Myth*, 210–28, except where otherwise cited.

male macaques living in nine different social groups were fed the same diet but for one crucial difference: groups received either no soy isoflavones or a dose of isoflavones, high or low, in the form of soy protein isolate. The results were pretty shocking:

> *In the monkeys fed the higher amount of isoflavones, frequencies of intense aggressive (67% higher) and submissive (203% higher) behavior were elevated relative to monkeys fed the control diet (P's < 0.05). In addition, the proportion of time spent by these monkeys in physical contact with other monkeys was reduced by 68%, time spent in proximity to other monkeys was reduced 50%, and time spent alone was increased 30% (P's < 0.02).* [149]

The authors conclude, then, that "long-term consumption of a diet rich in soy isoflavones can have marked influences on patterns of aggressive and social behavior." They note that the effect is likely to have been as a result of aromatization of male hormones, a process which is known to modulate aggressive behavior. Estrogen has a key role to play in this natural process, and so it's likely that the phytoestrogens in the soy were interfering in it. The study continues:

> *Estrogen produced by aromatization of gonadal androgen has an important facilitative role in male-typical aggressive behavior that is mediated through its interaction with estrogen receptors (ER) in the brain. Isoflavones found in soybeans and soy-based dietary supplements bind ER and have dose- and tissue-dependent effects on estrogen-mediated responses.*

In short, a simple dietary change turned the macaques into passive-aggressive, well, incel apes—Minassian monkeys, if

---

[149] Simon et al., "Increased aggressive behavior."

you will. The rediscovery of this study last year, which originally appears to have been through the fitness website Herculean Strength, was widely publicized. The study was featured on *Infowars* and also commented on by Joe Rogan, who said, "This explains Twitter," in an Instagram post. Of course, this is a study of monkeys and not humans, so the findings have to be treated with a certain amount of caution. But, as Rogan suggested, the parallels with observable human behavior are pretty uncanny. It would certainly be interesting to see whether research in humans would substantiate the study's findings. So maybe Plato's Socrates was wrong, then, about a vegetarian diet being essential to ensuring peace and accord among the workers of the ideal Republic. At the very least, he'd have to add soy to the list of prohibited foods as well.

As funny as the idea of incel apes may be, or of Plato banning soy, the well-attested effects of phytoestrogens on humans, especially soy, are no laughing matter. Soy has been shown to have serious effects on women's reproductive function. One study, for instance, revealed that administration of 60 grams of soy protein caused women's cycles to lengthen and reduced levels of luteinizing hormone and follicle-stimulating hormone drastically, bringing the women dangerously close to infertility. In the 1970s, the WHO conducted research to identify natural contraceptives as an alternative to the pill, including soy, flax, and red clover. Clover had been known to disrupt mammalian reproduction since the 1940s, when sheep were observed to suffer from "clover disease" as a result of grazing on the plant. The research was abandoned, however, when it was discovered that the side effects of these plants were similar to, and in some cases worse than, the pill itself. Soy isoflavones may also be responsible for pre-cancerous thickening of the uterus lining, known as endometrial hyperplasia, as shown in an Italian study. This led the Italian researchers to question "the long term safety of phytoestrogens with respect to the endometrium."

In men, phytoestrogen consumption can cause equally drastic changes, which result mainly from disruption of the male body's proper testosterone-estrogen ratio. The kind of changes this can bring on are illustrated nicely—or not so nicely—by an anecdotal study. A sixty-year-old man presented himself to doctors at an endocrinology clinic with a serious case of gynecomastia (formation of breast tissue), as well as erectile dysfunction and reduced libido.[150] The doctors were puzzled, because although laboratory assessments showed that he had serum concentrations of estrogen four times higher than the upper limit of the reference range, there were no physical abnormalities present in his testicles or elsewhere to account for this. Finally, things started to make sense when he revealed that he had been consuming more than 3 quarts of soy milk a day. As soon as he stopped drinking it, the breast tissue disappeared and his hormone levels returned to normal. Scientists have consistently reported lower testosterone and higher estrogen levels in men who consume foods rich in soy phytoestrogens, and have even been able to induce "testosterone deprivation" in animals simply by feeding them soy isoflavones.[151]

Babies are particularly at risk from soy formula. One study from Switzerland showed that infants fed soy formula instead of breast milk had between 13,000 and 22,000 times more serum estrogen in their bodies.[152] If you're having trouble imagining what that means, perhaps the following comparison might help. After adjustment for various factors such as weight of the baby and bioavailability and quantity of the phytoestrogens, a 13 pound baby on soy formula would be ingesting the equivalent of between four and five birth control pills a day. Yes, you read that right. And you think your GF behaves strangely on just one pill a day! Researchers have generally been coy, though, about the potential negative effects of these

---

[150] Martinex and Lewi, "An unusual case of gynecomastia."
[151] Daniel, *The Whole Soy Story*, 368.
[152] Setchell et al., "Isoflavone content of infant formulas."

concentrations of estrogenic substances, limiting themselves to making vague observations that they "may be sufficient to exert biological effects."[153] For anybody with even the most basic understanding of the role of hormones in development and sexual maturation, this is no news at all. It's yet another damning indictment of our failure, as a society, to protect the most vulnerable that we allow them to continue eating such products without fully knowing their effects.

There are other problems with soy too, beyond the anti-nutrients and phytoestrogens. Soy is a goitrogen, meaning that it can suppress your thyroid and cause permanent damage if enough of it is eaten:

> [T]he New York Times *has reported an epidemic of cretinism in impoverished rural areas of China where iodine deficiency is widespread and poverty forces people to eat more soy than the small quantities that are the norm. . . . In Japan, where soy consumption is the highest of any country in Asia, thyroid disease is widespread. After all, Hashimoto's thyroiditis, the autoimmune form of hyperthyroidism, was first detected in Japan, and the prevalence of thyroid disease there has motivated Japanese researchers to undertake important studies proving the adverse effects of soy foods on the thyroid gland.[154]*

A Japanese study performed on healthy adults showed that just 30 grams of soy a day for thirty days was a sufficient amount to cause thyroid disruption. As Lierre Keith puts it, "thirty grams of soy was a snack when I was a vegan."[155] Again, infants are deemed to be at particular risk of thyroid disease if fed soy, including soy formula, which contains servings well in

---

[153] For instance in Setchell et al., "Exposure of infants to phyto-oestrogens."
[154] Daniel, *Whole Soy Story*, 314.
[155] Keith, *Vegetarian Myth*, 213.

excess of 30 grams. The British Committee on Toxicity has already warned of the toxic effects of soy formula in this regard, as has the US Research Council.[156]

Since we're talking about the Planetary Health Diet, and not just plant-based diets per se, we must also reckon with the potential effects of GMO foods and the toxic chemical freight of the copious herbicides and pesticides used to treat them. I've already talked about both of these in the previous section of this chapter, but it's worth saying a little more here with a specific focus on the likely effects these things will have on us, rather than the environment.

The Showa Denko tragedy, mentioned in the introduction, is probably the clearest example to date of what can go wrong with GMOs for human consumption; although, in a sense, it is actually a "best-case"—or maybe a "least-worse-case"—scenario, for reasons we'll soon see.[157] At the end of the 1980s, the Japanese company Showa Denko decided to start manufacturing its tryptophan supplements using a novel method. Tryptophan is an essential amino acid that's found in normal food, but many people also consume it in supplement form. It is common for amino acids to be manufactured in micro-breweries using microbial cultures, which is exactly what Showa Denko was doing. One day, though, the company decided to splice new genes into the bacteria they were using, in order to increase the yields of tryptophan produced. In 1989, soon after the introduction of the new GMO tryptophan, between five and ten thousand people fell ill in the United States, the supplement's main market, with a vanishingly uncommon illness called eosinophilia-myalgia syndrome (EMS). In a matter of months, dozens had been killed, but the final death toll may now number in the hundreds. Thousands were permanently disabled. Although Showa Denko has always been adamant that it was not the genetically modified bacteria that caused the disaster, pointing instead to

---

[156] Ibid.
[157] In my discussion of the incident I am relying on Mann et al., "The Thalidomide of Genetic Engineering." unless otherwise stated.

a supposedly faulty carbon filter as a cause of some unspecified contamination, the evidence very strongly suggests that it was the genetic modification that was to blame. The fact that the authorities were content to accept Showa Denko's explanation, after the company had destroyed all samples of the bacteria they were using, is evidence only of the powerful interests involved. Even then, billions of dollars were at stake for biotech companies whose activities might have been curtailed by new regulations on genetic modification. In a human future predicated on the use of GMOs on a planetary scale, the barriers to the truth erected by the rich and powerful are likely to disappear up into the clouds.

When I say the Showa Denko incident represents a "least-worse-case" scenario, I mean that it was an unfortunate stroke of luck that the contamination had the particular effects it did. This has led at least one set of authors to refer to the Showa Denko incident as the "thalidomide of genetic engineering." In the same way that thalidomide might still be used if its effects had taken a more subtle form than the terrible birth defects it is famous for, so too Showa Denko might still be manufacturing its tryptophan in the same way if it hadn't brought on such an unusual illness. In both cases, though, the damage was of a kind that aroused interest straight away, although it still took eight years and tens of thousands of birth defects before thalidomide was finally removed from the European market in 1963.[158] It is very easy to imagine a scenario where genetically modified food has serious negative effects that go undiscovered simply because they don't stand out in the same way as children born with seal-limb syndrome. Elevated long-term rates of a particular cancer, for instance, or increased rates of auto-immune disorders might eventually grab the attention of medical professionals, but by that point causality would have become so diffuse that pinpointing the ultimate cause might be impossible. In the case of the Showa Denko tryptophan, it was

---

[158] Vargesson, "Thalidomide-induced teratogenesis."

easy enough for investigators to identify the fact that all of the sufferers had been taking the same supplement, and likewise in the case of thalidomide. But what if everybody—I mean ten billion people—is eating the same kinds of GMO foods? Where would we find the background or "control" group that might help us identify the ultimate cause?

While it certainly feels like a cop-out to say that we can't know what the effects of massively increased GMO consumption will be, we just can't. And we already know that DNA can pass whole from food into human blood "through an unknown mechanism," as a study in *PLOS One* showed.[159] The case of Showa Denko should, at least, make us think twice about whether genetic modification of food is a good idea. Not least of all because the kind of genetic engineering being used was of an extremely primitive nature—the alteration of just a single gene to increase the yield of an amino acid—compared to the incredibly complex new procedures, for instance using CRISPR technology. The complexity of the engineering, as well as the scale on which consumption of its products will take place, means the potential for harm is of a magnitude that at present we can only begin to imagine.

It's worth noting, since we're on the subject, that GMOs are already widely consumed in the US, often without the consumer's knowledge, and that this is a trend that will only grow in the near future if regulations are not brought in to stop it, or at least better inform consumers of what it is they're actually eating. Food that contains GMOs is even being labeled non-GMO, as producers exploit loopholes in labeling regulations in order to avoid using a term that still, quite rightly, has strong negative connotations for many members of the public. Companies are able to get away with claiming that compounds produced by genetically modified organisms are non-GMO, since the compounds themselves have not been altered. These compounds are often referred to as synthetic biology, or syn-bio,

---

[159] Spisák et al. "Complete Genes May Pass."

products. Brave Robot Ice Cream, for instance, contains a protein produced by genetically engineered yeast, but the ice cream is not labeled as containing GMOs. Probably the most well-known syn-bio product, though, is the Impossible Burger, which uses a genetically engineered substance known as "heme" (nothing to do with heme iron) to make the fake meat appear to bleed when cut or bitten into. Again, the product is not labeled as GMO.[160] Before novel ingredients, such as Impossible Burger's heme, are added to food in the US, they must achieve the designation of "Generally Recognized as Safe" (GRAS) from the FDA, but this process has many flaws. Not least of all, application for the status, and therefore disclosure of novel ingredients, is voluntary, and the company is allowed to supply its own research in support of the application.[161] It's not hard to see how such a system could be abused.

With regard to herbicides and pesticides, there's no question that eating non-organic produce, as all food in the Planetary Health Diet will be, is a significant source of exposure. A recent study out of Australia, for instance, showed that the "healthiest diet in the world," the so-called Mediterranean diet, can lead to a significant increase in consumption of toxic chemicals if the produce consumed is not organic.[162] On a non-organic Mediterranean diet, in which copious amounts of fruit, vegetables, and nuts are consumed, pesticide exposure can be three or more times higher than that of somebody on the archetypal unhealthy diet of processed food, red meat, sugar, and dairy and ten times higher than that of somebody on an organic version of the Mediterranean diet. (Organic produce, sadly, is often not totally free of toxic chemicals, since they may persist in the ground if an area is repurposed for organic growing, and "collateral damage" from spraying, as we saw in the case of dicamba and chlorpyrifos, is also common.) The researchers identified fruit, vegetables, and wholegrain cereals as the most

---

[160] Roseboro, "Synthetic biology products."
[161] *FoodPrint of Fake Meat.*
[162] Rempelos et al., "Diet and food type affect."

significant dietary contributors of pesticides. The study also demonstrates what I was saying about the difficulties posed when exposure or consumption becomes ubiquitous and the "control group" in society disappears. As the lead academic on the study puts it: "One of the difficulties of assessing the public health impacts of dietary exposure to pesticides is that once pesticides are widely used in food production everybody gets exposed."[163] That is the world of the Planetary Health Diet.

Let me just restate some of the negative human health effects that have been associated with glyphosate exposure in studies published during the last year: gut-flora disruptions associated with neurological and psychiatric diseases; and increased DNA methylation in post-menopausal women, a molecular change that can cause cancer and increase cellular aging; among others. Most lawsuits about glyphosate, including the 125,000 suits that were settled for nearly $11 billion in 2020, concern cancer, especially non-Hodgkin's lymphoma, although Bayer still denies that glyphosate is associated in any way with cancer.[164] Or what about chlorpyrifos? As we've already seen, studies link this pesticide with developmental abnormalities in the brains of babies, lowered IQ and cognitive development, autism, stunting, lung cancer, Parkinson's disease, and obesity. The truth is, even if we can't predict exactly what the negative effects of increased exposure to agricultural chemicals like glyphosate will be, we can be pretty sure, first, that there will be negative effects and, second, that they'll be more widespread than any we've seen to date. The question, then, is not if these effects will happen, but whether they can be properly assessed once all ten billion people on earth are consuming exactly the same chemical-laden food. This assumes there will even be a desire to do so, once the entire food chain is controlled by a handful of giant corporations.

---

[163] Southern Cross University, "Benefits of using organic food."
[164] BBC. "Bayer to pay $10.9bn."

So what will all this sub-optimal nutrition add up to for the citizens of "Welcome to 2030"? I think it should be pretty obvious that it's not going to be good. To give the devil his due once again, though, it's likely that some groups would actually benefit from adoption of the Planetary Health Diet, at least in the short term. First of all, and most obviously, there are those who at present have no food to eat. If you're starving in Africa, or anywhere else for that matter, a guaranteed supply of food, even if it looks nothing like the food humans need to thrive, is much better than nothing. According to the World Economic Forum, there were 820 million starving people worldwide in 2018.[165] Secondly, there are those who are overweight and obese. Certainly in the short term, they are also likely to benefit from adoption of the diet. And again, that's a lot of people: 1.9 billion overweight people worldwide in 2016, of whom 650 million were obese, according to the WHO.[166] As Diana Rodgers and Robb Wolf note, putting overweight people on a vegetarian or vegan diet has short-term benefits because it is basically like going on a fast, with the elimination of food types—especially sugar-heavy and processed foods—that would "immediately make anyone healthier." People who only eat junk food are likely to get more vitamins, minerals, and antioxidants than they were before, and as a result would feel better initially, when they change to a plant-based diet. In the long run, however, they'll be prey to the same deficiencies and problems all adherents of plant-based diets face.[167] Remember what I said in the introduction, too: we shouldn't be playing the numbers game with this diet, because that's exactly what the WEF and its supporters want us to do.

Let's put the starving and the overweight and obese to one side, then. As I mentioned earlier, when I outlined the Planetary Health Diet, I noted that the places where current dietary practices most diverge from the EAT Foundation's ideal are

---

[165] Lomborg, "Starvation still claims a child's life."
[166] World Health Organization, "Obesity and overweight."
[167] Rodgers and Wolf, *Sacred Cow*, 99.

Europe and America. These are the places where, obviously, we can expect adoption of the diet to have the greatest negative effects. We already have widespread literature on the negative effects of veganism and vegetarianism, by which I mean not only clinical and scientific accounts, but also biographical material from "survivors" (a term I generally hate) of those diets. This is one place we can look to get the most vivid idea of what it might be like for the rest of us to adopt the Planetary Health Diet.

*The Vegetarian Myth*, a book I have drawn liberally from, is not just a book about the rights and wrongs and the science of plant-based diets: it is also a moving personal testament to the absolute havoc—often irretrievable—that they can cause, as well as the cognitive dissonance involved in choosing to persist in that lifestyle, in spite of all the physical and mental discomfort it brings. Lierre Keith, the author, knew that the diet she was eating was sickening and killing her—this became apparent early on in her journey into veganhood, as a debilitating spine condition took hold—but she persisted for fifteen years before finally breaking and returning back to eating meat and animal products. The damage, though, can never be fully undone:

*My spine isn't coming back. But eating a diet of grass-fed animal products has repaired the damage a bit and made a dent in my pain level. My insulin receptors are also down for the count, but protein and fat keep my blood sugar stable and happy. I haven't missed a period in five years, though if I end up with cancer in my reproductive organs, I'm blaming soy. My stomach's okay—not great, but okay—as long as I take betaine hydrochloride with every meal. Between my spiritual practice and my nutri-*

*ent-dense diet, I am now depression-free, and I am thank-*
*ful every day. But the cold and exhaustion are perma-*
*nent.*[168]

I don't think it's hyperbolic to imagine that adoption of the
Planetary Health Diet will make a lot of people seriously unwell, both physically and mentally. Whether they will all be as
unwell as Lierre Keith was, I can't say for certain, but I think
there will be some quite dramatic effects at the population
level. Here, as a reminder, are some of the effects archaeologists have observed or inferred as a result of the Neolithic Revolution: physical shrinkage; nutritional deficiencies and stress
(iron deficiencies, rickets, tooth decay, etc.); reduced sexual dimorphism (differences in size and shape between males and females) and reproductive problems; and increased susceptibility
to illness and disease. It is entirely plausible that all of these
effects would be mirrored in the near future, if the majority of
the world's population adopts the Planetary Health Diet.

Let's look at physical stature first. "But, Egg, isn't it a bit
dramatic to imagine that people are all going to start shrinking? *Really?*" No, actually, it isn't. There's plenty of evidence,
some of which is very recent, for society-wide shrinkage as a
result of changing diet. When he visited the Outer Hebrides,
Weston Price noted that there had been a dramatic decrease in
height across Scotland as a result of the introduction of the sub-
optimal modern industrial diet:

> *I was concerned to obtain information from government*
> *officials relative to the incidence of tooth decay and the*
> *degenerative diseases in various parts of north Scotland.*
> *I was advised that in the last fifty years the average height*
> *of Scotch men in some parts decreased four inches, and*
> *that this had been coincident with the general change*

---

[168] Keith, *Vegetarian Myth*, 11.

*from high immunity to dental caries to a loss of immunity
in a great part of this general district.[169]*

We also know a lot about the mid-Victorian period in Britain,
a time when people were remarkably healthy. In fact, according to the authors of an article on the period, British subjects
of the time enjoyed "probably the best standards of health ever
enjoyed by a modern state."

> *Britain and its world-dominating empire were supported
> by a workforce, an army and a navy comprised of individ-
> uals who were healthier, fitter and stronger than we are
> today. They were almost entirely free of the degenerative
> diseases which maim and kill so many of us, and alt-
> hough it is commonly stated that this is because they all
> died young, the reverse is true; public records reveal that
> they lived as long—or longer than—we do in the 21st cen-
> tury.[170]*

What made the diet of the mid-Victorians so good was meat,
seafood, fruits, and vegetables, all of which were eaten in far
greater quantities than they had been before 1850. As Diana
Rodgers and Robb Wolf put it, "the hallmark of the mid-Victorian diet is an abundance of whole, largely unprocessed foods,
produced in a manner that goes far beyond our modern standards of 'organic' and grass fed."[171] A shift from a predominantly
grain-based diet brought with it massive increases in health
and longevity. But then, from about 1880, another, less-wel-
come shift took place—more or less the same shift Weston Price
was studying a little further down the road, so to speak. Brit-
ons began to eat more refined foods, including larger amounts
of sugar, flour, and canned meats and fewer vegetables, fruits,
fresh meat, and seafood. Their health suffered significantly,

---

[169] Price, *Nutrition and Physical Degeneration*, 57.
[170] The study is discussed in Rodgers and Wolf, *Sacred Cow*, 63–7.
[171] Rodgers and Wolf, *Sacred Cow*, 64.

and one of the main effects was, of course, stunting. It was so bad and so widespread that the British army had to lower its minimum height requirements for recruits.

Nutrition is a key factor in the global distribution of heights today. A huge study from 2017 showed that increased male height is associated with the "superior nutrition" of animal proteins, and in particular the protein from milk, eggs, and red meat.[172] The researchers used anthropometric data (body measurements) from 105 countries across Europe, the Middle East, North Africa, Asia, and Oceania, as well as data on average consumption of nearly thirty different kinds of protein sources. The results showed a clear correlation between average male height and average protein intake. They also revealed three broad types of diet: rice-based, wheat-based, and milk-based. Rice-based diets, associated with tropical Asia, produce the shortest statures of all, followed by wheat-based diets, which predominate in the Muslim countries of North Africa and the Middle East. Milk-based diets, typical of northern and central Europe, produce the tallest people in the world. The authors conclude:

> *[Plant-based diets] are not able to provide the optimal stimuli for physical growth, even if the intake of total protein and total energy poses no problem. In fact, we observed a difference of 10 cm (174 cm vs. 184 cm) between nations relying on the surplus of plant and animal proteins, respectively.*

They point, in particular, to the relatively low quality of plant protein, the presence of anti-nutrients, and the "disproportionate load of 'empty' calories from starch and oils that must be consumed per unit of a key nutrient."

Although the recommendations of the Planetary Health Diet don't go further than providing indicative relative caloric

---

[172] Grasgruber et al., "Major correlates of male height."

intakes—i.e. they don't also provide guidelines for protein consumption based on bodyweight—it's clear enough, since the protein is overwhelmingly plant-based, that it's going to be of an inferior quality and therefore an insufficient amount. So be under no illusions: the world of the Planetary Health Diet is not one in which you are going to be able to push the physical envelope. If you aren't even going to have enough protein to reach your proper height, you're not going to have enough to build a powerful physique either. We might speculate about what such a world would look like for athletes and sportsmen and -women. Would there be exemptions to ensure they got sufficient nutrition to compete at the highest levels? Or would standards just decline across the board? If the latter, there would no doubt be major gaslighting: "What do you mean the 100 meter record used to be 9.77 seconds!? The time to beat has always been 15 seconds!" But given how important sporting events are to ensuring a quiescent public—the bread and circuses of our day—I wouldn't be surprised if exemptions were made, one way or another.

Couple this with the hormonal effects of key nutrient and mineral deficiencies and consumption of phytoestrogens and things will look very bad indeed for men. This is another way of saying that sexual dimorphism, like in the Neolithic Revolution, is almost certainly going to decrease. Males and females are going to become more, rather than less, alike, as men's stature, hormone levels, and musculature decline. We should definitely expect reproductive problems, and not just those we might obviously anticipate as a result of reduced testosterone, such as decreased male fertility.[173] It might actually be the case that fewer men end up being born worldwide to mothers on the Planetary Health Diet. On average, there should be about 105 male babies born for every 100 female babies, but malnutrition has been identified as a cause of lower sex ratios, meaning that fewer male babies are born relative to female babies. A study

---

[173] See Swan and Colino, *Count Down*.

from 2000, which looked at six thousand pregnant women, found that a considerably lower number of male babies were born to the women who were vegetarian.[174] Vegetarian women were 23 percent less likely to give birth to a boy than women on an omnivorous diet. This is almost certainly the result of added physical stress due to the mother's diet, which threatens the viability of the fetus and can cause spontaneous abortion. Male babies seem to suffer more from an adverse fetal environment, as a number of studies have already observed. It's even been noted by demographers that, after "stressful" historical events like 9/11, the relative number of male births has decreased.[175]

Indeed, babies and children are likely to suffer most of all on the Planetary Health Diet. You may already be familiar with some of the horror stories associated with feeding children plant-based, and most of all vegan, diets. In 2019, for example, a vegan couple was jailed in Sweden, when their eighteen-month-old child was found in a state of extreme starvation.[176] The child's parents, who called themselves "nomads," had been feeding the baby breast milk, brown rice, and potatoes since birth, allegedly because the baby was suffering from "food allergies." (Breast milk from vegan women contains 69 percent less DHA, for instance, which is essential for proper brain formation of infants.)[177] Another similar recent case of an eighteen-month-old, from Florida, was even worse, because the poor child died.[178] The vegan parents, Sheila and Ryan O'Leary, had been feeding the child only breast milk and his three siblings only raw fruit and vegetables. The eldest child was least malnourished because she spent part of her time living with her biological father, who presumably fed her something more nutritious than rabbit food.

[174] Hudson and Buckley, "Vegetarian diets."
[175] Chebani, "Stress May Cause Spontaneous Abortions."
[176] Ibbetson, "Swedish couple who raised."
[177] Rodgers and Wolf, *Sacred Cow*, 105.
[178] Farberov, "US vegan parents who eat."

Although these are extreme cases, it's not for no reason that doctors in, for instance, Belgium have put forward proposals to make feeding babies vegan diets illegal. However, significant damage will already have been done to a baby if the mother followed a plant-based diet during the pregnancy, since the developing fetus depends for its nutrition almost entirely on what the mother is eating.[179] One recent study has revealed that children raised on vegan diets are over an inch shorter and have weaker bones than the average.[180] As a result of their findings, the study authors are unequivocal that children on vegan diets must be given long-term supplementation for vitamins D3 and B12, but this is really the tip of the iceberg in terms of nutrients vegan children lack. As French scientists noted:

*The vegan diet . . . raises questions about its benefits for a growing child: adequate caloric and protein intake, quality of essential amino acids, presence of essential fatty acids, inhibition of absorption of trace elements (including iodine, iron and zinc) and supply of various vitamins.[181]*

Really, this is just to reiterate what was said earlier about the whole host of nutritional deficiencies that all vegetarians and vegans face, with the caveat that these deficiencies are especially unkind to babies and children.

I think it's safe to say that we will see increased rates of disease too, and not just because of the various deficiencies associated with plant-based diets. Infectious diseases have made something of a roaring comeback in the last couple of years, if you hadn't noticed, and people would almost certainly be more susceptible to infection as a result of the various deficiencies they'd be running, like D3 and zinc. Vitamin D increases the effectiveness of immune-cell function and helps create barriers

---

[179] Rodgers and Wolf, *Sacred Cow*, 106.
[180] Desmond et al., "Growth, body composition, and cardiovascular."
[181] Rodgers and Wolf, *Sacred Cow*, 108–9.

to bacterial and viral infection.[182] Low vitamin D levels have been associated with higher risk of severe coronavirus symptoms, for instance.[183] I've run through the massive variety of chronic illnesses associated with consumption of PUFAs, phytoestrogens, and industrial herbicides and pesticides—everything from heart disease to cancer, and diabetes to autoimmune disorders. PUFAs are already consumed in vast quantities in the US—remember that soybean oil is the most widely consumed oil in the US today—but if everybody in the future derives all, or almost all, of their fat calories from vegetable and seed oils, we might reasonably expect these negative effects to become even more widespread. It also seems reasonable to expect some "known unknowns," to borrow Donald Rumsfeld's famous phrase, although we can't know exactly how many, and the problem of having no control group in society will make it much harder to identify these known unknowns, as was explained earlier. Nobody could have predicted, as we saw, that nearly ten thousand people would become ill with EMS until Showa Denko started using GMO tryptophan in its supplements. Do we really want to open that box on a worldwide scale?

.    .    .

So this is the diet, and the world, that the World Economic Forum has to offer us in the near future. A world where many of the worst trends of the present-day system of food production and consumption are not eliminated, but amplified. A world where your right to choose what goes into your body will disappear, and you will have no choice but to bear the negative effects, just like the wretched early farmers of the Neolithic Revolution. None of the claims made by the World Economic

---

[182] Cantorna et al., "Vitamin D and 1,25(OH)₂D."
[183] Karonova, et al., "Low 25(OH)D Level."

Forum or the EAT Foundation about the benefits of this globalist model for food stack up. Incoherence, however, won't stop this model from being made a reality. Only we can do that. But how?

# Part Two

## THE EGGS BENEDICT OPTION

# CHAPTER 3
# THE EGGS BENEDICT OPTION

So here we are. We now know everything we need to know about the Great Reset and how it will change the way we eat, and live, if it comes to pass. Now we can see that the comparisons I've made in the past with the Neolithic Revolution, which I've called "the original Great Reset," are not idle ones, but really do reveal how much we have to lose if we are forced to accept some version of the Planetary Health Diet. We will not be healthier; instead, we are likely to experience a wide variety of negative health effects, ranging from basic deficiencies to actual physical shrinkage, and we will surrender all control of the food system to corporations whose interests could not be further from our own. Eating, which many traditional cultures consider to be man's most fundamental form of engagement with the life-giving forces of mother nature, will no longer be something we have any power over.[184] Our alienation from the sacred foods our ancestors flourished on—which is already well advanced—will at last be complete. So what can we do to prevent this from happening?

I don't just mean that we should prevent the Great Reset from happening or create redoubts against it if it does happen,

---

[184] See for instance, Schmid, *Native Nutrition*, 49.

although those are both possibilities. I want to go much further and put forward an alternative vision to the Great Reset that we can strive for, something positive that can be constructed in its place and will make the world, or at the very least certain nations, look much more how we might like them to look than they do today.

As I've said in the introduction, following Alexander Dugin, the Great Reset is not really a definitive break with, but rather is an intensification of, the current global liberal system. Even if we prevent the Great Reset from taking place, the truth is that the global liberal system will still remain in place, with many of its tendencies still pointing in the direction of the Great Reset. Of course, things will not be as bad as they would be under the Great Reset, but that's hardly a recommendation—only a reprieve. We will still be living in a world where politicians and corporations pursue their own interests with no genuine concern for the lives or livelihoods of the people they claim to serve, a world where, instead of trusting and empowering individuals to look after themselves and their families, politicians and corporations foster sickness and dependency through a poisoned food supply and ad hoc medical treatments—and countless other evils too, all of which weaken individuals, their collective identities, and their traditions. Regardless of whether or not the Great Reset takes place, I think this is a perfect juncture for us to stop and think about the kind of nation, and the kind of world, we want to live in. Do we want to continue as things were before, or do we have the will and the vision to try something new? That is why I believe we should not be content just to prevent the Great Reset from happening, although that in itself will be an achievement.

I call my vision of politics "raw egg nationalism," and everything I say here is compatible—I think—with that vision to the extent that I have already laid it out. But I am going to go much further than I have ever gone before in laying out my vision of a nation built on the principles of raw egg nationalism. This is what I mean by the Eggs Benedict Option. Unlike Rod Dreher's egg-less Benedict Option, it doesn't involve a fanciful retreat in the face of encroaching darkness—as if the intentional Christian communities he proposes will simply be left alone by the heathens that surround them (fat chance, Rod!). Instead, today's Eggs Benedict Option will involve standing our ground, like men, and fighting for our birthright—our sacred nations— by pursuing a vigorous policy of nationalism and transforming the way the people of the nation produce and consume food. Neither without the other will work, as far as I see it.

Earlier I gave an account of the Neolithic Revolution and the transition to agricultural states because I wanted to draw some provocative comparisons between "the original Great Reset" and the present-day plans of Klaus Schwab and his fellow globalists. Hopefully, the similarities are plenty clear by now. Just for a moment, I want to return to the Neolithic Revolution to draw out one very obvious *dis*-similarity between then and now. The difference is this: in the Neolithic Revolution and its aftermath, there were other places to run to if you did not want to be a settled farmer living as a subject of a state, whereas now there is nowhere to go—not really—if you don't want to be a part of the Great Reset. The Schwab plan is a global one, meant to leave no life untouched if it succeeds. While it took thousands of years for the agricultural-state model created in the Neolithic to become the dominant global form, the globalists are already claiming that the world will look unrecognizable as soon as 2030.

Since we have an "original Great Reset," we might also talk of an "original Eggs Benedict Option." In the Neolithic, this was what James Scott calls "voluntary self-nomadization."[185] This involved, quite simply, downing tools and upping sticks to become a barbarian or nomad again—or, as the Neolithic Revolution advanced, for the very first time. Even before the existence of states, it was very common for sedentary sites to be abandoned and for the people to move on and settle somewhere else,

---

[185] Scott, *Against the Grain*, 219–56.

but the added pressures of population, coercion, and competition made the early states unstable to a much greater extent. Collapse could happen at any time, whether through the ravages of epidemic disease, revolt among the peasants, ecological changes leading to reduced agricultural productivity, or war with other states. When an early state began to unravel, populations that were previously forced to be settled agriculturalists could now choose not to be, and the evidence suggests that many were more than happy to vote with their feet as soon as the opportunity arose. And so what look to the historian and the archaeologist of today like little "dark ages," when written and physical records cease as a result of state collapse, may actually have been anything but dark ages for the peasants who were now free from the crushing exactions of state authority:

> *There may well be, then, a great deal to be said on behalf of classical dark ages in terms of human well-being. Much of the dispersion that characterizes them is likely to be a flight from war, taxes, epidemics, crop failures, and conscription. As such, it may stanch the worst losses that arise from concentrated sedentism under state rule.*[186]

Since the vast majority of the world's population remained non-state peoples until at least about AD 1600, if not later, going over to the barbarians remained an option for far longer and until far more recently than we might like to think. Herodotus, for instance, describes how certain Greeks might spend part of the year in the saddle among the famous nomadic Scythians, and self-barbarization was an option as much for the heavily pressed Roman cultivator in the late Empire as it was for the Chinese rice farmer if he could reach the nomadic horsemen of the Great Steppe. One pertinent fact that is worth remembering about the ancient world is that walls, and that includes the

---

[186] Scott, *Against the Grain*, 217.

Great Wall, were not just built to keep people out: they were also built to keep people *in*. One of the last groups to be able to continue this tradition of throwing off the garb of civilized life was the mountain men of the American frontier, whom I've discussed at length in an article in *Man's World*, my magazine. Venturing deep into the American wilderness, these hard European men took on the habits of the Native Americans as they hunted and trapped, living off game and buffalo and taking Indian women as wives. Scott calls this millennia-long period of movement outside the state "the Golden Age of the Barbarians," when vast spaces existed beyond state control and the settled centers of civilization lay before mobile horsemen like vast collections of tethered animals, ripe for the taking. Indeed, it's not for nothing that the Mongols chose to refer to settled grain-eating peasants using the same terminology they applied to the animals they herded, or that they treated them in the same dispassionate manner either.

Part of the reason why we don't hear this story told is because it flies so utterly in the face of the traditional narrative of civilisational progress. But, for many, the "trappings" of civilization really were just that—a trap. Today, with the total global hegemony of the state form, "self-nomadization" is impossible. This is the problem of "owned space," which Bronze Age Pervert puts at the heart of his exhortation to return to the Bronze Age Mindset. There are no latter-day Scythians to run away to in order to escape living in the bugman pod. As Benjamin Franklin famously put it, "We must, indeed, all hang together or, most assuredly, we shall all hang separately." But what does this hanging together actually amount to?

For Alexander Dugin, whose work helped define the nature of the Great Reset in the introduction, the proper response to the Great Reset must be of a very particular sort. Dugin asserts, first, that the response to the Great Reset must be a global one, because of the global nature of the plan, and, second, that the liberal nation-state form is not the answer because it is an integral part of the process that brought the

Great Reset into being in the first place. Globalism, in fact, is a "culmination" of liberal ideology, which is rooted in the medieval scholastic debate about the existence of universals, as I've discussed in the introduction. For Dugin, then, the only way to surpass globalism and the Great Reset is "the Great Awakening," a global front made up of various popular movements, from Trumpists in the US, via Orbanites in Hungary and Islamists in the Middle East, to the CCP in China.

Key to this Great Awakening is Russia, says Dugin, because of its dual nature—neither Europe, nor Asia, but both—and its staunch opposition to bourgeois liberal values, in favor of deep forms of collective identity: "the clan, folk, church, tradition, nation, and power."

> *Russians reject the Great Reset both from the Right and from the Left—and this, together with historical traditions, collective identity, and the perception of sovereignty and state freedom as the highest value, is not a momentary, but a long-term, fundamental feature of Russian civilisation.*[187]

The Russian experience, then, is instructive for all who want to escape the Great Reset, because it is a fundamental rejection of the values and forms that created it.

I think Dugin is absolutely right to point out that the reaction against globalism and the Great Reset is taking on a "glocal" form, to revive a hideous term that should probably have been left to rot. "Global," because resistance is to be found not just in a single region of the world but in every part, and yet "local" at the same time, because that resistance takes on a character that must necessarily be shaped and determined by local conditions. The Islamic response to globalism is of course going to be different from the Russian or the American, because each is drawing on a unique history and set of traditions. But

---

[187] Dugin, *The Great Awakening*, 39.

although the language, ideas, and practices used to express this resistance will vary, the practical effect is still the same: a wholehearted rejection of the terms of the Great Reset.

One of the key issues with this reaction is the extent to which it needs to be, or even can be, coordinated. How necessary is it for there to be a global "movement" against globalism? Calling the growing resistance to globalism "the Great Awakening" can only suggest a movement—for me, at least, the phrase immediately brings to mind the great religious revivals of the eighteenth and nineteenth centuries, but it may suggest something different to you. The phrase certainly suggests coordination. It is difficult, though, to see exactly what form that will take. For one thing, there are obviously serious differences of opinion between nations or civilizations—for instance, the Christian and the Islamic—which are just as likely to prevent cooperation as they are to make it possible. I think Dugin is definitely too optimistic about how much common cause national left and right movements can make with one another. While it might be possible for some national groups to support and coordinate with one another—for instance, right-populists in America and Hungary or America and Brazil—in other cases this will clearly not be possible. China and the Islamic regimes of the Middle East are the most obvious examples of groups Western nations are likely to have a hard time coming to terms with at all, in any form. Perhaps, at best, what will happen is that there will be a recognition of each nation or civilization's right to pursue its own destiny. A new "respect" on the international scene might be the first genuine attempt to honor the national right to self-determination, as enshrined in the UN Charter.

It is more likely, in my view, that certain individual nations, by which I really mean America, will make the greatest contribution to nailing the coffin lid shut on the Great Reset. The Trump presidency, for all its failures and missed opportunities, amply demonstrated just how much of a threat even a partially implemented America First agenda could be to the globalist plan. There is every reason to believe that a full-blooded commitment to America First under a leader who chose to surround himself with the right people, and knew who his enemies really were and took them more seriously than Trump did, would be a silver stake to the heart of the Great Reset, even without the efforts of other great nations like Russia and China, which, of course, is why it can't be allowed to happen—at any cost. The double-time dismantling of America that is taking place under Biden is being done with the clear aim of preventing a repeat of the 2016 election and a return to the popular politics of Trumpism. Nothing could be more obvious. In this there is hope as well as the most severe danger.

Still, I do think Dugin is right that the Russian example also has a very powerful role to play, although not necessarily for exactly the same reasons. The Russian model of agriculture, based around a division between household production for subsistence and industrial production for the market, provides a potential alternative to the globalist industrial system of agriculture that underpins the Great Reset. The benefits of such an alternative system, as we will see, extend far beyond simply the high-quality local food that it produces, and it could very well serve as a real embodiment of the tenets of the raw egg nationalist vision.

It is worth talking at a little length about the immediate practicalities of actually stopping the Great Reset, before I go into detail about the Eggs Benedict Option. One thing that seems crystal clear after the events of the past two years is that things are going to get worse, maybe much worse, before they get better. The madness of the last twenty-four months—the supply-chain breakdowns, product shortages, inflation, problems with the power network, war in Europe—is only going to continue and, unfortunately, deepen. We should be in no doubt that this is intentional. One development I've drawn my followers' attention to, both in my writings and on Twitter, is how Bill Gates has silently become the largest private landowner in the US. Over the course of the pandemic, he has snatched up tens of thousands of acres, putting his US holdings at over 240,000 acres in eighteen states from Washington to Florida. It is very likely that this pioneer of alternative food sources will use his immense concentration of agricultural land to help create forms of artificial scarcity that will drive prices of animal products through the roof. This will be only one part of the skulduggery aimed at making the changes of the Great Reset seem inevitable and as desirable as they can be, given the circumstances. As we have heard so many times before, they will tell us "there is no alternative."

Don't believe me? Try this recent *New York Times* article on for size, titled "You Want To Buy Meat? In This Economy?"

*Inflation has the potential to drive welcome change for the planet if Americans think differently about the way they eat. While hunger and food insecurity are a very real problem in the United States and globally, middle- and upper-class Americans still have more choices at the grocery store than perhaps any food shoppers in history. Climate change has motivated some to eat less resource-intensive meat and more vegetables, grains and legumes, but this movement has not reached the scale necessary to bring needed change — yet.*

In other words, let's hope inflation gets even worse. These people are salivating at the prospect of you being forced to change your diet. There is even praise for the Lever Act of 1917, which was enacted to allow the US government to requisition citizens' food and prevent hoarding. Door-to-door meat confiscations? Don't bet against it.

We are all going to have to face the prospect of finding it harder and harder to eat the foods we really want to eat. The price of animal products will almost certainly rise as their availability is made to decrease, by hook and by crook. The full Eggs Benedict Option is built around a radical reform of the industrial agricultural system at multiple levels, something that will of course take a significant amount of time and effort, and so this will not be much help in the immediate short term. My only counsel in the coming months and years is that you try to find ways to secure your access to the foods you want to eat. That might mean making friends with local farmers—which you should have been doing anyway!—and it might also mean beginning to produce your own food. A small amount of land, even a modest garden, can yield a surprising amount of high-quality produce, as the Russian system, discussed below, demonstrates. You might be extremely surprised by how little land you need to keep chickens, for instance. Even a few window boxes or just a sunny windowsill can be used to grow all the herbs you'll ever need and maybe some salad leaves as well. Since local subsistence production is the foundation of the Eggs Benedict Option, I'm advocating self-sufficiency anyway, but in the coming years, before the real fight against the Great Reset gains momentum, whatever preparations you can make may be the difference between compromising your diet and health or continuing to eat the life-giving foods that help make you a sovereign human.

There is, of course, also a tremendous amount of satisfaction to be had from producing your own food, as there is from any activity that demands care and meaningful attention in order to produce results. And that is before you even put the food you produced in your mouth. A store-bought tomato that has been chemically treated, picked well before it was ripe, and then artificially ripened in a warehouse with ethylene gas—well, do I really need to tell you that this "tomato" will taste nothing like a tomato that has ripened naturally on the vine in a sunny spot in your garden?

## *Eggs Benedict*

A book called *The Eggs Benedict Option*, by the author of the *Raw Egg Nationalism Cookbook* no less, would be a bit of a disappointment if it didn't contain a recipe for eggs Benedict, wouldn't it? Well, here it is: eggs Benedict, with five variations, including my own personal version: eggs Gironda.

Eggs Benedict is a classic breakfast/brunch dish consisting of a toasted English muffin topped with a thin slice of ham, poached egg, and Hollandaise sauce. A lot of people seem to think that making a Hollandaise sauce is incredibly hard, something only a trained chef could do, but really it's not that hard at all. Instead of using a saucepan to make the sauce, use a blender that has been warmed by being filled with hot water, then emptied and dried. Just follow the instructions carefully and you'll be fine.

Preparation: 20 minutes | Cooking: 20 minutes | Serves: 2

### Ingredients

For the Hollandaise
120 grams butter
1 large egg yolk
1 tablespoon lemon juice
Pinch of salt
Pinch of ground black or
  white pepper
Pinch of cayenne pepper

For the eggs
4 large eggs
2 English muffins
Butter (to butter the muffins)
4 thin slices of cooked ham
Paprika and chives, to garnish

First make the Hollandaise. Melt the butter in a pan until it is hot. Warm the blender bowl by filling it with hot water, then emptying and drying it. Add the egg yolk, lemon juice, salt, and both kinds of pepper, and blend at medium speed. Slowly add the hot melted butter with the machine still running until the mixture has emulsified.

Warm the sliced ham gently in the oven. Bring a large pot of water to a simmer (do not boil). Crack each egg and gently tip it into the water. Cook the eggs for 4 to 5 minutes then carefully remove them with a slotted spoon and transfer to a plate covered with a paper towel to absorb any excess water. Take another paper towel and gently pat the tops of the eggs dry as well. Slice the English muffins in half, then toast and butter them. Arrange each muffin on a plate and top each half with a slice of ham, then a poached egg, and finally some Hollandaise. Garnish with chopped chives and a fine dusting of paprika.

Want to try something a little different? Here are some variations on classic eggs Benedict:

Eggs Royale: Simply replace the ham with smoked salmon.

Eggs Florentine: Swap the ham with wilted spinach. Some restaurants also swap the Hollandaise for a Mornay sauce, a white sauce made with gruyère cheese.

Eggs Cochon: A Spanish-influenced dish from New Orleans. Swap the ham for braised pulled pork (a suckling pig is traditionally used). The muffin is often swapped for a buttermilk biscuit.

Eggs Neptune: A popular variation from New England. Use a generous amount of crab meat instead of ham.

Eggs Gironda: My homage to the patron saint of raw egg nationalism. Vince Gironda was a pioneer of high-fat, low-carb diets in bodybuilding, so to make eggs Gironda you should swap the muffin for a thick slice of blood sausage and the ham for some nice grilled bacon.

## Returning to the Land:
## The Russian Dacha Gardening System

Now it is time to consider what I like to call the "full" Eggs Benedict Option. This is what I see as a full response not just to the Great Reset, but to the problems of the modern industrial system of agriculture more generally. Indeed, this is an option we can pursue regardless of whether or not the threat of the Great Reset does materialize, since, as we've already seen, the Great Reset is really just an intensification of some of the worst aspects of the system we have today.

To implement this alternative system would not be easy, though. It would require tremendous will, both on the part of ordinary people and their political representatives, and it would take time, not least of all because we in the West, and especially in America, would have to undo a great many of our worst ingrown habits. But the potential benefits, well, they would be tremendous, and not limited to food. This new system could be the beginning of a totally new way of life, a new path that restores health and dignity to ordinary people, protects the earth, and restores man's sacred bonds to community and nation.

I want you to think. Imagine a system that first of all provided the people with plentiful, organic, ethically-produced food of the highest quality: meat, eggs, dairy, fruits, vegetables, and herbs, the whole caboodle. This would be pretty good on its own, right? But what if I told you that this system also required no centralized or complicated delivery and distribution mechanisms and that it did not need heavy machinery or government subsidies to make it work either? The system would be robust too, resistant to external shocks, including prolonged political crises. If you are thinking this sounds too good to be true, wait till I ask you to imagine how this system keeps ordinary people fit and healthy, as well as fostering local bonds between neighbors. Now, surely, I've stretched credulity well past breaking point! But, if I haven't, let me do so by adding one final benefit:

this system would draw the people back to the land, heightening their sense of place, purpose, and history—their deep identity, in short.

In truth, nothing about this system is improbable. It already exists *here*, in the world. And it exists in a place we're encouraged, at least by the mainstream media and the other mystifying emissaries of globohomo, to look at with the deepest distrust. I am talking, of course, about Russia. The system is known as "dacha gardening" or "food gardening." Here I'll describe in detail what the system looks like, how it functions, and, just as importantly, how we might begin to start emulating it ourselves. The account that follows will depend heavily on the excellent dissertation of Leonid Sharashkin, which is readily available on the internet.[188]

Let's begin with some facts. In 2004, thirty-five million Russian households, or approximately 66 percent, owned small garden plots that were used for growing food for subsistence and for the market.[189] Collectively, these garden plots were producing more than 50 percent of Russia's total agricultural output. It is worth putting this in context:

> *In 2006, 53% (by value) of the country's total agricultural output was from household plots which occupied only 2.9% of agricultural land, while the remaining 47% of output by commercial farming enterprises . . . and individual farmers, required 97.1% of agricultural lands.[190]*

What this amounts to is thirty-five million Russian households producing 92 percent of the potatoes produced nationally, 77 percent of the vegetables, 87 percent of the berries and fruit, 53 percent of the meat, 52 percent of the milk, and 27 percent

---

[188] Sharashkin, "Socioeconomic and Cultural Significance."
[189] This section draws on Chapter 1 of Sharashkin, "Socioeconomic and Cultural Significance." Individual quotations and notable statistics are given separate footnotes.
[190] Ibid., 12.

of the eggs.[191] And all this on less than 3 percent of the total
agricultural land in the country. That makes the household
system thirty-eight times more efficient than the government-
supported industrial system (i.e. household agriculture requires thirty-eight times less land to produce 1 ruble of output).

Given the growing interest in environmentally-friendly
farming methods, you would think researchers and advocates
would be crawling over one another to study Russia's household agriculture. While household agriculture is an important
part of a number of national economies, it is worth remembering that Russia is a fully industrialized nation of 150 million
people that has hypersonic weapons and still regularly sends
people into space. We are not talking about some small, out-of-
the way nation whose people live in a manner totally at odds
with modern realities—well, not totally, anyway.

The sad fact is, though, that the Russian system continues
to receive little recognition at all. Many researchers—who
should know better—still believe that it is a system that arose
and continues to exist due to hardship and deprivation, rather
than being a deep cultural form that provides numerous other
benefits beyond the high-quality food it produces. Most commentators and academics have chosen to focus on Russia's industrial farming system, at the expense of the household
economy, because the industrial production of grains and flax
provides, and has provided, most of their cash crop and export
commodities and is therefore of most importance to the state.
Added to this is the fact that the majority of growers (86.6 percent in 2006) grow purely for subsistence, and always have
done, meaning that their produce never hits the open market.
And even when the state-supported industrial farming system
in Russia came under enormous strain with the collapse of the
Soviet Union and the household system took up the slack ad-
mirably, researchers still did not pay much attention. The fact
that Russia did not experience a famine in the early 1990s was,

---

[191] Ibid., 14.

without a doubt, due to the existence of an alternative, locally-based system that could continue to supply ordinary people with food when the state was unable to. This is not hyperbole. To my knowledge, Sharashkin's dissertation remains the best resource for people wanting to understand this phenomenon.

What I won't be doing here is providing a how-to manual; I won't be telling you how to produce compost and manure in the manner of a household farmer, nor how to companion-plant trees and shrubs to maximize yields. No, there will be none of that. Instead, I want you to understand what the system is and what it does, before I discuss how we could learn from it here in the West.

Central to the system of Russian household or dacha gardening are small plots of land next to or near the homes of the rural dwellers who cultivate them, or at a distance from the town and city homes of urban owners. The majority of cultivators on this micro happen to be urban dwellers (over two-thirds of the Russian population live in towns and cities). The term "dacha should be noted, is never used to refer to the garden plot rural residents. A dacha, at least in Soviet times, was supposed to mean a country get-away reserved for recreation, while "garden" was the term for a plot used for agriculture, but there has since been a certain amount of definitional blurring. What matters, at base, is that ordinary Russians, in both the countryside and the city, tend to small plots of land in the countryside to produce food. These plots range in size from about 0.07 acres, in the case of a garden, to about 25 acres (10 hectares), for a separate subsidiary plot, although the average size of a subsidiary plot is around 1.25 acres. Dacha gardens are often organized into wider collectives, known as dacha cooperatives, dacha associations, or gardening associations, which create broader infrastructure for local gardeners.

Within Russia, at least, the enduring contribution of small-scale farmers to the national food economy has long been recognized. The Soviet agronomist Alexander Chayanov, for instance, wrote a famous study of peasant household agriculture (*Peasant Farm Organization*, 1925) that placed small-scale peasant cultivators front and center in Russian life, right back to the days of the earliest Russian polities. Interestingly, at the very time Chayanov was writing, Soviet reforms were introducing a split into the ancient Russian agricultural system for the first time, dividing it into two sectors: the first, an "official," modern, collectivized, industrial sector; and the second, a "private," household sector, independent of the state and geared towards subsistence. Under the new Soviet regime, subsistence-growing among the rural population never ceased—even at the height of the collectivization reforms—but it was forbidden to urban dwellers until the beginning of World War II, when the threat of food shortages began to loom.

As the collectivized sector grew and eventually, after hideous birthing pangs, began to outstrip the old Tsarist system, the private household sector grew as well. By the mid-1950s, household production accounted for 25 percent of the country's agricultural output. Despite its important contribution, however, the authorities gave the household system only sideways approval, fearful of encouraging any "capitalistic" tendencies that might be latent in the form. But by the 1980s, with Gorbachev's *perestroika* and then the collapse of the USSR, things really started to change, and quickly, as the official collective system retreated and opportunities for household cultivation increased dramatically. Between 1992 and 2000, the share of household agriculture increased from 32 percent to over 50 percent of national output. In truth, these figures are likely to be an underestimate of the contribution of households. First of all, they do not take into account wild foraging or hunting and fishing, all of which make a significant contribution to the Russian food economy. The official agricultural figures also include non-food crops, such as flax, so if these are removed, and only food crops are considered, the contribution of the household system to the food economy increases yet further. We've already seen that the production of certain food crops in the household system is incredibly high: 90 percent of all potatoes, for instance, and 80 percent of vegetables.

Household agriculture is spread across the entire country, whereas commercial agriculture is concentrated in the "black soil" or *chernozem* regions of southern European Russia. As a result, outside the black soil regions, the share of household agriculture is even higher, despite the fact that conditions in these other regions are nowhere near as favorable. In Vladimir, for instance, the region studied by Sharashkin, the share of household agriculture in the region's output was 57 percent, 6 percent higher than the national average.

The incredible productivity of household agriculture in Russia today—thirty-eight times that of industrial agriculture, a figure I like to repeat—is not without precedent. Russian historians have noted that, before World War I, peasants' private plots attached to their homes were as much as four times more productive than the fields outside the village. But how is such amazing productivity possible?

First, households make much better use of their land than industrial enterprises. Whereas households use 69 percent of their land and smaller, individual, family farmers use 67 percent, the big corporate farms use as little as 24 percent.[192]

Then there is the question of labor. On a per hectare basis, households put in far more labor than enterprises and, what's more, the quality of their labor is different, as you might expect. Householders *care* about their own plots in a way that no agricultural laborer would. This is a well-known phenomenon, with roots that stretch back to the days of serfdom. Serfs were known to care little for their lord's land, generally doing the minimum they needed to satisfy their obligations and then lavishing attention on their own plots of land. Similar foot-dragging behavior was common in the days of Soviet collectivism too. Tending the earth is, of course, hard physical work, but the

---

[192] Ibid., 16.

fact that householders put in more work on their plots than the monetary value of the crops they produce is a testament to the recreational and health benefits of doing the work. One study of four cities in Russia showed that urban gardeners spent, on average, $1,000 of their work time to produce $140 worth of produce.[193] It is worth noting that household gardening is not a source of employment, although it provides food for subsistence and for the market. Gardening is not undertaken instead of employment, and it does not in any way compete with the "official" economy, as some commentators seem to fear. Indeed, the growing season in central European Russia is only 110–120 days a year, i.e. around four months or a third of the year, so gardening could hardly function as full-time employment.

As a third reason, householders have a much higher level of integration in the use of their land. What this means, basically, is that they blend different species in a way that large commercial enterprises don't. Whereas the big enterprises tend to monoculture, garden plots are best characterized as "micro-scale agroforestry systems." Householders plant together a variety of annual crops, such as potatoes, with shrubs, such as berry canes, and trees—apples, plums, etc. Because of the small size of the plots, these crops must be placed closely to each other. Annuals, shrubs, and trees are planted together in a complementary way that makes best use of the space and of the characteristics of the crops being planted. For example, a low hedge of raspberry bushes can be placed alongside vegetable beds to provide shelter from the wind and to attract birds that will control pests. The interaction of the crops is also important, with the positioning of certain crops, such as vegetables, changing to accommodate the growth cycles of larger plants, such as shrubs and especially trees. Since I am talking a lot about fruit and vegetables, it is worth restating that household gardening is not just about plants, and many household gardeners also produce milk, eggs, meat, and other animal products.

---

[193] Ibid., 38.

Their incredible productivity is one of the most obvious advantages of Russian household gardens, but there are plenty of others, and they deserve consideration in detail. Another obvious advantage is the sustainability of the system. Census evidence shows that many local gardening associations formed by urban dwellers are already decades old, but even more impressive is the fact that rural subsidiary plots (plots attached to or near rural dwellings) have been in continuous use not just for decades but even centuries. There is no question that householders preserve the fertility of the land even as they benefit from it so richly.

Household gardening has low capital requirements. It requires little to no machinery to carry out, nor is there any need for long-distance transport to provide the necessary inputs or to move the products. The system is also subsidy-free. In 2004, for instance, commercial agriculture in Russia received subsidies of 78.2 billion rubles, which amounted to nearly 18 percent of its total output, whereas the household sector received no subsidies, despite being more productive. Even with these massive subsidies, commercial agriculture saw its share in the nation's agricultural output decrease from 67 percent in 1992 to 43 percent in 1994.[194]

Resistance to inflation is another benefit of the household gardening system. During the 1990s, after the collapse of the Soviet Union, Russia was subject to hyperinflation, but the price of many staples was kept relatively low because they were produced in the household and not the commercial sector. Between 1992 and 2004, for instance, the price of bread, a commercially produced food staple, increased 503 times, whereas the price of potatoes, over 90 percent of which are produced by households, increased only 232 times.[195]

The size of the household sector also serves to reduce Russia's dependency on food imports. Without such massive household production, imports of staple crops, which are minimal,

---

[194] Ibid., 37–8.
[195] Ibid., 38.

would have to be significantly larger. Even during the economic crisis of the 1990s, Russia was able to remain less dependent on food imports than other developed nations. Food security is highlighted as a growing issue for the future, especially as a result of climate change projections, but there can be little doubt that it is a good thing, per se, for a nation to be in control of its own food supply, as much as it can be.

Although I've already noted that the vast majority of household production is geared towards subsistence, the portion that does reach the market has some interesting characteristics. The majority of households that sell do so directly to the market. In Vladimir, according to Sharashkin, only 16 percent of sellers relied on wholesale channels rather than selling to the customer without the involvement of a middle man. Direct selling has a number of benefits for both buyer and seller: the buyer gets access to fresh, locally-produced food; and the seller receives full market price for their produce, maximizing their margins. Moves towards centralized processing of household produce have so far been resisted by buyer and seller alike.

No account of household gardening would be complete without mentioning the social and health benefits, both physical and mental, of this system. It has been estimated that the recreational value of household gardening far outstrips the value of the food produced. As well as providing a wide array of quite obvious psychological and physical benefits—calm and stress-relief; a sense of independence; regular, hard physical exertion—household gardens are places for family and friends, and much time is spent on the plots just socializing or relaxing, especially in good weather. The exchange of goods between household gardeners, often without the use of money, creates local networks of trust and cooperation that make for happier, more-closely-knit communities.

So these are the main nutritional, environmental, economic, and social benefits of the household system as it exists in Russia today. As well as being massively productive—far in excess of the industrial agricultural sector—and allowing ordinary people access to high-quality local produce, other benefits include: household gardening is sustainable in the long-term; has low capital requirements; does not need to be subsidized; protects consumers from inflation; and reduces the nation's dependency on imports. One of the most interesting aspects of the household movement that I've yet to cover, though, is its spiritual aspect. A new form of spirituality, which builds on the ancient history of small-scale cultivation in Russia, has seen growing popularity in recent decades, due to the growth of a movement known as "Anastasia."

The notion that agriculture has a unique spiritual component is a very ancient one, reflected in the deeper meaning of the words we use to describe it.

*Actually, the words* agriculture *and* culture *both derive from the Latin root* cult. Cult *(which in modern usage signifies a system of religious ritual or worship, often with negative connotations) stems from the Latin verb for* to till *or* to take care of the land *(it is for this reason that the first meaning of* culture *found in English dictionaries to this day is "cultivation of the soil"). This association with religion is not random. The fact that the Latin* cult *means both agriculture and religion reflects that originally, agriculture was viewed as a spiritual path, and the most direct interaction with God was seen not in any formal religious ritual familiar to us today, but through cultivation of the soil. Thus, the notion of the sacredness of the human-earth connection through agriculture is included even in the words we use today. Our distant forbearers made no distinction between agriculture and what we call today "religion," and did not separate the notion of "sacred" from "nature."*[196]

---

[196] Ibid., 67–8.

This notion is also present in ancient Slavic beliefs and pre-Christian customs, and it is to these sources that the Anastasia movement looks, primarily. It has exploded in popularity since the late 1990s, although not without a certain amount of pushback from the Russian Orthodox Church, the media, and the state.[197]

The name "Anastasia" is derived from the first of a series of books—the ten-book *Ringing Cedars of Russia* series—by the Russian writer and entrepreneur Vladimir Megre. The books have sold over eleven million copies in Russia alone, largely without the help of advertising. The central idea behind the movement, and his books, is to create an ancestral dwelling on a plot of ground where the next generation can be born and raised. The cardinal virtues of the movement are sustainability, self-reliance, and simple living, in harmony with nature and the eternal life-giving principle (*rod*). As Sharashkin explains, in ancient Slavic belief there is a deep association between family and kin and the wider social order and religion:

> *Both* family *and* kin *were viewed as part of and were inscribed in the natural cycle of conception, birth, growth, maturity, death, and re-birth (as observable in the annual cycle of nature, and, more specifically, in the agricultural cycle). Indeed, the Russian word for "family" (*sem'ia*) is almost undistinguishable from the word for "seed" (*semia*), while the word for "kin" (*rod*, which includes all the ancestors, the present generation, and all future descendants of a family) also signifies the* power of birth *at large (both in the human family and nature). In fact, little distinction was made between feminine fertility and the fertility of "Mother Earth" — both of which were held sacred (thus, a piece of turf or soil was traditionally used to administer an oath: it was first put on one's head, then*

---

[197] My discussion of the Anastasia movement is taken from Sharashkin, "Socioeconomic and Cultural Relevance," 235–42.

*eaten). . . . From the same root* rod- *stem such words as* rodit' *("to give birth"),* Rodina *("Motherland" or "birth-place"),* roditeli *("parents," lit. "the ones who give birth"),* rodnoi *("native," "one's own"),* rodnia *("relatives"),* plodorodie *("fertility," lit. "the bearing of fruit"),* rodnik *("water spring," i.e., where a stream is born),* Rod *(the cosmic life-giving principle, the origin of all life) and* priroda *("nature," lit. "attached to Rod"). Rod is symbolized by a circle divided into six segments — a symbol that has survived in Russian folk art to the present day.*[198]

Given that there are ten books in the series, it would be no simple task to summarize the beliefs of the movement neatly. The books are written in an enigmatic, mystical style, rather than as a systematic series of religious teachings. One of the central concepts of the movement is resurrection, as embodied in the rebirth of nature at spring each year. This rebirth is the product of the interplay between the earth, seen as feminine, and the growing power of the masculine sun. The concept of resurrection is personified in the ancient goddess of spring, Lelia, who later came to be known as Anastasia. Megre actually claims to have received the wisdom contained in the series directly from Anastasia, on a trading expedition through the Siberian taiga.

As well as outlining a philosophy of man living in harmony with nature, the movement advocates a new decentralized model for the national economy, with self-sufficient rural settlements as the primary unit. These settlements are composed of individual family homesteads or "family domains." Between 1996, when *Anastasia* was published, and 2014, the movement grew to at least two hundred of these rural settlements, spread across more than half of all the regions of Russia. While this eco-village movement is an outgrowth of the household garden-

---

[198] Sharashkin, "Socioeconomic and Cultural Relevance," 75–76.

ing system, there are some important differences. The minimum size for a homestead, in Merge's opinion, is 1 hectare, which is considerably larger than a typical dacha or household garden. This larger size is necessary to fulfil the founder's mission of creating communities that are self-sufficient not only in food but also in other crops like flax, timber, firewood, plants for medicinal use, and other products. Megre has stated that, if the household gardeners can be as productive as they are, working small plots in their spare time, then there is absolutely no reason why full-time cultivators on larger plots of land could not make household agriculture the foundation of the national economy.

What pushback the movement has received has largely been as a result of its embracing ancient pre-Christian beliefs and customs. Although the movement is not openly hostile to Russian Orthodoxy, and in fact includes a number of elements that are clearly drawn from the Russian Christian tradition, this has not stopped powerful figures from within the Orthodox Church from lobbying against the group, including to prevent government allocation of land for family homesteads. Many charge the movement with being a "cult." A Russian newspaper article in 2006 even went so far as to accuse Anastasia members of feeding their children to wild animals, echoing a charge laid at the feet of Slavic pagans centuries before by the Church. As Sharashkin explains, it's no wonder that the movement has faced such resistance, given the widely acknowledged persistence among the Russian people of pagan beliefs and customs, and of attempts to wipe them out.

Cult or not, it is clear that the Anastasia movement is the fullest conception that exists today of Russian household gardening as not just an economic movement, but a national and spiritual vocation. Although the values that animate the movement are present already in the practice of household gardening—whether we mean self-reliance and self-sufficiency or a deep connection to the soil of Mother Russia—it has taken a concerted effort, led by the enigmatic Megre and his books, to make them fully explicit and to market them as an actual way of life. What I take from this, above all, is the capacity for an apparently mundane practice like growing food for subsistence to become something much more, with the right kind of help. While I don't think the Anastasia movement can be dragged and dropped—there are already offshoots around the world—I do think that it can serve as an inspiration for something similar, even in the US. It is this possibility that I will consider next.

### High-Fructose Corn Syrup

One way to track the ascendancy of corn in the US food system over the decades is to look at sweeteners and, in particular, the rise of high-fructose corn syrup (HFCS), a substance that didn't exist before the 1970s but which has since become ubiquitous in American food, especially processed food, but also foods you would never expect to find sweetener in, like bread and ham. HFCS is by far and away "the most valuable product refined from corn, accounting for 530 million bushels every year."[199] Although the US FDA states that it is not aware of any evidence that HFCS is less safe than other sweeteners, this merely betrays the FDA's blithe attitude to health.[200] It's not so much what HFCS does, which is more or less the same as refined table sugar, but what has been done with it, that's the problem. The writer Michael Pollan and many others lay the blame for America's obesity crisis firmly at the door of the cheap sugar produced from corn and the cheap fat produced from soybean oil, both of which have been added to American food in ever greater quantities over the last four decades.

HFCS came to replace table sugar in the American food industry for a number of reasons, but primarily because there

---

[199] Pollan, *Omnivore's Dilemma*, 89.
[200] FDA, "High Fructose Corn Syrup."

was just so much cheap corn to be had, due to government subsidies that incentivize overproduction (see the main text). The process of creating HFCS was first marketed in the 1970s by the Clinton Corn Processing Company, in conjunction with the Japanese Agency of Industrial Science and Technology, which discovered an important enzyme that's used in the manufacturing process. Domestic production in the US grew from 2.2 million tons in 1980 to a height of 9.5 million tons in 1999.[201] Although about 90 percent of sweetener use outside the US is sucrose (i.e. table sugar), in the US the balance between HFCS and sucrose is about 50:50.[202] Brands like Coca Cola and Pepsi switched to HFCS in their drinks for the US market in the mid-1980s, but continue to use sucrose outside the US.[203] By 2006, average consumption of HFCS in the US had reached 66 pounds a year.[204]

HFCS is made by breaking down corn starch into glucose using enzymes, and then using another enzyme, D-xylose isomerase, to turn some of the glucose into fructose (the usual ratio is either 42 percent fructose or 55 percent, depending on the intended product). Before the creation of HFCS, fruit and grain products were the principal sources of fructose in people's diets, but now, with consumption of fruits and grains at a much lower level, HFCS is the primary source of fructose for most people in the US. Research suggests that there are some unique problems associated with excessive fructose consumption. Unlike glucose, which can immediately be used by the body's tissues, fructose has to be processed by the liver in order to be used and seems to encourage fat storage.[205] Fructose also stimulates areas of the brain associated with appetite control to a much lesser extent than glucose, making over-consumption more

---

[201] USDA, "High-Fructose Corn Syrup."
[202] White, "Straight talk about high-fructose."
[203] Daniels, "COKE, PEPSI TO USE."
[204] Pollan, *Omnivore's Dilemma*, 104.
[205] Maersk et al., "Sucrose-sweetened beverages."

likely.[206] HFCS consumption has been linked to insulin re-sistance and diabetes, as well as chronic inflammation and heart disease.[207]

Although it's true that table sugar also contains a signifi-cant quantity of fructose, meaning that it has the same effects as HFCS, this doesn't really explain why HFCS is so bad. To do that, we need to look at the context of HFCS consumption. HFCS is so bad because, despite being conceived as an alterna-tive to sugar, it hasn't actually replaced sugar consumption at all. Instead, the 60-odd pounds of HFCS that people are con-suming annually is *in addition* to the other forms of sugar they consume, which have also risen.[208] By constantly looking for new uses for corn, the producers have found, in HFCS, the per-fect means to sneak corn, and even more empty calories, into virtually every product on the supermarket shelves. Michael Pollan explains this nicely:

> *This is what makes high-fructose corn syrup such a clever thing to do with a bushel of corn: By inducing people to consume more calories than they otherwise might, it gets them to really chomp through the corn surplus. Corn sweetener is to the republic of fat what corn whiskey was to the alcoholic republic. Read the food labels in your kitchen and you'll find that HFCS has insinuated itself into every corner of the pantry: not just into our soft drinks and snack foods, where you would expect to find it, but into the ketchup and mustard, the breads and cereals, the relishes and crackers, the hot dogs and hams.[209]*

[206] Page et al., "Effects of fructose."
[207] Stanhope et al., "Consuming fructose-sweetened." and Rutledge and Adeli, "Fructose and the metabolic syndrome." and Malik et al., "Sugar-sweetened beverages."
[208] Pollan, *Omnivore's Dilemma,* 104.
[209] Ibid.

If you want a fun game to play the next time you go to the supermarket (I mean you, my American friends), pick a few random products and see if they contain HFCS. Chances are they will.

## Household Gardening beyond Russia

Could such a system work outside Russia? What about in the US—could a nationwide household gardening system work there? I really don't see why not.

Consider the following facts, as presented by Sharashkin. Russia has 18.8 million acres of household gardens, producing $14 billion of products a year. In the US, by contrast, there are 27.6 million acres of lawns, which support a lawn-care industry worth $30 billion a year.[210] On the basis of these figures alone, then, a US system of household agriculture, on the same scale as Russia's, certainly should not be seen as a pipe dream. There is more to it than the question of space, of course, but this is as good a place to start as any if we are to consider the practicalities of implementing such a system. Just like Russia, the US has abundant space, and not just space that could hypothetically be turned over to household agriculture, but space that is *already* owned by individuals and attached to their homes. So there is absolutely no reason why the government would need to get involved to distribute or even re-distribute land, although land purchases or even grants (something the US once did on a massive scale) could be a means to increase the amount of land open to small-scale production, and should by no means be off the table.

Another positive in favor of the US is the climate. The climate in Russia is far more challenging than that of the US, on the whole, and most of the US has a growing season that is far longer than the 110–120 days Russia has.

---

[210] Ibid., 243.

No, physical space and climate are not the real issues here. The real issues, it strikes me, would be issues of culture and political will. Both would need to change significantly if we wanted to get people to produce their own food and/or rely primarily on local networks to provide it. Among other things, people would have to accept a return to seasonal consumption, to purchasing certain kinds of good when they are in season (although use of equipment like polytunnels and heated greenhouses can provide some crops year-round in parts of the country that do not have the climate to do so normally), and they would also have to accept—perhaps the most bitter pill of all—that they have to devote a portion of their spare time not just to pursuits they "enjoy," like watching the television, but also to working in the garden. Truth is, though, Russians do not actually spend *that* much time working in the garden. During the growing season—a period of only four months, remember—Russian household gardeners spend an average of seventeen hours a week tending their gardens. If this sounds like a lot to you, take note of the fact that, according to the Nielsen media group, the average American spends thirty-two hours a week watching television.[211]

One interesting parallel Sharashkin draws toward the end of his thesis is between how, in times of crisis, people not just in Russia but also in the US and elsewhere in the Western world "suddenly recall where their food is coming from and turn to their local soil for subsistence." In particular, he points to the "Dig for Victory" campaigns that took place in the US and UK during the First and Second World Wars, when ordinary people were encouraged to plant gardens to aid in the war effort. During the Great Depression of the 1930s, twenty-three million American households are reckoned to have planted and tended food gardens. In the US, this was probably the last time when a notion of individual self-sufficiency was a genuinely important part of national policy.[212]

---

[211] Ibid., 243.
[212] Ibid., 243–45.

Although food gardening in the US declined massively after the end of the Second World War, it has not disappeared entirely. Food gardening still exists and often helps some of the poorest groups, even in urban areas, to live a better, healthier life. In deprived areas of Los Angeles, for instance, at least one study has shown that the produce from community gardens was able to make a serious contribution to food security for local residents, providing items for their diets that were not otherwise available and helping them to save as much as $600 a year on food purchases per growing season. Other studies have reported similar findings in places like urban New Jersey.[213]

I think that Sharashkin is right to look to the past for some deeper cultural context or tradition to sustain a household gardening system in the US. Any kind of major social change needs a compelling narrative to underpin it, to provide the motivation and the justification for the change, including any sacrifice, that needs to be made. Thankfully, the US has an incredibly rich history of individual initiative and small-scale agriculture that could be drawn upon to provide such a story. Remember that the US was once very much a nation of small, largely self-reliant farmers. Indeed, taming the earth and tilling the soil were once a central part of what it meant to be an American, perhaps even the formative experience that made Americans out of the various immigrants who had crossed the Atlantic to get there.

In 1893, the historian Fredrick Jackson Turner put forward a theory about the importance of the western frontier to American identity. The theory came to be known as the Turner Thesis, and it goes something like this. At each stage of its history, from the Thirteen Colonies, through the early days of the Republic and the first expansion across the Appalachians, to the settlement of the Midwest and the Great Plains, the needs and the conditions of the frontier made Americans, and America, what they were. As Turner famously put it:

---

[213] Ibid., 245.

> *American democracy was born of no theorist's dream; it was not carried in the Susan Constant to Virginia, nor in the Mayflower to Plymouth. It came out of the American forest, and it gained new strength each time it touched a new frontier.*[214]

Frontier life, for Turner, was an antidote to the old ways of Europe. In a land of near unlimited space that had to be claimed, tamed, and made productive by successive waves of frontiersmen, there was no place for the institutions that had defined the history of Europe, no need for aristocrats or kings, no need for armies or grand churches and hieratic pomp. The hard frontier life made for a vigorous, often violent, but ultimately egalitarian people, with little interest in the fineries of high culture and possessing a healthy anti-intellectualism.

Or, rather, the American frontier *had been* the antidote to the old ways of Europe. In 1890, three years before Turner wrote his famous thesis, the US census had officially announced the closing of the frontier. For Turner this represented a turning-point—*the* turning-point?—in the nation's history. With the frontier closed, but new waves of huddled masses arriving daily from Southern and Eastern Europe, what would the fate of the nation be without the time-honored way of making these people American? Would American democracy survive?

The Turner Thesis was extremely popular for some time, well into the mid- and even the late twentieth century. It became a common sentiment that America needed to find "new frontiers" if it was to remain a dynamic society, one which even shaped government policy. The notion of an unconquered frontier found its way into the policies and pronouncements of Franklin Delano Roosevelt and his New Deal, for instance. In a speech to celebrate the third anniversary of his social security policy, FDR said:

---

[214] Turner, *Frontier in American History*, 293.

*There is still today a frontier that remains unconquered—*
*an America unreclaimed. This is the great, the nation-*
*wide frontier of insecurity, of human want and fear. This*
*is the frontier—the America—we have set ourselves to re-*
*claim.*

Likewise, in his inauguration speech, John F. Kennedy also called upon the American people to "be pioneers on that New Frontier," which had now come to mean the frontier of scientific research and space exploration. The racial overtones and the emphasis on sacred soil of course began to rankle with academics, especially after World War II, but that did not stop the Turner Thesis from becoming a central part of the popular mythos of the US, seen in untold films, popular novels and histories, and every other kind of American cultural product you can imagine, from Yosemite Sam to the Marlboro Man.

Now I am not saying that the Turner Thesis, with its emphasis on the importance of frontiers, is the only narrative behind which Americans could rally if they sought to return to the land. It is just a powerful—and also plausible, or so I think—example of the kind of narrative that has enough depth and truth to it to serve that valuable purpose of providing unity, motivation, and direction for such a change. Because the fact remains, however much the academic "deboonkers" might kvetch and wail about blood and soil, that the Turner Thesis is very definitely true—certainly in the broad sense, and in much of the detail too. Frontiers, physical and mental, have exercised tremendous power over the destiny of America, and the notion of a new frontier—the fight against globalism?—could be just what the nation needs to reinvigorate itself.

There is a war of ideas that needs to be won, and such a narrative is precisely what is needed. One of the most pernicious ideas of our time is the idea, beloved especially by Turning Point conservacucks, that America itself is an idea. Charlie Kirk, founder of Turning Point USA, took this idea to its absurd final reduction when he claimed that, since America is nothing more than a "land of ideas," it would not make a difference if Americans were suddenly stranded on an island so long as they still had the Constitution! No nation is an idea, and that includes America, regardless of the importance of certain documents, and the ideas contained within them, to the nation's identity. This view of identity is so harmful in the American case because it allows massive demographic change to continue, change which has already fundamentally altered the nature of American society and threatens, if unchecked, to make it totally unrecognizable in the near-future. The American right needs a more tangible, grounded story of what it means to be an American, one that recognizes the unique contribution of America as a physical place, a land unlike any other, as well as the demographics that have traditionally comprised the American nation. In this regard, we could expect that the Eggs Benedict Option would not be for everyone in America today. So be it. This is not a bad thing. Any realistic right-winger will have to recognize sooner or later that there are parts of America that are lost to the nation—at least for now—whatever course of action is taken. What really matters is mobilizing the right people.

Another thing I am not saying is that this would not be a hugely formidable task. America is not Russia, and it does not have its unbroken thousand-year tradition of individual small-scale agriculture. While it might be possible for an American movement of renewal to emerge, like the Anastasia movement, spontaneously and without explicit political backing, it seems more likely to me that such a movement would have to be a political one, with the support of politicians. As far as I can see, political support would be absolutely vital for two reasons. First, because political organization, at the local and national level, would be the most direct way to build such a movement from scratch and spread its message. And second, because there would have to be significant changes to the law nationwide to make a system of household agriculture viable.

Recently, I've been reading a lot of Joel Salatin's work, and it is very instructive with regard to the way that the American system punishes the little man when it comes to agriculture. The title of perhaps his most famous essay is "Everything I Want to Do Is Illegal," and this later became the title of a compendium of essays on the same subject: how difficult it is for a small farmer to do things that should, at least in a sane country, be simple to do. Why can't a small farmer slaughter his own pigs? Why is raw milk so demonized? Why do business incentives and tax breaks for farmers always benefit the mega-players and push smaller players out of the market? I won't bore you by listing all the things that would need to change to make agriculture pay for small farmers too. Instead, I'll just say that if you want to learn more, you should pick up one of Salatin's books, not least of all because he actually makes interesting what might appear, on paper, to be extremely dull topics—yes, even the slaughtering of chickens and the need for local sawmills. The main takeaway, I think, is that for a system of widespread small-scale agriculture to be viable, there would have to be big changes to the laws regarding agriculture in the US, and these can only come as a result of political pressure. Politicians would have to make it easier not only for small-scale producers to produce the things they want to produce, but also to distribute their products—animal and plant—to others in the local area. Only a true form of political populism, which genuinely sought the wellbeing and livelihood of ordinary people, could break the corporate stranglehold on agriculture.

Even so, as the Russian household gardening system also reveals, we do not need to make an either/or choice between local people-centered production and a larger industrial system of agriculture. In fact, the two systems can exist side by side and complement each other, as they have done in Russia, and before that the Soviet Union, for decades. What we need, as many critics of the industrial agricultural system have repeatedly claimed, is a system or series of systems that operate on multiple scales. In the rare case of agriculture, at least, diversity really may be our greatest strength. That being the case, though, who says larger-scale agriculture couldn't change too?

### The Wider Promise of Regenerative Agriculture

What if the basic principles behind Russian household agriculture could be scaled up even further? What if we could replace the current industrial system of farming with one that doesn't deplete the earth but instead restores it, provides the highest quality nutrition, and benefits local communities and non-corporate producers (i.e. real farmers)? This would be a total departure from the current system, whose incentives are anything but high-quality nutrition and the health of individuals and local communities. This is the promise of what has come to be known as "regenerative agriculture," and I think it represents the perfect complement to an even more localized system of household farming.

As I've said already, the criticisms of the Great Reset system are also, to a large extent, criticisms that can be made of the current system of industrial food production. In many respects, the Great Reset in agriculture will simply be the worst excesses of today cranked up to eleven. Corporate consolidation towards monopoly; exploitation and, ultimately, destruction of smaller farmers; the use of toxic pesticides and herbicides; GMOs; relentless extraction with no concern for long-term consequences—all of these characteristics of the industrial farming system in 2022 point in the direction of the Great Reset and, even if the globalists are ultimately thwarted, will remain unless we do something about them.

Although Russian-style household agriculture can happily co-exist alongside industrial agriculture, there's no reason why industrial agriculture needs to look the way it does today, in Russia, the US, or anywhere else. It's not that we should do away with larger scale agriculture—as the Soviet case shows, having a food system that operates on multiple levels provides added resilience against shocks—but that we need to find a better way of doing it. And I don't just mean a "sustainable" alternative. "Sustainability" is one of the great buzzwords of today when it comes to, well, everything, but it actually serves to mask the nature of the problem, since it suggests that we just need to reach an ideal stage where we only take as much as we give, or vice versa. The hard reality is, as the earlier discussion of topsoil depletion made clear, we have diminished our crop land to the point that, if we aren't careful, we may make it unfit for farming forever. So what is regenerative agriculture, then?

Regenerative agriculture makes use of time-honored agricultural practices, such as no-till planting, cover-cropping, composting, and succession planting, to create agricultural systems that are not just sustainable, but actually increase soil health and biodiversity: they give back *more* than they take. They really do "regenerate," as the name suggests. The term "regenerative agriculture" appears to have originated in the 1980s, as a result of the Rodale Institute, an American nonprofit organization that supports research into organic farming. Robert Rodale, the founder, was in no doubt that sustainability was not the proper ideal for organic farming. He said:

> *By marching forward under the banner of sustainability we are, in effect, continuing to hamper ourselves by not accepting a challenging enough goal. I am not against the word sustainable, rather I favor regenerative agriculture.*[215]

After a flurry of publications in the 1980s, the term appears to have largely dropped out of use until the early noughties, when the Institute, and others, began promoting it again, with a par-

---

[215] *Sustainable Agriculture and Integrated Farming Systems*, 315.

ticular focus on climate change. There's now extensive literature on the topic, and the movement is receiving increasing amounts of attention. Joel Salatin has been on Joe Rogan; Allan Savory, founder of the Savory Institute, gave a TED Talk in 2013 on the potential of regenerative agriculture to fight climate change; and Gabe Brown, of Brown's Ranch, mentioned below, also gave a TED Talk on regenerative agriculture in 2016.

A variety of different definitions of the term "regenerative agriculture" are given or implied, but there are clear commonalities between all of them. Four of the most consistent principles of regenerative agriculture are commitments to: improve soil health and biodiversity; optimize resource use; mitigate the effects of climate change; and improve the quality and availability of water.[216]

What this means, invariably, is eliminating reliance on the products of agribusiness—grains for animal feed, fertilizers and chemicals for crops—and reducing the size of agricultural concerns. What this doesn't mean, however, is a single model to fit every context. Unlike the Planetary Health Diet model, which will impose a homogenous model on agricultural land the world over, regenerative agriculture is tailored to each individual context, so that different farms in different places will almost certainly look very different from one another. This really is the opposite of the Great Reset.

For example, at Great Plains Buffalo in South Dakota, Phil Jerde is restoring the ancient prairie land by moving buffalo across his land in a way that mimics how the great herds once moved across the plains.[217] He does this by rotating the animals frequently among small pastures, so that they stay tightly grouped together, trampling the ground and distributing their waste evenly. By rotating them regularly, the land and grass

---

[216] Schreefel et al., "Regenerative agriculture."
[217] These two examples are taken from Anderson, "Regenerative agriculture can make."

have plenty of time to recover. The effects have been remarkable. Over a period of ten years, desertified ground has become prairie again, water retention in the soil has greatly increased, Jerde's buffalo have never been healthier, and the overall biodiversity of the region, both plant and animal, has exploded.

The approach on Brown's Ranch, across the border in North Dakota, is very different. Here, Gabe Brown combines a variety of cropping techniques (cover cropping, multicropping, and intercropping) with mob grazing (in which large numbers of animals are grazed on a small amount of land for a short time, then rotated elsewhere) and no-till farming (planting without tilling). Although the methods are different from those of Great Plains Buffalo, the effects have been similarly remarkable. In around a decade, the Brown operation has restored organic-matter levels in the soil to levels most native prairie soils contained before the first settlers plowed them.

Much is made of the fact that many of the techniques of regenerative agriculture are well known to indigenous cultures. Here's the Regenerative Agriculture Foundation, for instance, via their website:

> *[Regenerative agriculture is] a vision for a future agriculture that combines indigenous knowledge with western science and technology, a future that re-establishes relationships between humans, crops, animals, soil, and ecosystems.*

The truth is that the essential principles were well known to us in the West too, before the so-called Green Revolution of the mid-twentieth century, which basically created the current industrial farming system as we know it, with the introduction of new high-yield crops, chemical fertilizers, herbicides and pesticides, and mechanization. We've just forgotten them. Well, some of us have, anyway. The case of Russian household agriculture shows that they have not been totally forgotten in

Russia, at least. Household gardeners use a wide variety of re-generative techniques to enhance soil fertility and increase yields, such as applying manure and compost and using crop rotation and co-planting.

One of the most interesting aspects of the regenerative farming model is how central animal agriculture, and grazing animals in particular, is to it. This is for a number of reasons. Joel Salatin refers to ruminants (i.e. grazing animals like cows and sheep) as "four-legged speed composters," which break down organic matter (i.e. grass) quicker than simple compost-ing and, through their waste, which is enhanced by bacteria from their stomachs, increase the amount of nutrients available to plants in the soil.[218] Animal manure reduces or elimi-nates the need for artificial fertilizers—which are manu-factured using fossil fuels, if that's something you're worried about—and in a well-managed grazing system, zero manpower or fuel is required to disperse the manure, since the animals do it themselves as they move around. Grazing animals can also be employed to manage weeds as part of a cover-cropping sys-tem, eliminating the need for herbicides.

We've already seen that a significant proportion, perhaps the majority, of all agricultural land in the world is not actually suited for grain agriculture anyway, but grazing animals could be used to manage crops as well. Livestock grazing can easily be integrated into crop production and, in fact, it already is, including in the US. Many beef-producers in the US graze their cattle on corn-stalk residues after the harvest, for instance, and wheat production on the southern plains is also heavily inte-grated with cattle grazing. Besides the high-quality animal protein it produces, this integration improves crop yields and reduces dependence on chemical products significantly, if not entirely. Again, it's worth saying that this is just how farms functioned before the Green Revolution.

---

[218] Rodgers and Wolf, *Sacred Cow*, 166.

The authors of *Sacred Cow*, Diana Rodgers and Robb Wolf, lay out a compelling case for using cattle to increase soil quality by eliminating all grain feeding of livestock in the US—and that includes pigs and chickens—and feeding cattle exclusively on grass. As they argue:

> *Beef raised on pasture and managed holistically could provide not only nutrient-dense protein but also a system of improved soil water capture, increased biodiversity, carbon sequestration, and long-term sustainability.*[219]

Not only do they demolish arguments that raising beef on grass is somehow wasteful and environmentally unfriendly, but they also show, with careful calculations, that all beef in the US today could be pastured from start to finish. While some beef is fully pastured, a significant proportion is finished in grain lots, where the cattle are fed grain to increase their weight rapidly. Note, however, that no cattle are exclusively fed grain, and in fact overfeeding cattle with grain can cause serious, even fatal problems for them.[220]

Reducing the dependence of animal agriculture on grains, especially corn, could have some quite amazing social, economic, and political effects, beyond simply opening up massive amounts of land for other uses. Corn is the commodity par excellence of industrial agriculture, and its overproduction in the United States, including for use as feed for livestock and for export, has determined the trajectory of much more than just agriculture, in the US and abroad.[221] Over the twentieth century, with its Green Revolution, corn yields were increased from twenty-five bushels an acre to more than 140. The US now produces more than ten billion bushels a year. The problem is that it just doesn't pay to grow corn, so production must be

---

[219] Ibid., 178–9.
[220] Ibid., 149–51.
[221] This account of corn production is taken from Keith, *Vegetarian Myth*, 109–112.

heavily subsidized. This pattern first arose in the aftermath of World War I, when European demand for American foodstuffs, including corn, which had massively increased due to the war, disappeared. This left American farmers with a huge surplus with no market for it, lowering prices significantly. Then came the Great Depression. Those farmers who didn't go bust were stuck in the unenviable position of having to produce more to meet their costs, which then drove prices even lower, meaning the farmers had to produce still more to meet the expanding shortfall, and so on—a true vicious cycle. The first federal subsidies for corn were not intended to make food available cheaply; they were supposed to keep farmers in business, plain and simple.

By the 1970s, however, things had changed, as the New Deal programs were dismantled in favor of programs that, in Michael Pollan's words, "instead of supporting farmers . . . [supported] corn at the expense of farmers."[222] Rather than the government buying up corn to prevent it from flooding the market and further depressing prices, or selling grain from its granary when adverse conditions pushed prices up, a system of direct payments was introduced. When prices fell too low, the government would simply pay the farmers. One effect of this has been to ensure that the market, in America and overseas, is constantly flooded with corn:

> *The result has been an unending river of corn, drowning our arteries and our insulin receptors, our rural communities, and poor subsistence economies the world over.*[223]

What these subsidies amount to, if you didn't know already or couldn't guess, is a massive annual payment, a kind of agricultural Danegeld, straight into the pockets of enormous grain cartels—Cargill, Monsanto, etc.—which are able to dictate that prices should be lower than production. And who makes up the

---

[222] Quoted in Rodgers and Wolf, *Sacred Cow*, 111.
[223] Keith, *Vegetarian Myth*, 111.

difference? Taxpayers, of course! Six companies control 75 percent of all the grain-handling facilities, and they are the ones that set the price for grain. As we've already seen in the case of the beef market, although farmers have a choice whether or not to accept that price, in reality their hands are tied. Accept or die.

This is the main reason why livestock in the US are fed corn, in what are known as concentrated animal feeding operations (CAFOs): because there's so much of it and it's so cheap. Cheap grain means cheap beef, chicken, and pork. The CAFO model, which ultimately benefits the big grain cartels, is further subsidized by the government, which provides tax relief and exemptions from environmental-protection laws, as well as developing a meat-grading system that awards the fat marbling produced by grain-fed beef the highest ranking.

It's hard to overestimate just how important corn is to the broader US industrial system. Here's a great quotation about corn from Michael Pollan:

*Everything about corn meshes smoothly with the gears of this giant machine; grass doesn't. Grain is the closest thing in nature to an industrial commodity: storable, portable, fungible, ever the same today as it was yesterday and will be tomorrow. Since it can be accumulated and traded, grain is a form of wealth. It is a weapon too. . . . The nations with the biggest surpluses of grain have always exerted power over the ones in short supply. Throughout history governments have encouraged their farmers to grow more than enough grain, to protect against famine, to free up labor for other purposes, to improve the trade balance, and generally to augment their power. . . . The real beneficiary of this crop is not America's eaters but its military-industrial complex. In an industrial economy, the growing of grain supports the larger economy: the chemical and biotech industries, the oil industry, Detroit, pharmaceuticals (without which*

*they couldn't keep animals healthy in CAFOs), agribusi-*
*ness, and the balance of trade. Growing corn helps drive*
*the very industrial complex that drives it. No wonder why*
*the government subsidizes it so lavishly.*[224]

While we're on the topic of what's wrong with corn, it's also worth stating that "corn production uses more herbicides and insecticides and causes more runoff and water pollution than any other crop."[225] The CAFO system, as well as causing untold misery for the animals that are trapped within it, especially chickens and pigs, is also responsible for significant pollution as a result of concentrated animal waste that contains pathogens, antibiotics, hormones, chemicals, and other toxic substances. About 80 percent of all antibiotics produced in the US are given to livestock and poultry, and the overwhelming majority, as much as 90 percent, of this figure goes to animals that are not sick. Rather, the antibiotics are used to increase growth rates yet further and to prevent sickness that would be caused by the hideously cramped conditions they live in. Antibiotic resistance among pathogens is a major concern today, not just for animals but for us as well, and is clearly exacerbated by the way animals are raised in CAFOs.

It's not hard to see, then, how reducing the production of and reliance on corn could go a long way towards helping redress the balance of agriculture, and so much more besides, in the US today. Diana Rodgers and Robb Wolf are in no doubt that pasturing all cattle throughout their life cycle in the US would bring significant benefits to smaller farmers and local communities, all at the expense of the giant companies that dominate agriculture today.[226] For one thing, rearing grass-fed cattle is much more profitable per acre than growing corn, even though it requires more labor. More labor means more jobs, too. If the government were to shift its support and subsidies away

---

[224] Pollan, *Omnivore's Dilemma*, 201.
[225] Rodgers and Wolf, *Sacred Cow*, 177.
[226] Ibid., 234–5.

from CAFO operations to ranchers and grazers who produce grass-fed beef—perhaps as incentives for environmental regeneration—the benefits for local economies, and communities, could be considerable. The corporatization of agriculture, which has seen small farms disappear by the thousands, has been a disaster for rural communities across the US. By reversing this trend, and favoring real producers, it's entirely possible that much of the vibrancy and hope that has been lost in rural life could be restored once again.

And that would surely have political effects too. The original American populism was a grass-based movement: small independent farmers fighting to sustain their way of life, and to limit the power of predatory institutions like the railroads and, of course, large corporations. In America today, a century later, corporations dominate economic, social, and cultural life in a way that the original populists could scarcely have imagined. The Great Reset would see that domination completed. A renewed populism, raised on grass and watered by the right government, could help ensure that corporations are kept in their place—as servants, not masters of the people—and are never able to consolidate their power in such a way again.

.    .    .

Russia provides an irrefutable example that a powerful industrialized nation can make small-scale local agriculture work on a national level. And by "work," I mean that it serves the needs and interests of ordinary people first and foremost. What's more, Russia is able to do it without the government investing any money or effort of its own, but simply by relying on the resourcefulness and the traditions of the people themselves. As Vladimir Megre, the founder of the Anastasia movement, has said, imagine what such a system could do if it had the explicit backing of the government! In a nation as favored by God as the United States, the possibilities for such a system far outstrip those of probably any other nation on the planet. The question is not whether it could work—the answer to that question is clear—but whether the people are tired enough of the current system and aware enough of the dire alternative that is being planned for them to make a change. We will see.

# CONCLUSION:

# WELCOME TO 2030—DÉJÀ VU?

*Welcome to 2030. Welcome to my nation—or should I say, "our nation." I own things. I own a car. I own a house. I own appliances, including a Weber Smokey Mountain grill, and clothes.*

*It might seem odd to you—if you're a globalist, I mean. Not that there are many of those around these days. The globalists wanted ordinary people to give up everything they own, to share everything in common. Transportation, accommodation, food, and all the things we need in our daily lives. They said that one by one all these things would become free, so it wouldn't make any sense for us to own much. They said we'd be living in a totally different kind of society by 2030. And, the truth is, we are, just not the kind of society they wanted us to live in.*

*In the beginning, the people started electing more and more politicians who knew what the globalists were up to. For the first time in a long time, the interests of the nation and the people were what mattered. We couldn't believe it. No more pointless wars! No more aid to foreign nations that actually hate our guts and conspire against us! These politicians knew that a nation is only as strong as the individuals it's comprised of, so they did all they could to make the little man as big as he possibly* could be. The corporations that sickened and hooked our children on their "medicines" were broken up, and the chief architects of these great crimes were made to answer for them. The evidence for what they'd done was overwhelming. All that was needed was someone with the will to come along and finally make them pay. The same thing happened to the corporations that poisoned our food and water. For the crimes of high-fructose corn syrup, glyphosate, and soybean oil, old forms of exemplary punishment were brought back.

Alongside all of this, there was a popular movement to get people to return to the land. People began turning their lawns and yards into fruit and vegetable patches, growing espaliered fruit and nut trees up against their fences and vines on south-facing walls. People realized how little land you need to keep chickens. Maybe you could even fit a goat in there too, for milk and as a living weed killer. People began to form clubs and associations where they planned what they would grow together and so they could exchange equipment, knowledge and, of course, their delicious home-grown organic produce. New laws made it possible to do things that had previously been damn near impossible. Selling raw milk was no longer illegal. In fact, it was encouraged by the newly created Secretary for Human Health and Flourishing. The right-wing bodybuilders emerged from long anonymity and led national fitness drives, showing the people how to exercise and eat properly. Not only did people become much healthier, but we also started to feel part of something again. The nation seemed to be a living, breathing thing we were all part of. We are pioneers of a new way of life, just like our forefathers.

Now that the big agricultural concerns were broken up, the tyranny of corn is at an end. The larger farms can produce real food again, using methods that don't strip the earth of its goodness and threaten to leave it barren forever. Buffalo roam the plains in huge numbers like they had before, guided by farmers who now know that those majestic animals should never have been allowed to leave. The immense suffering of the chickens *and pigs was brought to an end, not a moment too soon, and they were given space to be the creatures God intended them to be. The globalists had wanted people to give up the foods that made their ancestors fit and healthy, but instead the opposite happened: we came home.*

*Of course, the globalists didn't go down without a fight. They knew that it was all or nothing. They tried every trick in the book. Political scandal. False flags. Inflation and artificial scarcity. War. They even tried the pee-pee tape again! But nobody believed them, at least not the people that mattered. And so, in the end, the globalists were defeated.*

*We lost some people along the way. Those who decided that it had become too much, all these strong communities and people who actually love their nation. Those who felt obsolete and useless when* CNN *and the* New York Times *were outlawed. They live in Canada now.*

*Oh yes, I shouldn't forget this either. After many months of searching, a newly constituted elite special forces team caught up with Bill Gates, in one of his underground lairs somewhere in the South Pacific. The soldiers were armed to the teeth and ready for a fight, but despite all that money, which could have made him the equal of any potentate from history, Gates just gave himself up. When they captured him, he was still wearing that awful lilac sweater, still looking like the pregnant-man emoji. He's in Guantanamo now, awaiting trial.*

*All in all, it's a good life, much better than the path we were on, when it became so clear that we had to make a change or the globalists would do it for us. We had all these terrible things happening: obesity; cancer; xenoestrogens; microplastics everywhere; destruction of the environment; social unrest. We lost way too many people before we realized that we could do things differently. Turns out the old ways really are the best.*

·   ·   ·

Forgive me, I was daydreaming . . .

It's 2022. That means 2030 is less than eight years away. My hope, now that you've read this book, is that you understand in much greater detail exactly what this could mean if the enemies of human freedom actually get what they want.

In the first chapter, I told the story of the Neolithic Revolution at length because I believe it has much to tell us about the stakes of the dietary transformation the globalists have in store for us today. Far from being a happy tale of Progress, the transition to agriculture in the Near East and the emergence of the first grain states had very clear winners and losers. The winners, an elite minority, ruled over a mass of people who were weaker, shorter, and unhealthier than their hunter-gatherer ancestors. It should come as no surprise, then, that the early agriculturalists seem to have seized every opportunity to flee back to more "primitive" lifestyles, whether as a result of rebellion, war, or some other form of state collapse. The "Golden Age of Barbarians" posited by James Scott, when agriculturalists could simply run away to the other side if they chose, lasted millennia, until the state form finally achieved full political domination of the globe. Today, though, everywhere is owned space, and there is nowhere to run to avoid the new global serfdom we face.

In the next chapter, I outlined the WEF-sponsored Planetary Health Diet. This almost entirely plant-based diet is intended to be the first ever truly global diet. Everybody will be made to eat it—except, of course, the masters of the universe, who you can bet will continue to dine on the finest foods known to man. The Diet's proponents claim it will not only make us all healthier, but will also reduce the effects of man-made climate change and help us feed an expanded global population of ten billion. In truth, it will do nothing of the sort. Rather, the Planetary Health Diet will complete modern man's alienation from the life-giving foods that sustained his ancestors and make him prey to many of the same illnesses that hobbled the first agriculturalists. A new kind of total domestication, one that goes even deeper than that of the Neolithic Revolution, awaits us. The food supply will be controlled by a handful of stupidly wealthy corporations whose real interest is not the health of the people, or of the planet, but their own enrichment. The model of agriculture that will support the Planetary Health Diet is an intensification of the worst aspects of the current industrial system and will rely on genetically-modified crops that require vast quantities of chemical fertilizers and toxic herbicides and pesticides to produce the necessary yields. The Diet's focus on climate change is a smokescreen that obscures the potentially devastating environmental consequences of increasing our reliance on a form of agriculture that has already brought our soils to the point of exhaustion. And although it will be the globalists who experiment with new forms of genetic modification, we are the ones who will suffer the consequences.

In the final chapter, I presented my own response to the challenge of the Great Reset: the Eggs Benedict Option. Is it possible for us to pursue a vision of agriculture that puts the health of individuals and the nation first, and promises to restore rather than degrade the environment? I believe it is, as I've tried to show with the example of Russian household gardening and the new movement for regenerative agriculture. There is absolutely no reason to believe that a nationwide system of household gardening couldn't work in a country like the US, which enjoys many advantages the people of Russia could only dream of. The question isn't whether or not it could work, but whether the necessary will could be summoned to make people change their personal habits and to challenge the biases of the current political system, which so heavily favor big corporations. A renewed populism could do this and also make it possible for a different, better kind of agriculture to emerge on a larger scale. Regenerative agriculture goes beyond the paradigm of "sustainability" and promises to restore the environment at the same time as providing the highest quality nutrition. For such a system to work, it would require active

political support, so again this is where populism comes in. Instead of providing subsidies for endless amounts of corn that
nobody really needs, politicians could support subsidies for
farmers who make their farms regenerative ones. This would
help break the corporate stranglehold on agriculture and, in
addition to its positive health and environmental effects, could
do much to revitalize rural communities that have been devas-
tated by the corporatization of agriculture.

My focus here has been on the US and the benefits it could
reap from my proposals. But as I said in the introduction, I believe these changes could be implemented more broadly in
other nations as well. A system combining local production and
distribution of high-quality organic food with a larger regenerative system of agriculture would offer any nation resiliency
and food security at different scales. One thing that has been
amply illustrated by the recent supply-chain disruptions is
that the food-production and distribution systems of modern
nations are extremely vulnerable to shocks, and that it can
take months, or even years, for problems to be resolved fully.
Concentrations of power are never good, whether we're talking
agriculture and food, or the political system. Food security is
something that all governments should be taking very seriously now. But even governments that say they're doing just
that are still stuck in the frame of mind that has led us to this
moment of crisis.

Take the UK government, for instance. In 2016, in the wake
of the popular decision to leave the EU, which many predicted
could lead to chronic food shortages, the Conservative government commissioned an inquiry into a "National Food Strategy,"
and at the beginning of July last year it released its findings at
last. Surprise, surprise, the report proposes "solutions" that are
only likely to deepen the problems they are intended to solve.
The thinking seems to be that the problem isn't that we're relying solely on large-scale production and distribution systems,
but that somehow we aren't relying on them *enough*. And of

course we are asked to take the same drearily familiar "planetary" perspective, with man-made climate change as its lens, precisely the view that is used by Klaus Schwab and his acolytes to justify the sweeping changes of the Great Reset. It's time to think differently.

I'm not saying it will be easy. Nothing that's worth pursuing ever is. But the alternative is just too dreadful to contemplate. Nor am I saying that I have all of the answers. Much still needs to be thought out and thought through. Even if you don't agree with everything I've said, I hope you can agree with me on this, at least: that now is the perfect time for us to think about fundamental changes to the way we live and eat.

The globalists have their plan, and we need ours. We stand at a crossroads. Which way, Western man?

# BIBLIOGRAPHY

## Books Cited and for Further Reading

Daniel, Kaayla T. *The Whole Soy Story: The Dark Side of America's Favorite Health Food*. Washington, DC: NewTrends Publishing, 2005.

Dugin, Alexander. *The Great Awakening vs the Great Reset*. London: Arktos Media, 2021.

Enig, Mary G. *Know Your Fats: The Complete Primer for Understanding the Nutrition of Fats, Oils and Cholesterol*. Bethesda, MD: Bethesda Press, 2000.

Fallon, Sally and Mary G. Enig. *Nourishing Traditions: The Cookbook that Challenges Politically Correct Nutrition and Diet Dictocrats*, Revised Second Edition. Brandywine, MD: NewTrends Publishing, 2001.

Fallon Morell, Sally. "Ancient Dietary Wisdom for Tomorrow's Children" in *Doing Nutrition Differently: Critical Approaches to Diet and Dietary Intervention*. New York: Routledge, 2016.

Florida, Richard. *The Great Reset: How the Post-Crash Economy Will Change the Way We Live and Work*. New York: Harper Collins, 2010.

Gwynne, S.C. *Empire of the Summer Moon: Quanah Parker and the Rise and Fall of the Comanches, the Most Powerful Indian Tribe in American History*. New York: Scribner, 2010.

Keith, Lierre. *The Vegetarian Myth: Food, Justice, and Sustainability*. Crescent City, CA: Flashpoint Press, 2009.

Mithen, Stephen J. *After the Ice: A Global Human History, 20,000-5000 BC*. Cambridge, MA: Harvard University Press, 2003.

Perlmutter, David and Kristin Loberg, *Grain Brain: The Surprising Truth about Wheat, Carbs, and Sugar—Your Brain's Silent Killers*. New York: Little, Brown and Company, 2013.

Plato. *The Republic*. Reprint. London: Penguin World's Classics, 2017.

Pollan, Michael. *The Omnivore's Dilemma: A Natural History of Four Meals*. New York: Penguin Books, 2007.

Price, Weston A. *Nutrition and Physical Degeneration: A Comparison of Primitive and Modern Diets and Their Effects*. 1939. Reprint. Oxford: Benediction Classics, 2010.

Rectenwald, Michael. *Google Archipelago: The Digital Gulag and the Simulation of Freedom*. Nashville: New English Review Press, 2019.

Rodgers, Diana and Robb Wolf. *Sacred Cow: The Case for (Better) Meat: Why Well-Raised Meat Is Good for You and Good for the Planet*. Dallas, TX: BenBella Books, 2020.

Salatin, Joel. *Everything I Want To Do Is Illegal: War Stories from the Local Food Front*. Swoope, VA: Polyface, Inc., 2007.

Schmid, Ronald F. *Native Nutrition: Eating According to Ancestral Wisdom*. Rochester, VT: Healing Arts Press, 1994.

Schwab, Klaus and Nicholas Davis. *Shaping the Future of the Fourth Industrial Revolution*. New York: Currency, 2018.

Schwab, Klaus and Thierry Malleret. *COVID-19: The Great Reset*. Geneva: Forum Publishing, 2020.

Scott, James C. *Against the Grain: A Deep History of the Earliest States*. New Haven, Yale University Press: 2017.

Shanahan, Catherine. *Deep Nutrition: Why Your Genes Need Traditional Food*. New York: Flatiron Books, 2017.

Stoll, Steven. *Larding the Lean Earth: Soil and Society in Nineteenth-Century America*. New York: Hill and Wang, 2003.

Sutton, Anthony Cyril. *Wall Street and FDR: the True Story of How Franklin D. Roosevelt Colluded with Corporate America*. 1975. Reprint. West Hoathly: Clairview Books, 2013.

Swan, Shanna H., and Stacey Colino. *Count Down: How Our Modern Word Is Threatening Sperm Counts, Altering Male and Female Reproductive Development, and Imperiling the Future of the Human Race*. New York: Scribner, 2021.

Turner, Frederick Jackson. *The Frontier in American History*. 1893. Reprint. New York: Henry Holt and Company, 1921.

Weatherford, Jack. *Genghis Khan and the Making of the Modern World*. New York: Three Rivers Press, 2004.

## Cited Papers, Articles, and Other Sources

Agamben, Giorgio. "Communist Capitalism." *Ill Will*, December 15, 2020. https://illwill.com/communist-capitalism.

Alba, Davey. "The baseless 'Great Reset' conspiracy theory rises again." *The New York Times*, November 17, 2020. Updated December 23, 2020. nytimes.com/live/2020/11/17/world/covid-19-coronavirus#the-baseless-great-reset-conspiracy-theory-rises-again.

Allentoft, Morten E., Martin Sikora, Alba Refoyo-Martínez, Evan K. Irving-Pease, Anders Fischer, William Barrie, Andrés Ingason, et al. "Population Genomics of Stone Age Eurasia." Preprint. *bioRxiv* (2022). doi.org/10.1101/2022.05.04.490594.

Anderson, Ross. "How Engineering the Human Body Could Combat Climate Change." *The Atlantic*, March 12, 2012. https://www.theatlantic.com/technology/archive/2012/03/how-engineering-the-human-body-could-combat-climate-change/253981/.

Anderson, Stephanie. "Regenerative agriculture can make farmers stewards of the land again." *The Conversation*, February 11, 2019. theconversation.com/regenerative-agriculture-can-make-farmers-stewards-of-the-land-again-110570.

Andrews, Luke. "Up to TEN MILLION Americans may suffer from rare Alpha-gal Syndrome, which causes sufferers to develop an allergy to meat - limited surveillance and odd symptoms could mean many do not even know they have it." *Daily Mail*, May 9, 2022. dailymail.co.uk/health/article-10798033/Up-TEN-MILLION-Americans-suffer-rare-Alpha-gal-Syndrome.html.

Anti-Defamation League. "'The Great Reset' Conspiracy Flourishes Amid Continued Pandemic." Anti-Defamation League Blog, December 29, 2020. adl.org/blog/the-great-reset-conspiracy-flourishes-amid-continued-pandemic.

Associated Press. "Pesticide caused kids' brain damage, California lawsuits say." *New York Post*, July 13, 2021. nypost.com/2021/07/13/pesticide-caused-kids-brain-damage-california-lawsuits-say/.

Atchison, Jennifer, Lesley Head, and Alison Gates. "Wheat as food, wheat as industrial substance; comparative geographies of transformation and mobility." *Geoforum* 41, no. 2 (2010): 236-46. doi.org/10.1016/j.geoforum.2009.09.006.

Barlett, Donald L. and James B. Steele. "Monsanto's Harvest of Fear." *Vanity Fair*, April 2, 2008. vanityfair.com/news/2008/05/monsanto200805.

Barnett, Jacqueline A., Maya L. Bandy, and Deanna L. Gibson, "Is the Use of Glyphosate in Modern Agriculture Resulting in Increased Neuropsychiatric Conditions Through Modulation of the Gut-brain-microbiome Axis?" *Frontiers in Nutrition* 9 (2022). doi.org/10.3389/fnut.2022.827384.

BBC. "Bayer to pay $10.9bn to settle weedkiller cancer claims." *BBC News*, June 25, 2020. https://www.bbc.com/news/business-53174513.

BBC Monitoring and BBC Reality Check. "What is the Great Reset - and how did it get hijacked by conspiracy theories?" *BBC News*, June 24, 2021. bbc.com/news/blogs-trending-57532368.

Ben-Dor, Miki, Raphael Sirtoli, and Ran Barkai. "The evolution of the human trophic level during the Pleistocene." *American Jounral of Physical Anthropology* 175, no. S72 (2021): 27–56. doi.org/10.1002/ajpa.24247.

Bressan, Paola and Peter Kramer. "Bread and other edible agents of mental disease." *Frontiers in Human Neuroscience* (2016). doi.org/10.3389%2Ffnhum.2016.00130.

Campbell, David. "Towards a Less Irrelevant Socialism: Stakeholding as a 'Reform' of the Capitalist Economy." *Journal of Law and Society* 24, no. 1 (1997), 65–84. https://www.jstor.org/stable/1410603.

Cantorna, Margherita T., Lindsay Snyder, Yang-Ding Lin, and Linlin Yang. "Vitamin D and 1,25(OH)$_2$D Regulation of T cells." *Nutrients* 7, no. 4 (2015): 3011–21. doi.org/10.3390/nu7043011.

Center for Health Security. "Event 201." Accessed July 27, 2022. https://www.centerforhealthsecurity.org/our-work/exercises/event201/.

Chebani, Tampiwa. "Stress May Cause Spontaneous Abortions of Male Fetuses According to Study." *Gilmore Health News*, October 27, 2019. https://www.gilmorehealth.com/stress-may-cause-spontaneous-abortions-of-male-fetuses-according-to-study/.

Cofnas, Nathan. "Is vegetarianism healthy for children?" *Critical Reviews in Food Science and Nutrition* 59, no. 13 (2019): 2502–60. doi.org/10.1080/10408398.2018.1437024.

Cohen, Alexander and James Arkin. "Afghans Don't Like Soybeans, Despite $34 Million U.S. Program To Change Their Tastes." *Forbes*, July 24, 2014. forbes.com/sites/centerforpublicintegrity/2014/07/24/afghans-dont-like-soybeans-despite-a-big-u-s-push.

Creech, Elizabeth. "Discover the Cover: Managing Cover Crops to Suppress Weeds and Save Money on Herbicides." Farmers.gov Blog, July 24, 2018. farmers.gov/blog/conservation/discover-cover-managing-cover-crops-suppress-weeds-and-save-money-herbicides.

Daisley, Brendan A., Anna M. Chernyshova, Graham J. Thompson, and Emma Allen-Vercoe. "Deteriorating microbiomes in agriculture—the unintended effects of pesticides on microbial life." *Microbiome Research Reports* 1, no. 6 (January 25, 2022). dx.doi.org/10.20517/mrr.2021.08.

Dallas, David C., Megan R. Sanctuary, Yunyao Qu, Shabnam Haghighat Khajavi, Alexandria E. Van Zandt, Melissa Dyandra, Steven A. Frese, Daniela Barile, and J. Bruce German. "Personalizing protein nourishment." *Critical Reviews in Food Science and Nutrition* 57, no. 15 (May 23, 2017), 3313–31. doi.org/10.1080/10408398.2015.1117412.

Daniels, Lee A. "COKE, PEPSI TO USE MORE CORN SYRUP." *The New York Times*, November 7, 1984. nytimes.com/1984/11/07/business/coke-pepsi-to-use-more-corn-syrup.html.

Deol, Poonamjot, Elena Kozlova, Matthew Valdez, Catherine Ho, Ei-Wen Yang, Holly Richardson, and Gwendolyn Gonzalez, et al. "Dysregulation of hypothalamic gene expression and the oxytocinergic system by soybean oil diets in male mice." *Endocrinology* 161, no. 2 (2020). doi.org/10.1210/endocr/bqz044.

Desmond, Małgorzata A., Jakub G. Sobiecki, Maciej Jaworski, Paweł
Płudowski, Jolanta Antoniewicz, Meghan K. Shirley, and Simon Eaton, et
al. "Growth, body composition, and cardiovascular and nutritional risk of
5- to 10-y-old children consuming vegetarian, vegan, or omnivore diets."
*The American Journal of Clinical Nutrition* 113, no. 6 (2021): 1565–77.
doi.org/10.1093/ajcn/nqaa445.

Drury, Colin. "Should everyone have their own personal carbon quota? Calls
grow for emissions allowances." *The Independent*, November 13, 2021.
independent.co.uk/climate-change/news/personal-carbon-allowance-
trading-climate-crisis-b1956705.html.

EAT Advisory Board. "No Protection from Pandemics Unless we Fix our Food
Systems," an Open Letter to the G20. Eat Forum, 2020.
eatforum.org/learn-and-discover/no-protection-from-pandemics-unless-we-
fix-our-food-systems/.

Elmore, Bart. "The herbicide dicamba was supposed to solve farmers' weed
problems – instead, it's making farming harder for many of them." *The
Conversation*, January 26, 2022. https://theconversation.com/the-
herbicide-dicamba-was-supposed-to-solve-farmers-weed-problems-
instead-its-making-farming-harder-for-many-of-them-174181.

Engdahl, William. "Monsanto is 'like a mafia selling protection' to farmers."
*RT*, January 14, 2014. rt.com/op-ed/monsanto-is-like-mafia-584/.

Farberov, Snejana. "US vegan parents who eat only raw fruit and vegetables
are charged with MURDER for the starvation death of their 18-month-old
son who was found weighing only 17lbs." *Daily Mail*, December 19, 2019.
dailymail.co.uk/news/article-7810073/Vegan-parents-charged-murder-
baby-sons-starvation-death.html.

FDA. "High Fructose Corn Syrup Questions and Answers." Accessed July 23,
2022. fda.gov/food/food-additives-petitions/high-fructose-corn-syrup-
questions-and-answers.

*The FoodPrint of Fake Meat.* GRACE Communications Foundation. 2021.
foodprint.org/reports/the-foodprint-of-fake-meat/.

Frasetto, L.A., M. Schloetter, M. Mietus-Synder, R.C. Morris Jr., and A.
Sebastian. "Metabolic and physiologic improvements from consuming a
paleolithic, hunter-gatherer type diet." *European Journal of Clinical
Nutrition* 63 (2009): 947–55. doi.org/10.1038/ejcn.2009.4.

Fuchs, Benjamin, Miika Laihonen, Anne Muola, Kari Saikkonen, Petre I.
Dobrev, Radomira Vankova, and Marjo Helander. "A Glyphosate-Based
Herbicide in Soil Differentially Affects Hormonal Homeostasis and
Performance of Non-target Crop Plants." *Frontiers in Plant Science* 12
(2022). doi.org/10.3389/fpls.2021.787958.

Ghiraldi, Marluci, Beatriz G. Franco, Izabel C.F. Moraes, and Samantha C.
Pinho. "Emulsion-Filled Pectin Gels for Vehiculation of Vitamins D3 and
B12: From Structuring to the Development of Enriched Vegan Gummy
Candies." *ACS Food Science and Technology* 1, no. 10 (2021): 1945–52.
doi.org/10.1021/acsfoodscitech.1c00271.

Gilsing, A.M.J., F.L. Crowe, Z. Lloyd-Wright, T.A.B. Sanders, P.N. Appleby, N.E. Allen, and T.J. Key. "Serum concentrations of vitamin B12 and folate in British male omnivores, vegetarians and vegans: results from a cross-sectional analysis of the EPIC-Oxford cohort study." *European Journal of Clinical Nutrition* 64 (2010): 993–9. doi.org/10.1038/ejcn.2010.142.

Goodman, Peter S. "Record Beef Prices, but Ranchers Aren't Cashing In." *The New York Times*, December 27, 2021. Updated December 29, 2021. nytimes.com/2021/12/27/business/beef-prices-cattle-ranchers.html.

Grasgruber, P., M. Sebera, E. Hrazdíra, J. Cacek, T. Kalina. "Major correlates of male height: A study of 105 countries." *Economics and Human Biology* 21 (2016): 172–95. doi.org/10.1016/j.ehb.2016.01.005.

Greely, Henry T. "Are we ready for genetically modified animals?" World Economic Forum, January 19, 2016. weforum.org/agenda/2016/01/are-we-ready-for-genetically-modified-animals.

Griffin, Annaliese. "You Want to Buy Meat? In This Economy?" *The New York Times*, June 2, 2022. nytimes.com/2022/06/02/opinion/inflation-vegetarian-vegan.html.

Hämäläinen, E.K., H. Adlercreutz, P. Puska, and P. Pietinen. "Decrease of serum total and free testosterone during a low-fat high-fibre diet." *Journal of Steroid Biochemistry* 18, no. 3 (1983): 369–70. doi.org/10.1016/0022-4731(83)90117-6.

Hansen, Tue H., Marie T.B. Madsen, Niklas R. Jørgensen, Arieh S. Cohen, Torben Hansen, Henrik Vestergaard, Oluf Pedersen, and Kristine H. Allin. "Bone turnover, calcium homeostasis, and vitamin D status in Danish vegans." *European Journal of Clinical Nutrition* 72 (2018): 1045–54. doi.org/10.1038/s41430-017-0081-y.

Heap, Ian and Stephen O. Duke. "Overview of glyphosate-resistant weeds worldwide." *Pest Management Science* 74, no. 5 (2018): 1040–49. https://doi.org/10.1002/ps.4760.

Held, Lisa. "Bayer Forges Ahead with New Crops Resistant to 5 Herbicides." *Civil Eats*, July 1, 2020. civileats.com/2020/07/01/bayer-forges-ahead-with-new-crops-resistant-to-5-herbicides-glyphosate-dicamba-2-4-d-glufosinate-quizalofop/.

Herrmann, Wolfgang. "Vitamin B 12 Deficiency in Vegetarians." In *Vegetarian and Plant-Based Diets in Health and Disease Prevention*, edited by François Mariotti, 791–808. Amsterdam: Elsevier, 2017.

Holston, William E. "The Diet of the Mountain Men." *California Historical Society Quarterly* 42, no. 4 (1963): 301–9. justmeat.co/docs/the-diet-of-the-mountain-men-william-e-holsten.pdf.

Howard, Philip H. "Op-ed: Giant Meat and Dairy Companies Are Dominating the Plant-Based and Cellular Meat Market." *Civil Eats*, September 22, 2021. civileats.com/2021/09/22/op-ed-giant-meat-and-dairy-companies-are-dominating-the-plant-based-protein-market.

Hudnall, Hannah. "FACT CHECK: IS KLAUS SCHWAB RELATED TO THE ROTHSCHILD FAMILY?" *Check Your Fact*, January 18, 2022. checkyourfact.com/2022/01/28/fact-check-klaus-schwab-mother-rothschild/.

Hudson, P. and R. Buckley. "Vegetarian diets. Are they good for pregnant women and their babies?" *The Practising Midwife* 3, no. 7 (2000): 22–3. https://pubmed.ncbi.nlm.nih.gov/12026434/.

Ibbetson, Ross. "Swedish couple who raised their baby as a VEGAN are jailed for three months after the 18-month-old nearly starved to death." *Daily Mail*, May 23, 2019. dailymail.co.uk/news/article-7063219/Swedish-couple-raised-baby-VEGAN-jailed-nearly-starved-death.html

Iguacel, Isabel, María L. Miguel-Berges, Alejandro Gómez-Bruton, Luis A Moreno, and Cristina Julián. "Veganism, vegetarianism, bone mineral density, and fracture risk: a systematic review and meta-analysis." *Nutrition Reviews* 77, no. 1 (2019): 1–18. doi.org/10.1093/nutrit/nuy045.

Inman, Phillip. "Pandemic is chance to reset global economy, says Prince Charles." *The Guardian*, June 3, 2020. https://www.theguardian.com/uk-news/2020/jun/03/pandemic-is-chance-to-reset-global-economy-says-prince-charles.

Karonova, Tatiana L., Alena T. Andreeva, Ksenia A. Golovatuk, Ekaterina S. Bykova, Anna V. Simanenkova, Maria A. Vashukova, William B. Grant, and Evgeny V. Shlyakhto. "Low 25(OH)D Level Is Associated with Severe Course and Poor Prognosis in COVID-19." *Nutrients* 13, no. 9 (2021): 3021. doi.org/10.3390/nu13093021.

Kelland, Kate. "In glyphosate review, WHO cancer agency edited out 'non-carcinogenic' findings." *Reuters*, October 19, 2017. reuters.com/investigates/special-report/who-iarc-glyphosate/.

Kemp, Luke, Laura Adam, Christian R Boehm, Rainer Breitling, Rocco Casagrande, Malcolm Dando, and Appolinaire Djikeng, et al. "Point of View: Bioengineering horizon scan 2020." *Genetics and Genomics* (2020). doi.org/10.7554/eLife.54489.

Lambert, Charles, P. "Saturated fat ingestion regulates androgen concentrations and may influence lean body mass accrual." *The Journals of Gerontology: Series A* 63, no. 11 (2008): 1260–1261. doi.org/10.1093/gerona/63.11.1260.

Lee, Chang Woock, Teak V. Lee, Vincent C.W. Chen, Steve Bui, Steven E. Riechman. "Dietary Cholesterol Affects Skeletal Muscle Protein Synthesis Following Acute Resistance Exercise." *The FASEB Journal* 25, no. S1 (2011). doi.org/10.1096/fasebj.25.1_supplement.lb563.

Liao, Matthew S., Anders Sandberg, and Rebecca Roache. "Human Engineering and Climate Change." *Ethics, Policy & Environment* 15, no. 2 (2012): 206–21. doi.org/10.1080/21550085.2012.685574.

Lim, Meng Thiam, Bernice Jiaqi Pan, Darel Wee Kiat Toh, Clarinda Nataria Sutanto, and Jung Eun Kim. "Animal Protein versus Plant Protein in Supporting Lean Mass and Muscle Strength: A Systematic Review and Meta-Analysis of Randomized Controlled Trials," *Nutrients* 13, no. 2 (2021). doi.org/10.3390/nu13020661.

Lomborg, Bjorn. "Starvation still claims a child's life every 3 seconds – here's how we could change this." World Economic Forum, July 30, 2019. weforum.org/agenda/2019/07/820-million-starving-people-number-growing/.

London, Bianca. "Cockroach milk is being hailed the next big superfood, so would you dare to try it?" *Glamour*, January 2, 2020. https://www.glamourmagazine.co.uk/article/cockroach-milk-benefits.

Lucia, Rachel M., Wei-Lin Huang, Khyatiben V. Pathak, Marissa McGilvrey, Victoria David-Dirgo, Andrea Alvarez, Deborah Goodman, et al. "Association of Glyphosate Exposure with Blood DNA Methylation in a Cross-Sectional Study of Postmenopausal Women." *Environmental Health Perspective* 130, no. 4 (2022). doi.org/10.1289/EHP10174.

Maersk, Maria, Anita Belza, Hans Stødkilde-Jørgensen, Steffen Ringgaard, Elizaveta Chabanova, Henrik Thomsen, Steen B Pedersen, Arne Astrup, Bjørn Richelsen. "Sucrose-sweetened beverages increase fat storage in the liver, muscle, and visceral fat depot: a 6-mo randomized intervention study." *The American Journal of Clinical Nutrition* 95, no. 2 (2012): 283–9. doi.org/10.3945/ajcn.111.022533.

Malik, Vasanti S., Barry M. Popkin, George A. Bray, Jean-Pierre Després, Walter C. Willett, Frank B. Hu. "Sugar-sweetened beverages and risk of metabolic syndrome and type 2 diabetes: a meta-analysis." *Diabetes Care* 33, no. 11 (2010): 2477–83. doi.org/10.2337/dc10-1079.

Malkan, Stacy. "Chlorpyrifos: Common Pesticide Tied To Brain Damage in Children." Organic Consumers Association, October 22, 2020. organicconsumers.org/blog/chlorpyrifos-common-pesticide-tied-to-brain-damage-in-children.

Mamounis, Kyle J., Ali Yasrebi, and T.A. Roepke. "Linoleic acid causes greater weight gain than saturated fat without hypothalamic inflammation in the male mouse." *Journal of Nutritional Biochemistry* 40 (2017): 122–31. doi.org/10.1016/j.jnutbio.2016.10.016.

Mann, George V. "Diet-Heart: End of an Era." *The New England Journal of Medicine* 297 (1977): 644–50. doi.org/10.1056/NEJM197709222971206.

Mann, L.R.B., D. Straton, and W.E. Crist. "The Thalidomide of Genetic Engineering." Revised April 2001 from the GE issue of *Soil and Health* (1999). gmwatch.org/en/news/archive/2001/9344-the-thalidomide-of-genetic-engineering?tmpl=component.

Martinex, Jorge and Jack E. Lewi. "An unusual case of gynecomastia associated with soy product consumption." *Endocrine Practice* 14, no. 4 (2008): 415–18. doi.org/10.4158/EP.14.4.415.

Mattick, Carolyn S., Amy E. Landis, Braden R. Allenby, and Nicholas J. Genovese. "Anticipatory Life Cycle Analysis of In Vitro Biomass Cultivation for Cultured Meat Production in the United States." *Environmental Science and Technology* 49, no. 19 (September 2015): 11941–11949. https://doi.org/10.1021/acs.est.5b01614.

Mauldin, John. "Brace Yourself For 'The Great Reset.'" *Forbes*, May 31, 2017. https://www.forbes.com/sites/johnmauldin/2017/05/31/mauldin-brace-yourself-for-the-great-reset/?sh=1b6e3b9f5d38.

Mercola, Joseph. "Seeds of Evil: Monsanto and Genetic Engineering." Organic Consumers Association, February 10, 2014. organicconsumers.org/news/seeds-evil-monsanto-and-genetic-engineering.

Mero, Antti. "Leucine Supplementation and Intensive Training." *Sports Medicine* 27 (1999): 347–58. doi.org/10.2165/00007256-199927060-00001.

Motta, Erick V.S., J. Elijah Powell, and Nancy A. Moran. "Glyphosate induces immune dysregulation in honey bees." *Animal Microbiome* 4, no: 16 (2022). doi.org/10.1186/s42523-022-00165-0.

Naughton, Shaan S., Michael L. Mathai, Deanne H. Hryciw, Andrew J. McAinch. "Lineoleic acid and the pathogenesis of obesity." *Prostaglandins and Other Lipid Mediators* 125 (2016): 90–99. doi.org/10.1016/j.prostaglandins.2016.06.003.

Noor, Ramadhani, Utibe Effiong, and Lindiwe Majele Sibanda. "Can gene editing help tackle global hunger?" World Economic Forum, July 8, 2015. weforum.org/agenda/2015/07/can-gene-editing-help-tackle-global-hunger.

Nylka, Ruby. "More spent on low iron hospitalisations as meat intake declines." *National Health*, January 1, 2019. stuff.co.nz/national/health/108767316/more-spent-on-low-iron-hospitalisations-as-meat-intake-declines.

Page, Kathleen A., Owen Chan, Jagriti Arora, Renata Belfort-DeAguiar, James Dzuira, Brian Roehmholdt, Gary W. Cline, et al. "Effects of fructose vs glucose on regional cerebral blood flow in brain regions involved with appetite and reward pathways." *JAMA* 309, no. 1 (2013): 63–70. doi.org/10.1001/jama.2012.116975.

Parkin, Beth L. and S. Atwood. "Menu design approaches to promote sustainable vegetarian food choices when dining out." *Journal of Environmental Psychology* 79 (2022). doi.org/10.1016/j.jenvp.2021.101721.

Peat, Ray. "Aging, estrogen, and progesterone." RayPeat.com. raypeat.com/articles/aging/aging-estrogen-progesterone.shtml.

Philpott, Tom. "The Bloody Secret Behind Lab-Grown Meat." *Mother Jones*, March 2022. motherjones.com/environment/2022/03/lab-meat-fetal-bovine-serum-blood-slaughter-cultured/.

Ramsden, Christopher, Daisy Zamora, Sharon Majchrzak-Hong, Keturah R. Faurot, Steven K. Broste, Robert P. Frantz, John M. Davis, Amit Ringel, Chirayath M. Suchindran, and Joseph R Hibbeln. "Re-evaluation of the traditional diet-heart hypothesis: analysis of recovered data from Minnesota Coronary Experiment (1968–73)." *The BMJ* 353 (2016). doi.org/10.1136/bmj.i1246.

Rectenwald, Michael. "The Great Reset, Part III: Capitalism with Chinese Characteristics." Mises Institute's *Mises Wire*, January 1, 2021. https://mises.org/wire/great-reset-part-iii-capitalism-chinese-characteristics.

Rectenwald, Michael. "What Is the Great Reset?" Independent Institute, February 28, 2022. independent.org/publications/article.asp?id=14039&.

Rempelos, Leonidas, Juan Wang, Marcin Barański, Anthony Watson, Nikolaos Volakakis, Hans-Wolfgang Hoppe, and W. Nikolaus Kühn-Velten, et al. "Diet and food type affect urinary pesticide residue excretion profiles in healthy individuals: results of a randomized controlled dietary intervention trial." *The American Journal of Clinical Nutrition* 115, no. 2 (2022): 364–77. doi.org/10.1093/ajcn/nqab308.

Riechman, Steven E., Chang Woock Lee, Gentle Chikani, Vincent C.W. Chen, and Teak Veng Lee. "Cholesterol and Skeletal Muscle Health." In *A Balanced Omega-6/ Omega-3 Fatty Acid Ratio, Cholesterol and Coronary Heart Disease*, edited by A.P. Simopoulos and F. De Meester. *World Review of Nutrition and Dietetics* 100 (2009): 71–9.

Riechman, Steven E., Ryan D. Andrews, David A. MacLean, and Simon Sheather. "Statins and Dietary and Serum Cholesterol Are Associated With Increased Lean Mass Following Resistance Training." *The Journal of Gerontology. Series A: Biological and Medical Sciences* 62, no. 10 (2007), 1164–71. doi.org/10.1093/gerona/62.10.1164.

Rolland, Nathalie C.M., C. Rob Markus, and Mark J. Post. "The effect of information content on acceptance of cultured meat in a tasting context." *PLOS One* 15, no. 4 (2020). https://doi.org/10.1371/journal.pone.0231176.

Roosevelt, Franklin Delano. "Radio Address on the Third Anniversary of the Social Security Act. White House, Washington, D.C." August 15, 1938. Reproduced at The American Presidency Project. presidency.ucsb.edu/documents/radio-address-the-third-anniversary-the-social-security-act-white-house-washington-dc.

Roseboro, Ken. "Synthetic biology products entering the market unregulated, unlabeled—and even with non-GMO claims." *The Organic & Non-GMO Report*, September 7, 2021. non-gmoreport.com/articles/synthetic-biology-products-entering-the-market-unregulated-unlabeled-and-even-with-non-gmo-claims/.

Rutledge, Angela C. and Khosrow Adeli. "Fructose and the metabolic syndrome: pathophysiology and molecular mechanisms." *Nutrition Reviews* 65 (2007): S13–S23. doi.org/10.1111/j.1753-4887.2007.tb00322.x.

Sainato, Michael. "Billionaires add $1tn to net worth during pandemic as their workers struggle." *The Guardian*, January 15, 2021. theguardian.com/world/2021/jan/15/billionaires-net-worth-coronavirus-pandemic-jeff-bezos-elon-musk.

Sarwar, Ghulam. "The Protein Digestibility–Corrected Amino Acid Score Method Overestimates Quality of Proteins Containing Antinutritional Factors and of Poorly Digestible Proteins Supplemented with Limiting Amino Acids in Rats." *The Journal of Nutrition* 127, no. 5 (1997), 758–64. doi.org/10.1093/jn/127.5.758.

Schafer, Meredith G., Andrew A. Ross, Jason P. Londo, Connie A. Burdick, E. Henry Lee, Steven E. Travers, Peter K. Van de Water, Cynthia L. Sagers. "The Establishment of Genetically Engineered Canola Populations in the US." *PLOS One* 6, no. 10 (2011). https://doi.org/10.1371/journal.pone.0025736.

Schreefel, L., R.P.O. Schulte, I.J.M. de Boer, A. Pas Schrijver, H.H.E. van Zanten. "Regenerative agriculture—the soil is the base." *Global Food Security* 26 (2020). doi.org/10.1016/j.gfs.2020.100404.

Schwab, Tim. "Covid-19, trust, and Wellcome: how charity's pharma investments overlap with its research efforts." *The BMJ* 372, no. n556 (2021). https://doi.org/10.1136/bmj.n556.

Scrimshaw, Nevin S. "Iron deficiency." *Scientific American* 265, no. 4 (1991): 46–52. doi.org/10.1038/scientificamerican1091-46.

Setchell, Kenneth, Linda Zimmer-Nechemias, Jinnan Cai, and James E Heubi. "Exposure of infants to phyto-oestrogens from soy-based infant formula." *The Lancet* 350, no. 9070 (1997): P23–7. doi.org/10.1016/S0140-6736(96)09480-9.

Setchell, Kenneth, Linda Zimmer-Nechemias, Jinnan Cai, and James E. Heubi. "Isoflavone content of infant formulas and the metabolic fate of these phytoestrogens in early life." *American Journal of Clinical Nutrition* 68, no. 6 (1998): 1453S–61S. doi.org/10.1093/ajcn/68.6.1453S.

Sharashkin, Leonid. "The Socioeconomic and Cultural Significance of Food Gardening in the Vladimir Region of Russia." PhD diss., University of Missouri-Columbia, 2008. soilandhealth.org/wp-content/uploads/01aglibrary/010177.sharashkin.pdf.

Simon, Neal G., Jay R. Kaplan, Shan Hu, Thomas C. Register, Michael R. Adams. "Increased aggressive behavior and decreased affiliative behavior in adult male monkeys after long-term consumption of diets rich in soy protein and isoflavones." *Hormones and Behavior* 45, no. 4 (2004): 278–84. doi.org/10.1016/j.yhbeh.2003.12.005.

Solati, Zahra, Shima Jazayeri, Mehdi Tehrani-Doost, Salma Mahmoodianfard, and Mahmood Reza Gohari. "Zinc monotherapy increases serum brain-derived neurotrophic factor (BDNF) levels and decreases depressive symptoms in overweight or obese subjects: a double-blind, randomized, placebo-controlled trial." *Nutritional Neuroscience* 18, no. 4 (2015): 162–8. doi.org/10.1179/1476830513Y.0000000105.

Southern Cross University Media Release. "Benefits of using organic food in a traditional Mediterranean diet." *Scimex*, November 1, 2021. https://www.scimex.org/newsfeed/benefits-of-using-organic-food-in-a-traditional-mediterranean-diet.

Spisák, Sándor, Norbert Solymosi, Péter Ittzés, András Bodor, Dániel Kondor, Gábor Vattay, and Barbara K. Barták, et al. "Complete Genes May Pass from Food to Human Blood." *PLOS One* 8, no. 7 (2013). doi.org/10.1371/journal.pone.0069805.

Stanhope, Kimber L., Jean Marc Schwarz, Nancy L. Keim, Steven C. Griffen, Andrew A. Bremer, James L. Graham, Bonnie Hatcher, et al. "Consuming fructose-sweetened, not glucose-sweetened, beverages increases visceral adiposity and lipids and decreases insulin sensitivity in overweight/obese humans." *The Journal of Clinical Investigation* 119, no. 5 (2009): 1322–34. doi.org/10.1172/JCI37385.

Sundaram, Anjali. "Yelp data shows 60% of business closures due to the coronavirus pandemic are now permanent." *CNBC*, September 16, 2020. Updated December 11, 2020. cnbc.com/2020/09/16/yelp-data-shows-60percent-of-business-closures-due-to-the-coronavirus-pandemic-are-now-permanent.html.

*Sustainable Agriculture and Integrated Farming Systems: 1984 Conference Proceedings*, edited by Thomas C. Edens, Cynthia Fridgen, and Susan L. Battenfield. East Lansing, MI: Michigan State University Press, 1985.

Tian, Sinuo, Sen Yan, Zhiyuan Meng, Shiran Huang, Wei Sun, Ming Jia, Miaomiao Teng, Zhiqiang Zhou, Wentao Zhu. "New insights into bisphenols induced obesity in zebrafish (*Danio rerio*): Activation of cannabinoid receptor CB1." *Journal of Hazardous Materials* 418 (2021). doi.org/10.1016/j.jhazmat.2021.126100.

Tuikkala, Päivi, Sirpa Hartikainen, Maarit J. Korhonen, Piia Lavikainen, Raimo Kettunen, Raimo Sulkava, and Hannes Enlund. "Serum total cholesterol levels and all-cause mortality in a home-dwelling elderly population: a six-year follow-up." *Scandinavian Journal of Primary Health Care* 28, no. 2 (2010). doi.org/10.3109/02813432.2010.487371.

USDA Economic Research Service. "High-Fructose Corn Syrup Production and Prices." Accessed July 23, 2022. ers.usda.gov/topics/crops/sugar-sweeteners/background.aspx#hfcs.

Vargesson, Neil. "Thalidomide-induced teratogenesis: History and mechanisms." *Embryo Today: Reviews* 105, no. 2 (2015): 140–56. doi.org/10.1002/bdrc.21096.

Vedmore, Johnny. "Schwab Family Values." *Unlimited Hangout*, February 20, 2021. unlimitedhangout.com/2021/02/reportaje-investigativo/schwab-family-values/?lang=es.

van Vliet, Stephan, Evan L. Shy, Sidney Abou Sawan, Joseph W. Beals, Daniel W.D. West, Sarah K. Skinner, Alexander V. Ulanov, et al. "Consumption of whole eggs promotes greater stimulation of postexercise muscle protein synthesis than consumption of isonitrogenous amounts of egg whites in young men." *American Journal of Clinical Nutrition* 106, no. 6 (2017): 1401–12. doi.org/10.3945/ajcn.117.159855.

Waite, Richard, Craig Hanson, Tim Searchinger, and Janet Ranganathan. "This is how to sustainably feed 10 billion people by 2050." World Economic Forum, December 7, 2018. https://www.weforum.org/agenda/2018/12/how-to-sustainably-feed-10-billion-people-by-2050-in-21-charts/#:~:text=%20This%20is%20how%20to%20sustainably%20feed%2010,is%20mostly%20driven%20by%20population%20growth%2C...%20More%20.

Wang, Bo, Evangelia E. Tsakiridis, Shuman Zhang, Andrea Llanos, Eric M. Desjardins, Julian M. Yabut, Alexander E. Green, et al. "The pesticide chlorpyrifos promotes obesity by inhibiting diet-induced thermogenesis in brown adipose tissue." *Nature Communications* 12, no. 5163 (2021). doi.org/10.1038/s41467-021-25384-y.

White, John S. "Straight talk about high-fructose corn syrup: what it is and what it ain't." *The American Journal of Clinical Nutrition* 88, no. 6 (2008): 1716–21. doi.org/10.3945%2Fajcn.2008.25825b.

Whiting, Kate. "How soon will we be eating lab-grown meat?" World Economic Forum. October 16, 2020. weforum.org/agenda/2020/10/will-we-eat-lab-grown-meat-world-food-day/.

Whittaker, Joseph and Kexin Wu. "Low-fat diets and testosterone in men: Systematic review and meta-analysis of intervention studies." *The Journal of Steroid Biochemistry and Molecular Biology* 210 (2021). doi.org/10.1016/j.jsbmb.2021.105878.

"Who's on the Magic Mountain." *The Economist*, January 23, 2014. economist.com/international/2014/01/23/whos-on-the-magic-mountain.

Wilkin, Shevan, Alicia Ventresca Miller, Ricardo Fernandes, Robert Spengler, William T.T. Taylor, Dorcas R. Brown, David Reich, et al. "Dairying enabled Early Bronze Age Yamnaya steppe expansions." *Nature* 598 (2021): 629–33. doi.org/10.1038/s41586-021-03798-4.

Willett, Walter, et al. "Summary Report of the EAT-*Lancet* Commission." A summary of *Food in The Anthropocene: the EAT-Lancet Commission on Healthy Diets From Sustainable Food Systems*. The EAT-*Lancet* Commission, 2019. eatforum.org/content/uploads/2019/07/EAT-Lancet_Commission_Summary_Report.pdf.

World Economic Forum. "Artificial Intelligence for Agriculture Innovation, Community Paper." March 2021. https://www3.weforum.org/docs/WEF_Artificial_Intelligence_for_Agriculture_Innovation_2021.pdf.

World Economic Forum. "Klaus Schwab—World Economic Forum—Davos Conversation." July 17, 2007. YouTube video, 2:24. youtube.com/watch?v=oN-zUjf-MAw&t=1s.

World Economic Forum. "Meat: the Future series: Alternative Proteins." January 2019. weforum.org/docs/WEF_White_Paper_Alternative_Proteins.pdf.

World Health Organization. "Obesity and overweight." June 9, 2021. who.int/news-room/fact-sheets/detail/obesity-and-overweight.

World Science Festival. "Could We Make Humans Smaller Than Cats?" December 9, 2016. YouTube video, 3:37. youtube.com/watch?v=ZxqvNqy3flI.

Ye, Tian and Anna S. Mattila. "The Effect of ad appeals and message framing on consumer response to plant-based menu items." *International Journal of Hospitality Management* 95 (2021). doi.org/10.1016/j.ijhm.2021.102917.

Yi, Sang-Wook, Jee-Jeon Yi, and Heechoul Ohrr. "Total cholesterol and all-cause mortality by sex and age: a prospective cohort study among 12.8 million adults." *Scientific Reports* 9, no. 1596 (2019). doi.org/10.1038/s41598-018-38461-y.

Zureik, M, D. Courbon, and P. Ducimetière. "Decline in serum total cholesterol and the risk of death from cancer." *Epidemiology* 8, no. 2 (1997), 137–43. https://pubmed.ncbi.nlm.nih.gov/9229204/.

# ABOUT THE AUTHOR

With his breakout smash cookbook, *Raw Egg Nationalism in Theory and Practice,* which is now available in hardback from Antelope Hill Publishing, anon Twitter sensation RAW EGG NATIONALIST introduced the world to raw egg nationalism. By combining irreverent humor with culinary expertise, the wisdom of Golden Age bodybuilders, and redpill nutrition and politics, RAW EGG NATIONALIST created a cookbook unlike any other—one that's been seen in the hands of Alex Jones, Owen Shroyer, Jack Posobiec, Noor Bin Ladin, and many others. He has since written two other books (*Three Lives of Golden Age Bodybuilders* and *Draw Me a Gironda*), founded the men's magazine *MAN'S WORLD*, written essays for *American Mind*, and made numerous interview and podcast appearances, including in the Tucker Carlson documentary *The End of Men*. He is currently working on the second *MAN'S WORLD Annual*, which will be available at the end of the year. The first, containing all the best content from the magazine's first year, is available now from Antelope Hill Publishing.

For links to all of his work and appearances, visit lnk.bio/ raweggnationalist.

CPSIA information can be obtained
at www.ICGtesting.com
Printed in the USA
BVHW041537091022
648785BV00001B/7